Philosophy and Politics - Critical Explorations

Volume 6

The purpose of Philosophy and Politics - Critical Explorations is to publish high quality volumes that reflect original research pursued at the juncture of philosophy and politics. Over the past 20 years new important areas of inquiry at the crossroads of philosophy and politics have undergone impressive developments or have emerged anew. Among these, new approaches to human rights, transitional justice, religion and politics and especially the challenges of a post-secular society, global justice, public reason, global constitutionalism, multiple democracies, political liberalism and deliberative democracy can be included. Philosophy and Politics - Critical Explorations addresses each and any of these interrelated yet distinct fields as valuable manuscripts and proposal become available, with the aim of both being the forum where single breakthrough studies in one specific subject can be published and at the same time the areas of overlap and the intersecting themes across the various areas can be composed in the coherent image of a highly dynamic disciplinary continent. Some of the studies published are bold theoretical explorations of one specific theme, and thus primarily addressed to specialists, whereas others are suitable for a broader readership and possibly for wide adoption in graduate courses. The series includes monographs focusing on a specific topic, as well as collections of articles covering a theme or collections of articles by one author. Contributions to this series come from scholars on every continent and from a variety of scholarly orientations.

More information about this series at http://www.springer.com/series/13508

Daniele Santoro • Manohar Kumar

Speaking Truth to Power – A Theory of Whistleblowing

 Springer

Daniele Santoro
Centre for Ethics, Politics, and Society,
ILCH
University of Minho
Braga, Portugal

Manohar Kumar
Department of Social Sciences and
Humanities
Indraprastha Institute of Information
Technology, Delhi
New Delhi, India

ISSN 2352-8370   ISSN 2352-8389   (electronic)
Philosophy and Politics - Critical Explorations
ISBN 978-3-319-90721-5   ISBN 978-3-319-90723-9   (eBook)
https://doi.org/10.1007/978-3-319-90723-9

Library of Congress Control Number: 2018951057

Printed on acid-free paper

This Springer imprint is published by the registered company Springer International Publishing AG
part of Springer Nature.
The registered company address is: Gewerbestrasse 11, 6330 Cham, Switzerland

Preface

This is a coauthored book whose origin dates back to 2012, when both authors worked at Luiss University. Wikileaks had already published back in 2010 the "Afghan War Diary" and the "Iraq War Logs," but Chelsea Manning was still unknown as the source of the leaks, Julian Assange not yet caged in the Ecuadorian Embassy in London, and Edward Snowden still an employee of a contractor working for the US National Security Agency. We had already been following the development of the Wikileaks releases when the Snowden affair exploded in June 2013. The role of secrecy in democracy caught our attention at that point both as scholars and as citizens. We have changed several places and affiliations since then, but we have kept working together on the project of a joint book on these topics. The book reflects our initial motivation. We were not so much concerned with the biographies of whistleblowers, but with the political significance of the NSA disclosures. For us, the Snowden affair represented the closing of a circle that had started in the aftermath of 9/11, when a new securitization paradigm had imposed itself in domestic and international politics, and secret programs had become predominant in the security agenda. We believe that the political significance of whistleblowers is to have exposed to the public for the first time after 9/11 the consequences people had to pay in the name of security. This book argues that whistleblowing is a form of civil dissent by agents who remind us, against the opinion of the majority, that the ultimate aim of a constitutional democracy is to protect the rights of the governed.

Braga, Portugal   Daniele Santoro
New Delhi, India   Manohar Kumar

Acknowledgments

As any book, also this one would not have been possible without the help and support of many people and institutions. We are particularly grateful to Alessandro Ferrara and David Rasmussen, editors of the series in which this book appears, for their encouragement and support. We had many discussions with Sandro, whose philosophical wisdom helped us to better place the discussion of whistleblowing within the debate on dissent.

The Centre for Ethics, Politics, and Society, where Daniele works, has been very supportive during the period in which the book was written. João Cardoso Rosas, João Ribeiro Mendes, Alexandra Abranches, David Alvarez, Roberto Merrill, and the other members of the Centre have been very kind with comments and suggestions on several topics discussed here. Daniele thanks also the Aix-Marseille Institute for Advanced Studies (IMèRA), the Chaire Hoover d'éthique économique et sociale – UCLouvain, and the National Research Council of Italy, where he carried out part of this project during fellowship appointments.

We also thank the Indian Institute of Technology (IIT), Delhi, and the Aix-Marseille School of Economics, where Manohar held appointments as a postdoctoral researcher during the past 3 years. He wishes in particular to mention Arudra Burra, Bijoy Boruah, Sanil V, and Ravinder Kaur of IIT Delhi, and Feriel Kandil of Aix-Marseille for their support. Since March 2018 Manohar has joined the Center for IT and Society (IIIT Delhi) – Department of Social Sciences and Humanities.

Selected topics of this book have been presented at conferences in Alghero, Prague, Louvain, Stirling, London, Manchester, Braga, and Lisbon.

We are particularly grateful to the audiences of the following seminars and workshops for their comments on earlier drafts of Chaps. 3, 4, and 5: the Tata Institute of Social Sciences, December 2012; the Manipal Centre for Philosophy and Humanities, September 2014; the panel on Whistleblowing, Conscience and Conscientious Objection in Contemporary Public Life, sponsored by the President of Ireland's Ethics Initiative in Dublin, November 2014; the "Mercoledì Filosofici del Maino," University of Pavia, February 2015; the workshop "Civil Disobedience Beyond the State II," Berlin, May 2015; the Seminaire Vivès and the Mardis Intimes of the Chaire Hoover, Louvain, April and June 2015; the Tuesday Seminar,

Department of Humanities and Social Sciences, IIT Delhi, August 2015, April and September 2016; the Workshop on Disagreements and Disobedience, University of Milan, November 2015; the Pavia Workshop on Political Corruption, December 2015; the Summer School on Equality and Citizenship, the University of Rijeka, Croatia, June 2016; the Edinburgh Workshop on Disobedience and Political Protest, June 2016; the Economic Philosophy Seminar, GREQAM, Aix Marseille University, April 2017; the Workshop "Corruption, Democracy, and Whistleblowing," Aix-Marseille University, November 2017.

We wish to thank in particular for their thoughtful suggestions and discussions: Daniele Archibugi, Elvio Baccarini, Ali Emre Benli, Bruno Bernardi, Boran Berčić, Antonella Besussi, Enrico Biale, Giulia Bistagnino, Michele Bocchiola, Eric. C. Boot, Jonathan Bruno, Ian Carter, Robin Celikates, Emanuela Ceva, François Chateauraynaud, Matthew Christman, Maeve Cooke, Katrin Deckert, Daniele Cozzoli, Rowan Craft, Candice Delmas, Chiara Destri, Alessandra Facchi, Mark Fenster, Maria Paola Ferretti, Thomas Ferretti, Guy Fletcher, Corrado Fumagalli, Elisabetta Galeotti, Axel Gosseries, Graham Hubbs, Feriel Kandil, Ashwani Kumar, Volker Kaul, William Kornblum, Mark Knights, Ashwani Kumar, Maxime Lambrecht, David Leskowitz, Federica Liveriero, Michele Loi, Sebastiano Maffettone, Domenico Melidoro, Tim Meyers, Dorota Mokrosinska, Evgenia Mylonaki, Gianfranco Pellegrino, John Pitseys, Hervé Pourtois, Najat Rahaman, Nicola Riva, Sebastian Rudas, Marc Sangnier, Roberta Sala, Ingrid Salvatore, William Scheuermann, David Schimdtz, William Smith, Aakash Singh Rathore, Rahul Sagar, Zofia Stemplowska, Daniel Tkatch, Philippe Van Parijs, Stefano Vaselli, Mark E. Warren, Danielle Zwarthoed, and Theresa Züger.

We are grateful to two anonymous reviewers for their detailed reading of the manuscript and for their insightful comments on the original manuscript. A special thanks also to Alberto Patania, Upasana Sinha, Manisha Lath, and Sebastian Rudas who have read the text and suggested stylistic improvements.

Finally, we thank Diana Nijenhuijzen, Assistant Editor of the Social Sciences and Humanities Department of Springer, and Neil Olivier, for their editorial support and patience of conceding us more extensions than we would have imagined when we started writing the book.

Some of the topics of this book have been explored in other common writings. Chapter 5 is an expanded version of "A Justification of Whistleblowing," published in *Philosophy & Social Criticism*, (43/7) in June 2017. Here we analyze far more in detail the conditions of permissibility for whistleblowing formulated in that paper and clarify how it fits within a conception of the public interest. Chapter 3 draws partially on a yet unpublished paper on liberty, state secrecy, and what we call the right of assessment, whose seminal work set us on the path to whistleblowing. The historical reconstruction in the first part of Chap. 2, the discussion of the justification and limits of secrecy in Chap. 3 (especially sects. 3.3–3.6), and of informational asymmetry in Chap. 5 are materials partially borrowed from Manohar's dissertation 'For Whom the Whistle Blow? Secrecy, Civil Disobedience, and Democratic Accountability' and extensively revised for this book. The dissertation is available in the Luiss eprints repository.

The conclusion contains a brief discussion of the right to protection for whistle-blowers, a topic that we have explored more in detail in another joint paper entitled 'A Right to Protection of Whistleblowers', which recently appeared in the collected volume *Claiming Citizenship. Rights in Europe. Emerging Challenges and Political Agents* (pp. 186–203) edited by Daniele Archibugi and Ali Emre Benli for Routledge.

One last thought to our significant others, for the lovely support and patience during the many periods when we took time off from our family duties to gather on the manuscript. Daniele dedicates this book to Marta. May her also grow brave to speak out over the fence. Manohar dedicates it to his parents for their immense faith in him and for completing half a century of togetherness.

Daniele Santoro's position is funded by the Fundação para Ciencia e Tecnologia (FCT -SFRH/BPD/108669/2015).

Manohar Kumar's AMSE position was funded under the project Change of Direction. Fostering Whistleblowing in the Fight against Corruption co-funded by the Internal Security Fund of the European Union (Grant Number: HOME/2014/ISFP/AG/EFCE/7233).

Contents

Chapter 1
Introduction

Keywords Dissent · Plan of the book · Theory of whistleblowing · Secrecy · Security

1.1 The Political Context of Whistleblowing Disclosures

Whistleblowing is the act of disclosinginformation from public or private organizations with the purpose of revealing gross violations of citizens' rights, failures of government accountability, or corruption in public or private bodies that are of immediate or potential danger to the public interest. In this book we argue that whistleblowing is crucial for democracy because it contributes to institutional transparency and is a safeguard against the potential abuse of government and corporate power. Its motivating idea is that whistleblowing is a form of civil dissent, that is a conscientious act against the corporate and public powers when they endanger the public interest of democratic communities.

A growing amount of whistleblowing disclosures have characterized the international political scene since the early 2010s. Wikileaks first, and Snowden later have exposed to the public scrutiny the extent to which the US government has been collecting personal data of their citizens and foreign nationals. As a consequence, whistleblowing has received wide public attention and has sparked a debate between advocates of civil liberties and patriots of surveillance worried of a world marred by terrorism. The response from the state authorities thus far has been to curb these dissenting voices through a spate of anti-terror legislation. Often these measures have been used not just to single out individuals who may pose a national security

© Springer International Publishing AG, part of Springer Nature 2018
D. Santoro, M. Kumar, *Speaking Truth to Power – A Theory of Whistleblowing*,
Philosophy and Politics - Critical Explorations 6,
https://doi.org/10.1007/978-3-319-90723-9_1

threat, but also to suppress criticism of those anti-terrorism policies. Although whistleblowers face serious retaliations when they unveil the plunder of public resources, they are exposed to even worse conditions when they reveal state secrets. It is quite evident that governments are not happy with unauthorized disclosures. They cry out for punishment and prosecute whistleblowers for theft of government material, danger to national security, and even for setting a bad example. This led to extreme polarization in the early reactions to Wikileaks. For the advocates of national security Wikileaks was a cradle of spies, traitors, thieves, the worst league possible of human beings you may want to have around. On the other side, supporters of anti-surveillance movements, Anonymous, and hacktivists of different guise had united behind the 'the right to know' campaign in defense of Assange. We also supported the 'right to know' movement, but Wikileaks' intransigence was a bit troublesome to us. What if, in the name of truth, other less crystalline agendas were being pushed forward? Our fears became true later on in 2016, when the release of the Democratic National Committee emails were exploited to build the campaign against 'crooked Hillary.' One does not have to be a supporter of Hillary Clinton to see that those files had had some influence in obscene results of the ensuing elections. Can truths of public relevance be at the same time against the public interest? The puzzle was one of the animating ideas of the book.

The case of Edward Snowden was arguably less puzzling than Wikileaks', less shady at least. When the story came out in *The Guardian* in June 2013, it was alarming but limited in scope. Glenn Greenwald's article revealed that the National Security Agency had been collecting the phone records of millions of American customers of Verizon, a major telecom provider, after a secret court order issued months before. In a crescendo of new revelations, the public opinion found out that other companies and internet providers were also requested access to their customers' data. The phantom echelon program, called PRISM, was the first proof of an ongoing mass-surveillance operation affecting both US and foreign citizens. The NSA revelations were a tale of two betrayals. One was the betrayal of the US government against unaware citizens; the other was the betrayal of the source of those leaks against the government. Edward Snowden publicly revealed his identity a week after the Guardian had published the first article on PRISM. The vicissitudes of those frantic days is beautifully told in Laura Poitras' documentary *Citizenfour,* with original footage of the interviews by Greenwald and Ewen MacAskill held in a Hong Kong hotel with the NSA contractor. However, in the light of the much bigger betrayal by the government, Snowden's appeared more justifiable in the eyes of most part of the public opinion. It was the biggest leak of government secrecy since the Pentagon Papers. Snowden the whistleblower had become an international hero, a young and well-spoken David against the strongarm Goliath of the US security apparatus. The story since then is still unfolding. In this book we formulate a theory of whistleblowing to understand this kind of public disclosures and articulate the set of rights which define the scope of its constitutional legitimacy. Our purpose is to provide a framework of analysis for the many issues that whistleblowing poses to democracy.

1.2   A Theory of Whistleblowing

Only recently political philosophy has started to pay due attention to ethical and political relevance of whistleblowing. The best scholarship till recently could only be found in business ethics and among legal scholars. Scholars in these fields have insisted on the moral dimensions of loyalty, responsibility, and conscientiousness, but other equally important questions have received less attention: what role do individuals working within state institutions have in upholding just institutions? What makes an act of whistleblowing successful? Should an act of whistleblowing be penalized? Which criteria justify the act? In sum, there is a general lack of a normative understanding of whistleblowing that political philosophy should undertake.

   Little effort has also been made to understand whistleblowing as an act of dissent. Another important aim of this book is to contribute to this debate by shifting the attention from the procedures of consent formation to the constitutional mechanisms that guarantee the expression of dissent. We believe that one of the core principles of constitutional democracies is to protect the expression of dissent, and the way democratic institutions are responsive to dissent determines the quality of democracy and, ultimately, its legitimacy. What place dissenters have within a society, whether they enjoy personal safety, legal protection and are provided with channels of disclosure are hallmarks of a good democracy, and of its justice.

   We pay attention in this book to constitutional democracies, privileging the non-ideal conditions of the regimes in which dissent takes place. The reason for this choice is twofold. First, the changing nature of dissent in society is a reflection of the changing problems democratic societies face. Since whistleblowing is a specific form of dissent in historical democratic societies, its function is eminently practical; a democratic engagement in response to contingent needs for democratic accountability and transparency. As the forms of governmental control evolve —especially in the digital world—these forms of engagement also change, and new practice of dissent emerge, from acts of digital disobedience to the so-called political hacktivism.

   Second, within the so-called conditions of ideal theory, the right to dissent is not prima facie justified. People can legitimately exercise forms of dissent when the state is largely non-compliant with the principles of justice. For instance, for Joseph Raz the right to civil disobedience is limited to only those cases when citizens are denied the right to political participation. He argues that in the liberal state 'there can be no right to civil disobedience which derives from a general right to political participation' because 'the right to political activity is, by hypothesis, adequately protected by law' (1979: 273). But liberal states do not always ensure the right to participation. This may happen in many ways, sometimes by legal means which harden the conditions for the exercise of a right. The case is exemplified by the literacy tests put into place during the Jim Crow era in the United States, or by systems of mandatory voter registration. We see here a material infringement of the constitutional voter rights and a curtailment of a meaningful political participation. When the recognition of the right to political participation is a *fictio iuris*, denying citizens the right to express dissent for unjust laws deprives them twice of their rights. In a way, the very idea that democracy is the power of the people is a theoretical construction. However, governmental practices can be inspired by democratic models which serve as normative ideals for those practices and can be judged according to their degree of compliance with those models.[1]

How are dissent and democracy related then? As we said, our focus in this book is to clarify how whistleblowing reinforces the democratic standards of decision-making in non-ideal circumstances. The current debate is evasive on this point. According to some democratic theorists, democracy is an ideal of self-government which shapes both the procedures of decision-making and the outcomes of those decisions (see Brettschneider 2007: 3). Democracy is intrinsically valuable because only democratic procedures can effectively realize these values and no non-democratic or illiberal means can be justified in the name of democracy. Just like we hardly believe that a person can be virtuous when she acts viciously in the pursuit of a noble aim, in the same manner we should be skeptical of methods apt to realize a democratic goal that dodge democratic procedures. According to others, democracy is only extrinsically valuable: democracy is just one mode of realizing critical public values—typically liberty, equality, or a blend of both—but these values are only contingently dependent on the process of realizing them. If we were able to devise a better method, then we should abandon the democratic decision-making. Through the lenses of this debate, whistleblowing can be conceived of as either contributing to re-establish and reinforce democratic procedures of accountability and transparency, or as a form of dissent that overrides democratic decisions in the name of other values, such as public equality.[2] In the first case, democracy and dissent are closely related, and the protection of dissent should be one of its aims. In the second case, actual democratic regimes could still guarantee the expression of dissent in the name of other values, such as the protection of minorities or of diversity, but not necessarily those values which democracy is meant to realize. Democracy and dissent would be contingently connected, but the protection of dissent would not be a condition for the legitimacy of democracy, nor vice versa. We believe that in either case, whistleblowing still confers legitimacy to constitutional democracies by protecting the values that underpin the constitutional rights and the public interest of

---

[1] Whether a normative theory of justice should be ideal or instead account for the non-ideal circumstances of its implementation is an issue many authors have discussed in recent years. On one account, theories of justice should have an aspirational aim, for their conceptual function is not to recommend how people and institutions should behave, but to define the standards through which people and institutions can be judged, and possibly improved (see Estlund 2014). On a different account, the aim of ideal theories is not aspirational, let alone 'realistic,' but conceptual: to establish principles of justice independently from their practical goals, where principles do not depend on facts of the matter concerning human behavior (see Cohen 2003). When the problem concerns the concept of democracy, it seems difficult to imagine a purely conceptual model of democracy that does not have any practical goal. In this book, we will leave aside the debate on ideal and non-ideal theory to focus instead on standards of judgment for actual governmental practices.

[2] See for instance Christiano (2008) who defends an interpretation along these lines.

democratic polities. As it will become clear in what follows, this is not a trivial answer. When the system of checks and balances fail to curb the power of the executive, especially under conditions of unregulated secrecy, whistleblowers act in the name of the general public, and help to re-establish the democratic values embedded in the procedures. But whistleblowers can also play a non procedural role when governments, supported by the popular opinion, target minority groups in the name of majoritarian interests. In such cases, public interest disclosures are adversarial claims, as they call for the respect of rights over more popular demands.

1.3   Plan of the Book

First, something about how the book is organized. The distinction that we draw between civic and political whistleblowing is crucial to the structure of the book. Chapters 2 and 3 discuss the civic aspects in detail, while the remaining of the book is more concerned with government disclosures motivated by political purposes. Chapters 2, 4 and 6 can be also read independently of each other, while Chaps. 3 and 5 are closely related. Considered together, they provide a public interest justification for whistleblowing disclosures.

We start by offering in Chap. 2 a general overview of the history, the concept, and the functions of whistleblowing. We first reconstruct the historical context of the concept and practice of whistleblowing, paying particular attention to the concept of parrhesia, and then address some figures whose acts of dissent can be inscribed within a militant conception of democracy. Along with this reconstruction, we will explore the ideals of publicity.

In the second part, we present the current state of whistleblowing theory and review some justifications of whistleblowing proposed in the literature (the standard theory, complicity, the moral choice view, integrity, civic duty, and the question of loyalty). This discussion is instrumental to the last part of the chapter, where we provide a comprehensive definition of whistleblowing and discuss its constitutive elements. The crucial point of this section is the distinction we draw between two different forms of whistleblowing: *political and civic.* Roughly, political whistleblowing is the unlawful disclosure of government classified information, while civic whistleblowing refers to the disclosure of information intended to report cases of corruption in the private and public sector. The distinction between civic and political whistleblowing sets the plan for the rest of the book.

Chapter 3 defends the role of *civic* whistleblowing in the fight against corruption. We argue that such a function should be adequately understood within a conception of public interest. To this purpose, we analyze the notion of public interest, arguing that whistleblowing contributes to the public interest when it unveils crimes that cause an unfair allocation of the burdens of cooperation. This chapter too is divided into three parts. First, we review other existing conceptions on the injustice of political corruption and provide a working definition that will in turn be helpful for the second part, in which we offer two possible characterizations of public interest. The first characterization is based on the aggregation of non-competing individual interests, while the second will be cast in terms of all-purposive rights. In the final part of the chapter, we argue that the rights-based view of public interest captures an essential feature of the injustice of political corruption, namely that it affects citizens' agency to enjoy their rights. We suggest that the injustice of corruption does not primarily consist in disrupting the demands of accountability and the value of equality in citizens' social relationships, but in interfering with legitimate entitlements citizens have in virtue of their citizenship status.

A justification of whistleblowing is necessarily associated with the limits of institutional practices of secrecy, be its usurpation of power to serve private interests or the illegitimate restrictions of rights and liberties. Understanding political whistleblowing demands looking at how secrecy affects the democratic control of national security and the rights of individuals and groups. Chapter 4 will explore the role of political whistleblowing within the context of governmental secrecy. It provides an analysis of the impact that state secrecy has on the rights of individuals and the democratic structures of accountability. We start from the debate on the balance between liberty and security and move towards a critique of the idea that a balance is always justified. Then, we analyze the role that secrecy plays in matters of national security. In the second part of the chapter, we pay attention to the effects of unrestrained secrecy on rights and provide an alternative account of civil liberties. Finally, we introduce the notion of epistemic entitlement of rights and argue that secrecy is legitimate within a constitutional democracy when citizens enjoy a specific right (we call it the right of assessment) to be informed in due course in which circumstances their civil liberties are limited or restricted.

What does justify whistleblowing? Chapter 5 represents the core of our normative proposal. Although the proposal in this chapter is sufficiently comprehensive to hold for both civic and political whistleblowing, our main interest rests in political disclosures, because its justification is more demanding. To this purpose, we first discuss some arguments against political whistleblowing: it is a breach of a professional obligation that erodes trust; it is unpatriotic and an act of treason that harms national security; it is a form of vigilante justice that disrespects public procedures of accountability and operates with very partial information. We defend political whistleblowing from these charges and then move to define the circumstances of information asymmetry that lead to disclosures. Information asymmetry holds when an organization withholds confidential or secret information from public access. A whistleblower is an agent (an employee or public official) who, having privileged access to this information, is in the position to disclose it. When the information is *intentionally* withheld by the organization from public access either to protect an illegitimate interest or against the legitimate interests of the public, the whistleblower has a reason to disclose. We then present a justification of whistleblowing disclosures based on three permissibility conditions: communicative constraints, intent, and public interest.

Is political whistleblowing a form of dissent? The concern of the last chapter is to explain why political whistleblowing is a full-fledged form of political dissent. We discuss various forms of dissent and maintain that whistleblowing is neither a case of conscientious objection nor a case of civil disobedience. It is not conscientious objection, for concerns of public interest that are essential to justify whistleblowing are only incidental to conscientious objection. We argue instead that political whistleblowing is a distinctive act of civil dissent against the threat of unruled government secrecy. It is distinctive in character because, despite sharing some features of civil disobedience, its intended aim is limited to enhancing public awareness, not necessarily advancing a political or moral agenda. It is distinctive in character because it is a non evasive act of disobedience that, among other features, does not fall under the liberal principle of the fidelity to the law. However, it is a 'civil' act, an act of citizenship, addressing the public in a non-coercive and non-violent manner, whose disobedience of the law is justified only in the name of fundamental rights and of the democratic values of openness, accountability, and equal consideration of interests. In conclusion, political whistleblowing is a civil opposition against government secrecy whose civil commitment is measured by the willingness of whistleblowers to stand up against the government interests.

References

Brettschneider, Corey. 2007. *Democratic Rights. The Substance of Self-Government*. Princeton/Oxford: Princeton University Press.

Christiano, Thomas. 2008. *The Constitution of Equality. Democratic Authority and Its Limits*. New York: Oxford University Press.

Cohen, Gerald A. 2003. Facts and Principles. *Philosophy and Public Affairs* 31 (3): 211–245.

Estlund, David. 2014. Utopopobia. *Philosophy and Public Affairs* 42 (2): 113–134.

Raz, Joseph. 1979. *The Authority of Law: Essays on Law and Morality*. Oxford: Oxford University Press.

Chapter 2
What Is Whistleblowing?

Abstract The practice of fearless speech occupies a distinctive yet neglected role within the history of political thought. In this chapter we contextualize whistleblowing within such a tradition and define its proper scope. In the first part we offer an introduction on the origin of the term and a discussion of some early cases. We pay particular attention to the ancient Greek practice of parrhesia, and then situate whistleblowing within the debate on publicity. In the second part of the chapter we turn to the current debate on the morality of whistleblowing and review some conceptions proposed in the literature: the standard theory, complicity, the moral choice view, integrity, civic duty, and the question of loyalty. In the final part we lay down the features of a comprehensive definition. We introduce an important distinction between political and civic whistleblowing, provide a detailed account of both forms, and clear some confusions that have emerged in the recent literature.

Keywords Civic whistleblowing · Political whistleblowing · Parrhesia · Publicity · Moral choice · Complicity · Integrity · Civic duty

In its most general sense, whistleblowing is an act of public disclosure of information concerning wrongdoings that harm the public interest of a society. The exact etymology of the term is unknown, but it is likely to have emerged from two separate but related activities: first, from the practice in nineteenth century Britain when unarmed police men or bobbies blew the whistle to alert citizens in order to apprehend and chase a shoplifter or a pickpocket (Branch 1979: 237, cited in Johnson 2003: 4); second, from the practice of referees who blew the whistle to call a foul on the players (Hoffman and McNulty 2010). In this respect, the analogy with policemen and referees is instructive of the two functions of whistleblowing: as those who give the alarm; and as guardians of fair play ensuring conformity with the rules of

© Springer International Publishing AG, part of Springer Nature 2018
D. Santoro, M. Kumar, *Speaking Truth to Power – A Theory of Whistleblowing*,
Philosophy and Politics - Critical Explorations 6,
https://doi.org/10.1007/978-3-319-90723-9_2

the game.[1] The contemporary understanding of the term has partly inherited its original meaning. Contemporary whistleblowers signal wrongdoings within the organization they are usually part of.[2]

Given these semantic roots, it should not be surprising that whistleblowing is a metaphorical term: no paraphrase seems to define the term without losing part of its meaning. In part, the difficulty of semantic reduction may depend on the lack of agreement on which features should define the concept of whistleblowing. For another however, whistleblowing seems not to be a purely descriptive term. Like 'courageous' or 'coward', whistleblowing is a term that carries a moral evaluation, and part of what speakers describe as 'whistleblowing' depends on how they judge whistleblowers within the discursive context where the term is used. Evaluative differences can also explain the persistent disagreement between advocates and detractors of whistleblowers; between those who salute whistleblowers as civil heroes and those who deem them spies at the service of the enemy.

Despite the metaphorical and evaluative connotations of the term, we believe that whistleblowing is susceptible to a more precise analysis. The aim of the book is to vindicate its conceptual independence and lay the bases for a normative theory of whistleblowing. A normative theory comprises two fundamental aspects: a definition and conception of whistleblowing. A definition of whistleblowing refers the set of rules for the correct application of the term. It is not a definition of the empirical aspects of whistleblowing, such as the psychological motives that lead to a disclosure. It is instead a definition of the conceptual role the term 'whistleblowing' plays within a discursive practice.[3]

A 'conception' of whistleblowing is given by set of moral and political ideals that justify the concept of whistleblowing. In this chapter we will discuss some of them, and elaborate our conception in Chaps. 3, 5, and 6. Our fundamental tenet is that whistleblowing is a distinctive form of civil dissent, related to and yet independent of other forms of political agency, such as civil disobedience and conscientious objection.[4]

---

[1] The first and narrower sense of whistleblowing is somewhat retained by the French expression 'lanceur d'alerte', literally 'those who give the alarm'. Giving the alarm is quite different from calling a foul, and may also be done preemptively, before something bad happens. See Chateauraynaud (2013) on the definition of lanceur d'alerte.

[2] Robert Ann Johnson suggests that the term 'whistleblower' was also common to distinguish dissidents who revealed inside information about their organization from those insiders who belonged to the mafia groups or erstwhile communists who were informants of congressional committees (Johnson 2003: 4).

[3] To elucidate: a proper definition of the term 'lion' will include some constitutive properties, for instance that lions are mammals. Any improper use of the term 'lion', as in the sentence 'lions lay eggs' will violate the correct use of the term 'lion' in virtue of the properties of being a lion. Likewise, we define 'whistleblowing' as 'an act of public disclosure' such that disclosures that fail to be public, will not qualify as acts of whistleblowing.

[4] The distinction between concept and conception that we draw here is loosely Rawlsian (See Rawls 1955). Deborah Johnson has argued against the correlation between definition and justification. She suggests that 'reasons for acting, the degree of certainty that the whistleblower has about the wrongdoing and whether or not the whistleblower has tried to remedy the wrongdoing by

In what follows we will reconstruct the historical roots of whistleblowing from its origins to the current debate, and pay attention to the principle of publicity that has so much significance for the whistleblowers' claims of transparency. In the second part of the chapter we will focus on the definition of whistleblowing, describe its constitutive elements and distinguish it from other cognate notions that sometimes overlap and with whom whistleblowing is often confused.

2.1 The Legacy of Whistleblowers

As a term, whistleblowing derives from the noun 'whistleblower', which emerged in the 1950s as a slang word to designate individuals who exposed some dishonest practices in the organization they worked for.[5] We must credit Ralph Nader, the well-known American environmental activist, for being the first one to offer a definition of whistleblowing. Nader defined whistleblowing as:

> an act of a man or woman who, believing that the public interest overrides the interest of the organization he serves, blows the whistle that the organization is involved in corrupt, illegal, fraudulent or harmful activity (cited in Vandekerckhove 2006: 8).[6]

Although whistleblowing as a term may have appeared only in 1950s, the act of standing up against wrong practices in an organization has a much older history. Some argue that Thomas Paine should be considered the first American

---

internal mechanisms. ... will bear on our understanding of when whistleblowing is permissible and when it is morally obligatory, but these factors should not be confused with definitional features' (cited in Dandekar 1991: 91). We agree that these features are part of an understanding of whistleblowing, but we fail to see how they are unrelated to a definition of what whistleblowing is. If Johnson were right, we should say that the phenomenal properties of water (its viscosity, change of physical state...) are independent of the fact that water is H_2O.

[5] See Barrett (2006: 290–91), Lozano et al., Winton (2007). The most succinct definition is in the Oxford American English Dictionary, in which a whistleblower is defined as someone 'who informs on a person or organization engaged in an illicit activity'. The British English version of the Oxford dictionary is slightly different: whistleblower is someone 'who informs on a person or organization regarded as engaging in an unlawful or immoral activity.' Here also 'immoral' activities are subject to disclosure, although it is not clear what the term 'immoral' stands for. We will see that the nature of the activity is an essential element of a definition, and that none of the above is sufficient to capture the distinctiveness of the term.

[6] The occasion was a conference on professional responsibility in 1972 (Johnson 2003: 4; Bollier 2002). Wim Vandekerckhove cites an interesting case of an early warning against whistleblowing in a 1971 address by James Roche, then chairman of the board of General Motors, who warned: 'Some critics are now busy eroding another support of free enterprise—the loyalty of a management team, with its unifying values of cooperative work. Some of the enemies of business now encourage an employee to be disloyal to the enterprise. They want to create suspicion and disharmony, and pry into the proprietary interests of the business. However this is labelled—industrial espionage, whistle blowing, or professional responsibility—it is another tactic for spreading disunity and creating conflict (Roche 1971: 445, cited in Vandekerckhove 2006: 8).

whistleblower in virtue of his role in the Silas Deane affair.[7] Silas Deane was an American citizen sent to France by the Congress as a representative of the American Colonies in Europe. He carried secret instructions to sell American goods to Europe and procure guns and ammunitions for the war. In addition, he was supposed to enlist French help (who were unaligned) in the war. He managed to do so with the help of Caron de Beaumarchais and the French king, who sent armaments meant as a gift to help the war effort. But Deane and Beaumarchais charged the Congress for the shipments withholding the information of the gift. This became a controversial issue in the Congress and Deane defended his action in a series of letters to the Pennsylvania Packet. Paine, who was privy to the ongoing process in the congress, revealed it to the public, in the same newspaper through a series of letters (Winter 2010).[8]

A second landmark case of whistleblowing occurred in 1777 just a few months after signing of the American Declaration of Independence (Kohn 2011). A group of ten sailors and Marine gathered to discuss their concerns regarding the inhuman and barbarous treatment of captured British soldiers by the commander of the Continental Navy, Commodore Esek Hopkins. John Grannis, a Marine captain, selected as a representative of the ten men, submitted a petition to the congress regarding their concern with the activities of the commander. This petition led to the suspension of Hopkins who retaliated by filing a libel suit against the whistleblowers. The libel led to the jailing of two of them—Samuel Shaw and Richard Marven. In a petition to the congress on July 23, 1778 they pleaded that they did what they believed to be right and their duty (ibid.). This case led to the promulgation of the first American whistleblowers protection law, which was passed unopposed. The law read:

> That it is the duty of all persons in the service of the United States, as well as all other inhabitants thereof, to give the earliest information to Congress or any other proper authority of any misconduct, frauds or misdemeanors committed by any officers or persons in the service of these states, which may come to their knowledge (Legislation of July 30, 1778).

The congress even supported the whistleblowers financially in the case which they won later.

Another case that hit the front pages was that of Roger Casement (Dickey 2013). Casement, born in Ireland, arrived in Congo in 1880s as purser, surveyor, and engaged in many other jobs. In 1900 he was engaged with British Consular services and was asked to investigate the excesses of the Belgians in Belgian Congo. In 1904 he produced a report that bore testimony to these excesses perpetrated against the

---

[7] For a detailed narrative, see Larry Winter in his blog entry on the Deane's affair (2010). See also the entry on Silas Deane on *Encyclopedia.com*. One may wonder if whistleblowing existed before the term was coined. An answer to this question is that a concept does not exist outside some acceptance within a linguistic community. Thus, since whistleblowing was not conceptualized at the time of the Deane's affair, it would be futile to describe Paine as a whistleblower. However, this view would rule out cases with similar looking features just for a matter of terminology, which sounds odd. Concepts can be employed to analyze aspects of the past by using epistemic and hermeneutic resources available in the present.

[8] See Thomas Paine (1906), especially the chapter 'The affair of Silas Deane'.

native population by the colonialists. He wrote about the torture, mutilations, rape, and existence of slavery practices among other things. In the words of Edmund Dene Morel, a shipping official in Congo, the revelations removed the veil 'from the most gigantic fraud and wickedness which our generation had ever known' (ibid.).[9] He exposed, in the words of Colin Dickey, the doublespeak of King Leopold, who in the colony 'employed various euphemistic names and organizations (including The Congo Free State and The Commission for the Protection of the Natives) to give his actions a veneer of respectability' (ibid.). The affair was unmasked by Casement 'through clear, unequivocal description, direct testimony, lengthy quotations and interviews, and facts' (ibid.). As W.G. Sebald writes:

> Casement made it perfectly clear that hundreds of thousands of slave labourers were being worked to death every year by their white overseers, and that mutilation, by severing hands and feet, and execution by revolver, were among the everyday punitive measures of maintaining discipline in Congo (2002: 127).

The report sparked a human rights campaign against the Belgian monarchy. In addition to his report on Congo, Casement was also instrumental in publishing the Putumayo report that exposed the torture, terror, and forced labour of local Indians that made the rubber plantations in the Amazon Basin profitable. Casement had gone on a British consular service to the Amazon in 1909 after a public outcry against the exploitation in the rubber industry, following the publication of a series of articles in the London Magazine *Truth* by the American Engineer Walter Hardenburg.[10] Hardenburg had highlighted the immense brutality that the Indians faced in the Amazon Basin at the hands of the rubber companies in the form of torture, castrations, killing for amusement etc. (Taussig 1984). This act led John Tully to describe Hardenburg as a whistleblower (2011: 86).

Perhaps the most remarkable case of whistleblowing in history is Daniel Ellsberg's. Ellsberg was employed with the RAND corporation where he worked on what came to be known as the Pentagon Papers.[11] The study was commissioned by Robert McNamara, the Secretary of Defense, for the purpose of documenting the Vietnam War. In 1969 Ellsberg photocopied the 7000 page document and revealed it to the Senate Foreign Relations Committee and, in 1971, to The New York Times, The Washington Post, and 17 other newspapers. The papers revealed that the US had enlarged the scale of the war and built up the conflict without the knowledge of the public and the media. For his disclosures, Ellsberg was criminally charged on accounts of espionage, conspiracy, and stealing government property. The charges were later dropped when it was discovered that a secret White House team sought

---

[9] Morel also published a series of books documenting the atrocities in Congo. See Morel (1905) and (1907).

[10] Hardenburg's chronicle can be found in Ernest and Enock (1912) and Ernest and Casement (1912).

[11] The official title of the study was: *United States–Vietnam Relations, 1945-1967: A Study Prepared by the Department of Defense*. For more on the Pentagon Papers see Sheehan (1971), and Ellsberg (2003).

to publicly discredit Ellsberg by burglarizing the office of his psychiatrist in order to find personal information about him.

In the midst of the hot debate following the publication of Papers, Hannah Arendt wrote a essay for *New York Review of Books,* one of the first defenses of whistleblowing against the modern power of unrestrained secrecy (Arendt 1972). Arendt argued that the Papers did not only show that the Administration had deceived the American public and the Congress, but also the extent to which falsehood was allowed to 'proliferate throughout the rank of all governmental services, military and civilian'(1972: 4, 14). With evidence from the intelligence community systematically ignored in favor of lying and deliberate deception, the Papers revealed that '…all decisions in this disastrous enterprise were made in full cognizance of that fact that they probably could not be carried out: hence goals had constantly to be shifted' (ibid.), to save in the end the image of United States as the dominant power (ibid.: 17). Interestingly, Arendt was also the first to address the problem of the so-called post-truth. She argued that the lack of public assessment wipes out the facts from the consideration of politics, leading to self-deception in the government: 'not only are the people and their elected representatives denied access…, but also the actors themselves, who receive top clearance to learn all the relevant facts, remain blissfully unaware of them (ibid.: 30). Dealing with a mass of documents, most of which have no reason to be classified, government actors have no inclination nor time to go 'hunting for pertinent facts' (ibid.).

A myriad of cases, some more, some less known, crowd into the history of whistleblowing disclosures after the Pentagon papers. Names like Edward Snowden, Julian Assange, and Chelsea Manning have become iconic figures world-wide. Their stories are in the wider public domain, and we will not retell them here.[12] A less known history that is worth recounting is the more ancient practice of speaking truth to the power.

2.2   Parrhesia

Whistleblowing in its historical origin is a form of fearless speech that disclosed misdeeds in governments and organizations. The whistleblower is a truth-teller who believes to posses a truth of a larger social value, and since speaking the truth is demanding and courageous, whistleblowers live in fear of reprisals, risk for their career, liberty, and even life. Courage, fearlessness, and risk were also common among the ancient engagers in the practice of 'speaking the truth', parrhesia, a form

---

[12] Excellent books and even major movies have come out on the topic. The best book on the Snowden's affair are Greenwald (2014) and Harding (2014). Oliver Stone's movie *Snowden* (2016), based on Harding's book, was a major hit in the theaters. By far, the best reconstruction of the Snowden's affair is *Citizenfour* (2014), a documentary directed by Laura Poitras during the early days of Snowden's escape to Hong Kong. Featuring Snowden himself, along with journalists Glenn Greenwald and Ewen MacAskill, the movie won the 2015 Oscar for the best documentary.

of political agency that has come to the attention of scholars thanks to the later work of Michel Foucault.[13]

Parrhesia was a form of speech where the speaker addressed an audience in full sincerity, without the use of rhetoric or any form of manipulation (Foucault 2001: 12). Foucault argues that [t]he *parrhesiastes* is not only sincere and says what is his opinion, but his opinion is also the truth' (ibid.: 14). For the person practicing parrhesia there is no distinction between truth and what she believes, *episteme* and *doxa*. The practice of parrhesia arises in the cultural context of the Greece of the fifth century BC and represents an epistemological attitude unlike most of the modern accounts of truth based on the Platonic tripartite definition of knowledge as justified true belief.[14] Foucault argues that, for the classic Greek thought, the coincidence between belief and truth is not a result of a mental activity but of a verbal one, i.e. parrhesia (ibid.). Truth is something which one possess by the virtue of having certain moral qualities. The sincerity in speaking truth is demonstrated by the courage of speech that is contrary to the belief held by the majority (ibid.: 18). Therefore, parrhesia is a specific verbal activity characterized by 'frankness instead of persuasion, truth instead of falsehood or silence, the risk of death instead of life and security, criticism instead of flattery, and moral duty instead of self-interest and moral apathy (ibid.: 19–20). Ultimately, it is a form of criticism against the powerful in a situation where the speaker or confessor is in a position of inferiority with respect to the interlocutor. The parrhesiastes is always less powerful than the one with whom he or she speaks (ibid.: 17).

Unlike parrhesia, for the modern epistemological sensibility the mere possession of moral qualities and virtues is not sufficient to qualify a person as a truth-teller. Evidence that can survive scrutiny, and the test of reasons, are also required. A whistleblower can be a parrhesiastes only when the speech is backed by facts supporting the accusation. However, whistleblowing shares with parrhesia the moral ideals of truth-telling, courage, non-compulsion, sense of duty, and helping others. Like parrhesia, whistleblowing carries personal and professional risk. Whistleblowers have to overcome the fear of reprisals (Martin 2007),[15] of losing their jobs (Alford 2002; Johnson 2003), of being demoted or denied promotions (ibid.).[16] In some

---

[13] The original Greek term is παρρησῐᾱ (from πᾶς (*pâs*), 'all, every', and ῥῆσις (*rhêsis*), 'utterance, speech.') The Liddell and Scott's *Greek–English Lexicon* defines parrhesia as: '1. outspokenness, frankness, freedom of speech. [...] 2. in bad sense, licence of tongue' (Liddell & Scott 1996). Foucault discussed parrhesia in a series of lectures at the University of California at Berkeley in 1983 (Foucault 2001). He reminds us that the word appeared for the first time in Euripides and became common in the Greek 'world of letters' by the end of the Fifth Century BC (ibid.: 11). An increasing number of authors have discussed the similarities between whistleblowing and parrhesia in contemporary business ethics. See Andrade (2015), Karfakis and Kokkinidis (2011), Lewis and Vandekerckhove (2011), Mansbach (2009, 2011), Nayar (2010); Weiskopf and Willmott (2013); Weiskopf and Tobias-Miersch (2016).

[14] The classic locus of the tripartite definition is Plato's *Theaetetus* (1992: 201c, 202d).

[15] See also Glazer and Glazer (1989) and Neary (1992).

[16] See also Near and Miceli (1986), and Martin and Rifkin (2004).

cases they face assaults, imprisonment, or frame-ups, and are sometimes even accused of mental instability (Mansbach 2009) through the diagnosis of physicians connivent with the organization (Rothschild and Miethe 1994 in Mansbach 2011: 20). Sissela Bok noticed that, already in the 1970s, civil servants were asked to undergo psycho attitudinal tests in an attempt to discredit them (Bok 1980: 278–79). If not the accusation of being mad, they face character assassination and discredit of their motives. Edward Snowden and Chelsea Manning are exemplary cases: the former was accused of being a treasonous spy, while the latter's gender identity was publicly debated (Amoureux 2015: 136). Whistleblowers are often treated not as a truth-teller, but as a problem to be handled, or suppressed if not handled.[17] Despite all this, whistleblowers still engage in fearless speech as the ancient parrhesiastes, often sharing with them moral virtues and the epistemic commitment of lifting the veil of falsehood and deception. Like the ancient parrhesiastes, they are often alone in a hostile environment, where compliance is often synonymous with subordination and oppression.

2.3   Publicity

The ancient tradition of parrhesia was essentially a practice of transparency. Parrhesiastes opposed the men of established power by speaking the truth to them. Contemporary whistleblowers share the same practice. Transparency allows citizens to make informed choices when voting, and to participate in the deliberative sphere of decision making. Transparency in political affairs also contributes to realize the idea of popular sovereignty by informing citizens on which decisions are taken on their behalf, and thus build trust in the government over time. Transparency in the modern constitutional state implies also the publicity of government's acts.[18] Government publicity ensures the accountability of public officials, and that publicly stated goals are met in a just manner by taking into consideration the interests of the citizens.[19] In this section, we explore some of the most influential conceptions on publicity. Our purpose is to clarify how whistleblowing contributes to realize the publicity conditions of a transparent government.

The original point of reference in the modern discussion on publicity is Kant's *Towards A Perpetual Peace*. In the Second Appendix, Kant states that publicness is

---

[17] Brian Martin speaks of a 'suppression of dissent' in the case of those environmentalists in liberal democratic regimes who seek to expose research practices in the industry. See Martin (1981, 1996).

[18] The converse implication is not always true: public can also be interpreted as a property of acts of public officials, regardless whether they are transparent to the public at large. Waldron (2001) shows how even a Hobbesian sovereign is committed to publicity, but not transparency.

[19] For the economic benefit of state transparency, see Sen (1980) who argues that countries with free press do not face famines since the press is able to draw attention to citizens under a state of duress. Stiglitz (2002) argues that less information asymmetry in state affairs allows the citizens to put pressure on their governments for their legitimate demands.

a formal attribute of the law. What he means is that the law, if it is to be in accordance with morality, must be publicly known (in the sense of being publicly promulgated), since without such an attribute 'there can be no justice…and therefore no right' (1991: 125).[20] Kant states that the public quality of the law is an attribute that can be easily proved by every concerned citizen by 'a readily applicable criterion which can be discovered *a priori* within reason itself' (ibid.). The criterion is formulated as a test for the legitimacy of political maxims, what he calls the 'transcendental formula of public law':

> All actions affecting the rights of other human beings are wrong if their maxim is not compatible with their being made public (ibid.: 129).

The 'actions relating to the rights of other men' are what we may call public policies (see Luban 1996: 155), while the maxim is an instantiation of the policy in a particular circumstance. Kant argues that the principle concerns both the moral quality of the agent's intention underlying the maxim, and the rights of citizens affected by the application of the policy. Kant specifies two conditions of publicity that make a policy unjust:

> For a maxim which I may not *declare openly* without thereby frustrating my own intention, or which must at all costs be *kept secret* if it is to succeed, or which I cannot *publicly acknowledge* without thereby inevitably arousing the resistance of everyone to my plans, can only have stirred up this necessary and general (hence *a priori* foreseeable) opposition against me because it is itself unjust and thus constitutes a threat to everyone (Kant 1991: 126; emphasis in the original).[21]

Let's look more closely at these conditions: a policy is unjust (and thus constitute a threat) for every citizen affected by the policy *if*: (i) its public disclosure is incompatible with the intentions the agent has for endorsing the maxim, and thus the success of the policy depends on it being kept secret, *or* (ii) its public acknowledgment will arise resistance from anybody whose rights are affected by that policy. The first condition can be interpreted in various ways. It can be read as a performative contradiction between the intended aim of the maxim and the act of public disclosure, or as a case of self-defeat, that is when making the maxim public leads inevitably to the failure of the policy (Luban 1996: 172). It can also be read as an injunction of political morality that appears to be close to the categorical imperative: one cannot

---

[20] Notice that Kant's interpretation does not reflect the meaning of 'public law'. Public law, as canonically defined in the *Digest of Justinian*, includes the set of laws that regulate the relationship between the state and citizens, while the Private Law concerns the laws that regulate the relationships between citizen and citizen. Luban argues that 'Roman lawyers named such law "public" not because it is publicly promulgated, but because it concerns matters of public interest' (1996: 177).

[21] The conjunction 'or' seems to be used here inclusively, i.e. one condition is sufficient to rule out the maxim as just, but two or more of these conditions may apply at the same time.

rationally will a maxim to be universal and be secret at the same time. According to this reading, universalizability implies publicity.[22]

The second condition concerns the public affected by a policy. Here too we can read this condition in different ways: as saying that a maxim that cannot be made public will be extremely unpopular (Luban 1996: 173), or as an ideal condition in which all rational beings 'serve as judges of the acceptability of a proposed maxim, for only rational agents will necessarily and universally oppose all maxims which threaten their freedom' (K. Davis 1991: 413).

There are two important aspects of the principle of publicity, one clearly stated by Kant, the other more controversial. Kant makes it clear that the test does not say that the maxims that pass the test are right, but only that those that do not pass the test are wrong. It is a *negative* test—Kant writes—serving 'only as a means of detecting what is *not* right in relation to others.' (1991: 126; see also Gosseries and Parr 2017: Section 1.1). Since the test is part of the practical reasoning of a rational agent, it follows that the policy is *not unjust* if the agent has no reason to foresee that any of these conditions apply.

The second aspect concerns the ideal or actual status of the principle. Several writers believe that the test is merely hypothetical, no more than a thought experiment.[23] We can find support for this argument in the interpretation of the conditions discussed above as ideal constraints on publicity: only a perfectly rational agent may act in accordance with publicity, and only an ideal and rational public can judge when the policy is acceptable.[24] Moreover, 'any outcome of actual publicity would inevitably remain at best a rough approximation of what the test would lead us to with an ideal public' (Gosseries and Parr: ibid.). Therefore, we should conclude that the test does not imply 'a moral requirement that every political action actually be publicized,' but only that its maxim should be able to withstand full public knowledge. (Luban 1996: 156).

We agree that Kant did not intend to defend publicity as 'being actually publicized.' Nowhere in the *Perpetual Peace* he says that, and moreover the inference would amount to a logical mistake: the fact that a maxim passes the test of publicity does not imply that the maxim *must* be made public, but only that it should be *possible* to make it public.

---

[22] Gosseries and Parr (2017: Section 1.1) argue that the Kantian test is the equivalent in the political sphere of the categorical imperative. On the same point, Rawls writes that '[p]ublicity is clearly implied in Kant's notion of the moral law' (1999: 115f). Luban's rendering of the derivation is straightforward: 'If I could not publicize my maxim, I surely could not "will that it would become an universal law", for that should be tantamount to willing that it be made public' (1996: 181). However, he takes the textual evidence from the *Perpetual Peace* not to give a definitive answer to the question whether Kant makes a derivation from universalizability to publicity. He rather believes that 'the most plausible answer is that Kant did not distinguish between the universalizability and publicity components of the moral law' (ibid.).

[23] Gosseries and Parr (2017: 1.1), K. Davis (1991: 413), Luban (1996: 156) all agree on this point.

[24] Kevin Davis is the main proponent of this view: 'The only public capable of fulfilling the role as the standard to be used in the principle of publicity is the one of rational agents who demand nothing more than action which respects the right of humanity' (K. Davis 1992: 180, also cited in Gosseries and Parr: ibid.).

More contentious is the reading of publicity as an ideal condition: here the point does not seem to be that a just maxim must be publicized, but that the test can only be applied in ideal circumstances of rationality. According to this interpretation, the test presumes that the agent must reason from the highest point of view regarding his intentions, and foresee the acceptance or rejection of the maxim by a public in ideal conditions of rationality. Despite its scholarly support, this view seems implausible to us. First, it implies that the test is hard, if not impossible to apply, and thus pointless. Second, Kant explicitly says the formula is 'a readily applicable criterion,' which means that it should serve as an *actual test for publicity*, which is different from a *test for actual publicity*. Even if we cannot make a maxim actually public, we can still judge the maxim under the test to determine its capacity of being made public, its publicness as Kant calls it. In fact, as Kant reminds at the beginning of the Second Appendix, publicness is the only formal attribute of the public law, in the sense that it is the only attribute that remains essential to its lawfulness after we have abstracted from other material aspects of the law. In other words, for Kant publicness is an actual property of the public law. The view of publicity as an ideal condition is also quite remote from the moral and political purpose of Kant's project in the Perpetual Peace. It amounts to a conception that can at best engage with public policies only at a generic level, not with its specifics or its application.[25]

In our judgement, the best interpretation of the test is counterfactual. The test asks: if certain conditions of rationality are obtained (which do not obtain in actual conditions), would this maxim be compatible with publicity? The purpose of the test so conceived is to judge whether the law has in fact the attribute of publicness, which can only be detected under counterfactual conditions. We are persuaded that this is the best interpretation of the idea that for Kant the principle determines whether a maxim can withstand the test of publicity.

Who has the prerogative to judge if a policy can withstand the test? As we said, the formula applies to every rational agent, and it could be employed by any concerned person to test her intuition about public matters. That said, we must assume that in the non-ideal conditions of a constitutional democracy, the duty of publicity rests primarily on legislators when they design, propose, and vote a public policy, as well as on public officials when they apply it. How does the test apply to them? We may say that, in designing a policy, legislators and public officials should reason according to the conditions spelled out above: would a law made public contradict the intention of the legislator in designing it? And would the policy find the agreement of every citizen affected by it if they were fully informed of its provisions?

Let's consider first the case of public officials who are called to enact or enforce a secret policy. The whistleblower is a case in point. As part of the due process of deliberation before disclosure, the agent should ask if a secret policy on which she has privileged information would be compatible with its publicity. As we saw, the

---

[25] Luban (1996: 169) argues that since the principle of publicity focuses on maxims, which are general rules of action, the deliberation concerns the level of policies, while their specifics might be kept secret.

question concerns both the intention of the agent if it was made public, and whether she can envisage a full informed public to agree with the policy. It is possible for the would-be whistleblower to accept both the first condition (her reason for accepting a secret policy would be still compatible with its publicity), and foresee that an informed public would agree with the policy staying secret, if they were properly informed. In such a case the agent could refrain from disclosing the information and still pass the test. Of course, a whistleblower who applies the test and actually blows the whistle must have reached a different conclusion: first, that the secrecy of the policy is incompatible with her endorsement of it (the disclosure is a consequence of the fact that she would not support the secret policy if it was made public), and second that if the policy was made public, it would necessarily meet the resistance of the public.

A different, equally interesting, case concerns the legislator. The Kantian test in this case prompts a question about political morality: it involves the political reasoning of the moral politician, as Kant calls the politician sincerely inspired by moral ideals, and of the political moralist, who rather bends her moral principles to the convenience of the political situation. The test of publicity clearly imposes a stringent obligation on the moral politician to foresee whether every citizen affected by the policy would agree with her that passing a secret policy will not threaten their rights. However, public officials cannot always be trusted. They may deceive themselves,[26] or act with malice to make people believe that a secret policy is in everybody's interest when in fact it is not. This is the case of the political moralist. It is a platitude that cases of political convenience are far more common than cases of political morality. Yet, the Kantian test for publicity may serve here a pragmatic, if not a moral purpose. The test requires to judge whether a policy made public would frustrate its purposes, or be conducive to its own defeat. In this regard, we may conclude that, while the scope of the Kantian test is limited in circumstances of realpolitik, it yet retains some of its heuristic force.

Bentham's view of publicity differs substantially from Kant's. First, while for Kant publicity potentially concerns every citizen affected by a secret policy, for Bentham the acts that should fall within the scope of publicity are primarily those of a political assembly—the Parliament. In this sense, the application of publicity has the more limited scope of parliamentary procedures. Second, while for Kant publicity is a negative and hypothetical test that confers *ex post* legitimacy to policies, for Bentham publicity is a condition of actual assembly procedures. In *An Essay on Political Tactics* (Bentham 1838), he argues that the function of publicity is to ensure the accountability and control of the elected members of an assembly. He considers different reasons in favor of publicity. The first is

> …[t]o constrain the members of the assembly to perform their duty. The greater the number of temptations which the exercise of political power is exposed, the more necessary is it to give to who possess it, the most powerful reasons for resisting them. But there is no reason more constant and more universal than superintendence of the public (1838: 310).

---

[26] They might 'persuade themselves that their subjective motivations are unimpeachable, even if it appears to others that they had acted on disreputable reasons' (Chambers 2004: 169).

Bentham's point here is particularly ingenuous: publicity is an incentive to self-regulation against the temptations of political power. Moreover, publicity has a general legitimizing function for the government because it also contributes to 'secure the confidence of the people and their assent to the measures of the legislature' (ibid.). Few pages later, in replying to possible arguments against publicity, he also considers the objection that a system of publicity is a system of distrust: '[w]hom ought we to distrust'—he asks—'if not those to whom is committed great authority, with great temptations to abuse it?' (ibid.: 314). Since the power of public officials increase the possibility of misusing the public office for private gains (sometimes even escaping public scrutiny or prosecution), it is only through publicity—a dread of public judgement, and respect for public opinion—that state officials can be held accountable (ibid.).

Bentham also makes two additional considerations about the epistemic value of publicity. Publicity enables 'the governors to know of the wishes of the governed' (ibid.: 311), and 'is absolutely necessary to enable the electors to act from knowledge' (ibid.: 312); moreover, it provides 'the assembly with the means of profiting by the information of the public' (ibid.).

How much does Bentham concede to secrecy? He recognizes three exceptions to the rule of publicity: when publicity is expected to favor the enemy; to cause unnecessary injury to innocent persons; and to inflict an excessive punishment on the guilty (ibid.: 315). Therefore, unlike Kant, Bentham concedes that the 'law of publicity' cannot be absolute. These exceptions are based on his skepticism for the capacity of the legislator to foresee the consequences of unconditional publicity: 'it is impossible to foresee all the circumstances in which an assembly may find itself placed,' and there are no rules that can be 'formed for a state of trouble and peril' (1838: 315). Clearly this was not a concern for Kant.[27]

Gutmann and Thompson have argued that the Benthamite demands of publicity are not morally binding on public officials if they do not adhere to the utilitarian principle (1996: 98). This judgement may hold in general, but it seems to overlook the fact that Bentham also provides reasons for the epistemic value of an informed public that are independent of utilitarian considerations. When citizens fail to judge in a fair and accurate manner, their mistake is more often due to the concealment of important information rather than to their incapacity.[28] Therefore, to allow common

---

[27] It is arguable how the three exceptions mentioned by Bentham would apply to the Kantian test of publicity. Unnecessary injury and excessive punishment seem to be irrelevant to Kant's idea of publicity. For Kant publicity is not sufficient to make a law just. Since these cases constitute a violation of the 'rights of men', the maxim prescribing these actions would be unjust, no matter whether the maxim is made public. The case of favoring the enemy is more contentious. Bentham has probably in mind here the potential danger to national security due to a domestic enemy or to a foreign state. In the Second Appendix to *Perpetual Peace*, Kant is only concerned with the latter. In this context, he seems to justify secrecy to protect the state from the enemy, but only because international law as such may be incompatible with publicity.

[28] "[Y]ou are incapable of judging, because you are ignorant; and you shall remain ignorant, that you may be incapable of judging' (Bentham 1838: 313).

citizens to form a competent judgement, they need a sufficient amount of information (ibid.: 312–13).

In conclusion, although secrecy may be needed sometimes, it should be avoided as a general practice of politics, because it 'is an instrument of conspiracy; it ought not, therefore, to be the system of a regular government' (Bentham 1838: 315).

Similar considerations about the epistemic value of publicity can be found in John Stuart Mill's *Considerations on Representative Government* (Mill 1977). Mill argues that although publicity is per se 'no impediment to evil nor stimulus to good if the public will not look at what is done'… 'without publicity, how could they either check or encourage what they were not permitted to see?' (1977: 391). Like Bentham, Mill takes publicity to be both a principle of legitimation and a mechanism of popular control of the government. As a principle of legitimation, publicity is a requirement for the representation of the people in the affairs of the state, making them participants in the government and 'sharers in the instruction and mental exercise derivable from it' (ibid.: 436). As a mechanism of control, publicity is a method for the representative assembly to

> watch and control the government: to throw the light of publicity on its acts: to compel a full exposition and justification of all of them which any one considers questionable; to censure them if found condemnable, and, if the men who compose the government abuse their trust, or fulfil it in a manner which conflicts with the deliberate sense of the nation, to expel them from office, and either expressly or virtually appoint their successors (ibid.: 432).

Along with Kant and Bentham, Mill's conception of publicity provides a historical framework for one of the tenets of the morality of whistleblowing, the claim that accountability is an essential mechanism for a well-functioning democratic process. By ensuring access to information, otherwise unavailable through other means, whistleblowers make governments accountable to the public opinion. It is less clear whether whistleblowing contributes, as well, to the legitimating function of democratic government. Admittedly, the argument that whistleblowers cause distrust and suspicion towards the government has some plausibility. At the same time, we should be careful in equating distrust with lack of legitimation. Distrust towards the private interests of public officials is a reason for establishing norms of public control but, once in place, those norms legitimize the institutions that enforce them. Distrust can also foster, not only erode, legitimation. Whistleblowing cannot be a regular practice, but when the general norms of public control are malfunctioning, or do not exist, unauthorized disclosures can play the subsidiary role of public accountability. In this sense, whistleblowing contributes to the legitimacy of public institutions not only by the mere act of disclosure, but also when public institutions devise measures of legal protection for whistleblowers that serve this subsidiary role.

John Rawls' discussion of publicity departs from the previous considerations. He shares with Kant the idea that justice requires publicity, but unlike Kant publicity, for him, is not a property of maxims, but of the basic institutions of society. Moreover, unlike Bentham and Mill, he is not primarily concerned with the legitimation of acts of real-world governments; nor he considers publicity as a method of control of the executive power. Instead, publicity is a formal and procedural aspect of the justification of the principles of justice.

This conception is originally presented in *A Theory of Justice* (1999). In this work, Rawls argues that publicity is a property of (the system of) rules that constitute the basic structure of society (the object of the theory). The publicity of these rules consists in the fact that they are effectively known or available to be known by every member, and its justification follows from the equal claim every member has to know what to expect from the institutions regulating social cooperation. Consequently, publicity ensures that those engaged in an institution know what 'limitations on conduct to expect of one another and what kinds of actions are permissible'(ibid.: 49). Such knowledge for Rawls is common to all, that is everyone engaged in an institution is aware of 'what the rules demand of him and of the others. He also knows that the others know this and that they know that he knows this, and so on' (ibid.: 48–9). This conception of publicity is subject to a refinement in *Political Liberalism* (2005), where he details out the role of publicity in the constructivist justification of a political conception of justice.[29] He calls it full publicity.

Rawls argues that publicity has a narrow and a wider role. The narrow role is 'restricted to achieving the more or less minimum conditions of effective social cooperation, for example, to specifying standards to settle competing claims to setting up rules of coordinating and stabilizing social arrangements. Public norms are regarded as inhibiting self- or group-centered tendencies' (ibid.: 71). Only full publicity is part of the wider role of a political conception. It concerns a well-ordered society, that is a society effectively regulated by the principles of justice[30]: 'to realize the full publicity condition is to realize a social world within which the ideal of citizenship can be learned and may elicit an effective desire to be that kind of person' (ibid.).

---

[29] Here he distinguishes between three levels of publicity: the first level is 'when society is effectively regulated by public principles of justice: citizens accept and know that others likewise accept those principles, and this knowledge in turn is publicly recognized' (Rawls 2005: 66). At the second level, 'publicity concerns the general beliefs in the light of which first principles of justice themselves can be accepted, that is, the general beliefs about human nature and the way political and social institutions generally work, and indeed all such beliefs relevant to political justice' (ibid.). These beliefs are roughly agreed upon by citizens in a well ordered society 'because they can be supported (as at the first level) by publicly shared methods of inquiry and forms of reasoning' (ibid.: 67). These two levels can be modeled within the framework of the original position under a veil of ignorance. The third level 'includes everything that we would say—you and I— when we set up justice as fairness and reflect why we proceed in one way rather than another. At this level I suppose this full justification also to be publicly known, or better, at least to be publicly available' (ibid.). At this level publicity is a condition that must be satisfied by 'a political conception of justice for reasonable and rational citizens who are free and equal' (ibid.).

[30] A well-ordered society is a society effectively regulated by the principles of justice: every social member accepts and knows that the others accept, and the basic institutions act according to those principles (Rawls 1999: 397).

Of the two versions, only the first one is relevant to the present discussion. Whistleblowing disclosures at this level are symptomatic of a divergence between the rules governing social institutions and the actual practices within such institutions. They can also help to restore public norms against the prevalence of private interests. However, whistleblowing has a public role exclusively in non well-ordered societies, where the principles of justice are not satisfied by the social institutions. The function and justification of whistleblowing emerge only in the non-ideal conditions of justice where full publicity is not satisfied. Of course, full publicity can serve as a regulative ideal, or as a standard of judgment for societies in partial compliance with justice. In this sense, there is room for a normative justification of whistleblowing within the ideal/non-ideal theory debate on justice. But, the question itself 'is whistleblowing justifiable in a well-ordered society?' does not even admit an answer, because whistleblowers are not part of a social world inhabited by ideal citizens.

Perhaps one of the most comprehensive views of publicity in the literature of the last 20 years is Amy Gutmann and Dennis Thompson's *Democracy and Disagreement* (1996). Here they argue that reciprocity and democratic value of openness and transparency demands public reasons by both officials and citizens. The core of their proposal is that public policies are justifiable only if they have gone through a process of public deliberation. Public deliberation may also justify secret or confidential policies, but their necessity cannot be determined by public officials alone; it must also include the larger public and those who are affected by such policies (Gutmann and Thompson 1996: 104). Their proposal is to subject secrecy policies to a double deliberative evaluation. The test involves a two-order deliberation: the first in which a secret is justified only if it 'promotes deliberation on the merits of a public policy'. Merit here refers to whether a certain policy is of general or national interest. Informed citizens involved in public deliberation at this level can agree that keeping certain information confidential contributes to their well-being, as well to democratic stability. A policy can be justified at this level with larger consensus, especially in times of emergency when confidentiality is essential to make security measures effective. The second-order deliberation is satisfied only if citizens and their representatives have been able to deliberate at the first level, and consider whether keeping a policy secret affects negatively the 'deliberations on the merit of the public policy'(ibid.: 117). Deliberation at this level does not concern the content of the policy, but whether the procedures favor the first-order deliberation. For instance, information concerning why the introduction of a new policy should be classified, as well as the risk that could follow if the policy was made public, are considerations that enhance the epistemic capacity of citizens to decide whether the policy should be secreted. As an example, they suggest the case of the deployment of unmarked cars by the police. Details of the operations can remain covert insofar as there is a public knowledge of the deployment. 'The fact that the details of the policy are secret—they argue—is not itself a secret' (ibid.), but citizens must be able to judge the policy in advance and review its details post implementation (ibid.). If citizens involved in the deliberation are deprived of sufficient time and information to evaluate the content of the policy, their deliberative capacity is frustrated, and the quality of first-order deliberation is negatively affected. The details of a policy and its particular application in a given context can be secret only insofar as the policy itself is not secret.

Secrecy policies that pass the double evaluation are therefore public in the sense specified by the theory: they are an outcome of a public deliberation, and their procedures contribute to a better public deliberation. Not all forms of secrecy are public in this double sense. Consider the cases of deceptive and deep secrecy. Deceptive secrets are those intended to make citizens believe something known to be false (ibid.). Deep secrets instead are those whose very existence is hidden from the citizens (ibid.: 121).[31] If we accept the double deliberative standard, neither deceptive nor deep secrecy can ever be justified, because they frustrate the purpose of the second-order deliberation.

We may ask, at this point, whether whistleblowing disclosures contribute to the publicity standards of the theory. For the sake of the argument, we consider only those cases where deliberation concerns the opportunity to implement a secrecy measure or to classify a certain information. The first consideration we should make is that whistleblowers are not participants in the debate: they do not take part in the exchange of reasons in the discussion, nor they deliberate as part of a deliberative body. They deliberate in private, not in public.

The second consideration concerns the deliberative contribution of whistleblowers. Let us assume that a stand-alone whistleblower reflects on the opportunity to disclose information regarding a policy she believes to be of public interest, and while she does so there is a concomitant deliberative forum that is called upon to decide whether some covert investigation allowed by the same policy should remain classified. Take as an example the case of a new anti-terrorism policy to be implemented following a terrorist attack. We may imagine that the whistleblower has come in possession of critical information that the agency in charge of the investigation is abusing its power by profiling a specific group in an anti-terrorism operation that requires covert action, gathering sensitive data of some persons without probable cause, bugging their houses, and even conducting unwarranted searches. While the deliberative assembly is discussing whether to keep this policy in place, the whistleblower decides to go public and release the information of the abuses. How is the assembly affected by the decision? One way to look at this situation is this: the whistleblower affects the decision of the assembly by providing an information that will influence the opinion against the policy without her being part of the deliberation itself. We should then conclude that the decision of the whistleblower to leak a confidential information does not serve the deliberative purpose of a reasoned and informed decision. Not so fast though. Consider the case in which a secret policy can be effective only if the agency in charge of its implementation exercises

---

[31] Gutmann and Thompson distinguish deceptive and deep secrecy from 'shallow' secrecy. Shallow is a secret whose existence, but not the actual information, is known to citizens (ibid.: 121). While shallow secrets allow for a certain form of accountability, deep and deceptive secrets often end up compromising the democratic norms of deliberation, publicity, participation, and accountability, and thus are hard to justify.

a discretionary power of investigation that goes completely under the radar. This is a policy containing deeply secrets provisos. In such circumstances, the leak will provide an information especially relevant for the higher-order deliberation. Among the aspects of the policy on which the assembly should deliberate, there is also how to keep control of covert operations that might trespass the limit of the law. But deep secrets deprive the assembly of any possibility to gain access to information about abuses, because the assembly would be unaware of them. Its deliberative power would be compromised.

Whistleblowing is about circumstances that often escape public notice and scrutiny because of the veil of secrecy surrounding them. In some circumstances, even when the need for secrecy is agreed among citizens and legislators, secrecy might preclude accountability and empower those who control information.

In conclusion, whistleblowing disclosures can affect public deliberation in opposite ways. Whistleblowers may cut across the deliberative debate without subjecting their reasons to common criticism, but they can also provide critical information that a deliberative assembly could not otherwise take into account. If whistleblowing in one sense disregards the value of common deliberation on which policies to classify, in another it is instrumental to the public aim of the best informed deliberation.

2.4   The Current State of Whistleblowing Theory

The literature on whistleblowing of the last 30 years has mainly focused on the so-called corporate whistleblowers, although the varieties of practices falling under the term often include whistleblowers in the public sector, including those disclosing information of national security. Despite its growing momentum in the public discourse, a unifying analysis seems to be still missing, inducing the common confusion with spying, squealing, sneaking (M. Davis 2003: 539; Jubb 1999: 77). In this section we discuss the main attempts to provide a general account of whistleblowing. In the next section we present a general definition and assess it against the background of the current debate.

2.4.1   The Moral Choice View

Whistleblowers are often caught in dilemmas between conflicting civic and organizational duties, between integrity and loyalty, and often their good faith is questioned. Sissela Bok (1980) was the first author to point out the predicament whistleblowers face in their moral choices. She argues that whistleblowers must evaluate three aspects of their action: the accuracy of judgement, the breach of loyalty, and accusation. These aspects 'impose certain requirements: of accuracy and judgment in dissent; of exploring alternative ways to cope with improprieties, thus minimizing the breach of loyalty; and of fairness in accusation' (1980: 285).

The first aspect concerns the accuracy of judgment about facts on which they dissent. Since whistleblowing is in the benefit of the public, whistleblowers are obliged to ascertain the 'nature of this benefit, and to consider also the possible harm that may come from speaking out: harm to persons or institutions, and ultimately to the public interest itself' (ibid.). They are required to 'assure themselves of the accuracy of their reports, checking and rechecking the facts before speaking out; specify the degree to which there is genuine impropriety; consider how imminent is the threat they see, how serious, and how closely linked to those accused of neglect or abuse' (ibid.). Public disclosures should only be made when the facts warrant it.

Once the facts have been ascertained, whistleblowers must ensure that the existing alternatives for change have been explored and rejected before breaching their duty of loyalty. Alternatives may be rejected 'if they simply do not apply to the problem at hand, or when there is not time to go through routine channels, or when the institution is so corrupt or coercive that steps will be taken to silence the whistleblower should he try the regular channels first' (ibid.: 286). When possible alternatives have been ruled out, the considerations of public interest for breaching the role obligations become preponderant, and no oath or promise of confidentiality can be excused 'for complicity in covering up a crime or a violation of the public's trust' (ibid.).[32]

The third aspect concerns the possible accusation against the possibility of self-gain from disclosures or bias against persons. The whistleblower must exercise fairness in judgement and guard against any personal motives that influence a disclosure. The motivation should be backed by concerns of public interest and awareness of 'any motive that might skew their message; a desire for self-defense in a difficult bureaucratic situation, perhaps, or the urge to seek revenge, or inflated expectations regarding the effect that their message will have on the situation' (ibid.: 287). Along with self-guard, fairness also demands that the whistleblower should identify herself publicly and accept responsibility for disclosures. The publicity requirement becomes more binding if the allegations are derogatory or serious in nature. Most importantly, revealing one's identity allows for fact-checking, examination of evidence and motives and enables the accused to defend themselves (ibid.). That said, she concedes that the risk of retaliation may require, in some instances, anonymous disclosures. But anonymous disclosures usually raise suspicion in the public opinion, with the consequent risk of not being taken seriously. Moreover, anonymity imposes a strong obligation 'to let the accused know of the accusation leveled, and to produce independent evidence that can be checked' (ibid.: 287). Given that disclosures can often be grounded in bias or motivated by desires of self-gain even

---

[32] The oath of confidentiality can be overridden—Bok also argues—if the specific obligations 'were obtained under duress, or through deceit. They can be overridden, too, if they promise something that is in itself wrong or unlawful' (Bok 1980: 286).

when they are in the public interest, it is important for whistleblowers to consult and seek advice to reduce any bias or error in moral choice (ibid.: 288).

For the Moral Choice View whistleblowing is essentially a problem of practical deliberation (see Brenkert 2010). Bok is less concerned with a principled justification. Her merit is instead to present a step by step guide for action, a blueprint for educational purposes. Bok also has the merit of pointing out that it is in the agent's best judgement to decide when a disclosure is in the public interest. However, her argument lacks sufficient depth. There is little understanding of what the notion of public interest should designate. Disagreements about the definition of public interest may arise because of ambiguity, vagueness, or because public interest is an essentially contested concept.[33] None of these options seem to apply to Bok's use of public interest. Bok seems instead to have in mind that what justifies a disclosure is the whistleblower's personal conviction of what is the public interest. But consider the example of a classified information containing evidence of wrongdoing. For an employee, the fact that the information is classified may be a sufficient reason to think that its secrecy is in the public interest. For another, it is the evidence of a wrongdoing that justifies the disclosure in the public interest. The disagreement here is on which facts count in the decision. The two employees could even agree on what public interest is, but disagree on the facts that are relevant to uphold the public interest. The person's best judgement cannot be based exclusively on what she personally believes to be in the public interest. We need also an account of the facts relevant for the public interest.

2.4.2   The Standard Theory

Bok's work on secrecy and lying in the early 1980s contributed to create the new field of applied philosophy, opening up a space for discussion between professional philosophers and business scholars. It is not surprising that her early work on whistleblowing had a large echo in business ethics. Richard De George (1990, 2014) was among the first to formulate a comprehensive account—now called *standard*—in business ethics.[34] For De George, employees should be rarely obliged to blow the whistle, and no demand should be put on them to become a hero. The obligations raised by cases of whistleblowing rest instead with the corporations; they should establish channels of disclosures or communication. Yet, in absence of such procedures, circumstances may arise that force employees to disclose information outside

---

[33] We will discuss these cases in Chap. 3. For a reference on vagueness and how it is distinguished from ambiguity, see Sorensen (2016) and Williamson (1994). On essentially contested concepts, see Gallie (1956), and Waldron (2002) for an application to the law.

[34] Standard theory is the term used by Michael Davis (1996) to describe De George's account.

institutional channels. In these circumstances, whistleblowing is a moral obligation 'to prevent serious harm to others if they can do so with little cost to themselves' (2014: 321). De George distinguishes two levels of justification. The first is the level of permissibility.

1. The firm, through its product or policy, will do serious and considerable harm to employees or to the public, whether in the person of the user of its product, an innocent bystander, or the general public;
2. Once the employees identify a serious threat to the user of a product or to the general public, they should report it to their immediate superior and make their moral concern known;
3. If one's immediate superior does nothing effective about the concern or complaint, the employee should exhaust the internal procedures and possibilities within the firm. This usually will involve taking the matter up the managerial ladder and, if necessary—and possible—to the board of directors (De George 2014: 327–29).

Whistleblowing is morally required when in addition to the above three conditions the following two obtain:

4. The whistleblower must have, or have accessible, documented evidence that would convince a reasonable, impartial observer that one's view of the situation is correct, and that the company's product or practice poses a serious and likely danger to the public or user of the product;
5. The employee must have good reasons to believe that by going public the necessary changes will be brought about. The chance of being successful must be worth the risk one takes and the danger to which one is exposed (ibid.: 330–32).

The Standard Account is a form of constrained consequentialism. It is a consequentialist view because the justification of disclosure rests in the assessment of the harm, not on the intent of the disclosure. Whistleblowing is justified when the harms caused by the firm are sufficiently serious to trump the obligation of loyalty to the company. It is constrained by evidence and reason: harms need to be properly assessed, and all internal procedures of disclosures should be exhausted, before the employee considers external reporting based on the reasonable belief that the disclosure would lead to the possibility of change.

De George's account has been criticized for its demandingness. Michael Hoffman and Mark Schwartz argue that an assessment of the seriousness of the harm is 'too difficult, onerous, or subjective a criterion' (2014: 341). They suggest that it is difficult for an employee to ascertain 'what might be "serious" harm due to the lack of awareness of all of the potential implications of even minor misconduct, or whether the minor misconduct might actually represent the tip of major wrongdoing or a scandal' (ibid.). They propose to extend De George's account to make whistleblowing morally required 'for any observed misconduct with any degree of potential harm, leaving the recipients of the whistleblower's information (e.g. government regulators, the media, or special interest groups) with the responsibility to determine whether the reported activity is "serious" enough to render appropriate action to be taken'(ibid.). They suggest that the wrongdoer should be warned before undertaking any disclosure, but insist on loosening the evidence requirement and replace it with the obligation to provide 'reasonable evidence or belief based on first-hand knowledge.' As for the idea that the whistleblower should believe the disclosure will be 'making a difference', they suggest that this criterion should be discarded altogether. They conclude that in absence of anti-retaliation policies, there is no obligation to blow the whistle (ibid.: 344). Whistleblowing, in this revised account, is morally obligatory only when two conditions obtain: first, public disclosures should be legally protected; second, the role obligations of the employee make it a duty to prevent harms to the society (ibid.: 345).

In our view, the revised account correctly insists that it is beyond reasonability to ask the whistleblower to have good reasons to believe the disclosure will bring about a change. Whistleblowers should be responsible for an effective communication to the authority or the public at large, but they alone cannot ensure that the necessary changes will be made. Once the disclosure is made, and all available evidence passed over, it is incumbent upon the investigative agencies to follow up. However, they also introduce the more controversial requirement of advance warning. Why should the potential perpetrators of the wrongdoing be given advance warning, when they have all the reasons to stop the disclosure? This requirement seems rather counterproductive, even more when the party is in a position of influence, and can affect the investigation process or even stall the process of disclosure. It also undermines the very effort to come out in public, especially when personal risks of retaliation are high.

2.4.3   Complicity

Michael Davis has argued that the focus on harm prevention excludes actions generally considered to be whistleblowing (M. Davis 1996: 10). His complicity account is meant to shift the focus from the prevention of the harm to the responsibility in the wrongdoing. Under a complicity account, whistleblowing is obligatory when it is the only way to avoid the blame of being a contributor to the wrongdoing. Complicity, argues M. Davis, 'invokes a more demanding obligation than the ability to prevent harm does' because individuals are obliged to avoid doing moral wrongs, including remaining silent on 'facts necessary to correct a serious injustice' (ibid.: 10, 12). More precisely, under Davis' account, a person is morally required to disclose to the public when: what she reveals derives from her work for an organization; she is a voluntary member of that organization; she believes that the organization, although legitimate, is engaged in serious moral wrongdoing; she believes that her work for the organization contributes (more or less directly) to the wrong unless she publicly reveals what she knows (ibid.: 11).[35]

---

[35] Davis adds also the clause that the person must not only hold a sincere belief that the organization is committing a wrongdoing, but she must also be justified in holding the belief.

Notice that complicity does not demand 'enough evidence to convince others of the wrong in question.' Convincing others, or 'just being able to convince them, is not, as such, an element in the justification of whistle-blowing'. Rather, it requires 'the whistleblower be *justified* in her beliefs about the organization's wrongdoing and her part in it, but also that she be *right* about them' (ibid.: 13, emphasis in the original).

David Kline (2006) has argued that the complicity account fails to recognize the public and the civic dimension of whistleblowing. By emphasizing the contributory role of the whistleblower—he argues—M. Davis fails to appreciate the fact that a person does not need to fear the blameworthiness of complicity to decide to go public (ibid.: 261). He cites the example of Jeffrey Wigand, who disclosed information regarding the addictive nature of smoking while conducting research on safe cigarettes. Wigand had not causally contributed to the wrong he blew the whistle on. A person can blow the whistle not merely to avoid personal complicity, but when she becomes aware of a wrongdoing, whether she contributes to it or not (ibid.: 262).

In the same vein, Peter Jubb (1999) has also defended a view of whistleblowing based on its contributory role. However, his focus is not avoiding complicity per se, but the role of whistleblowers in redressing wrongs. Jubb argues that we should distinguish between a backward-looking and a forward-looking account of complicity. On the backward-looking view, 'X…is morally responsible for a wrong committed by Y if X's own earlier action contributes causally to Y's wrongdoing'. Since X and Y share the moral responsibility for Y's conduct, 'X can then be held morally at fault if Y's wrongdoing is a foreseeable consequence of his action' (1999: 82). However, causal responsibility is only one way people can be held responsible. On the forward-looking account instead a person does not need to causally contribute to someone else's wrong to be held responsible, as long as she can act after becoming aware of the wrong. The person can be judged morally culpable for *her* own action by remaining silent, thus condoning someone else's wrong and showing lack of respect for the victims and condoning the wrong (ibid.: 82).

In our opinion, the force of the complicity argument rests on the philosophical thesis that there is no sound distinction between action and omission. The thesis has an obvious ethical significance: a person who omits to act to prevent some bad consequences is equally responsible as if she had caused those consequences by acting. The same idea applies to the case of complicity: both the claim that a person is responsible when she does not report a wrong she has causally contributed to, and the further claim that not avoiding harm is tantamount to contributing to the cause follow from the thesis. Once we assume this thesis as a premise, it is easy to see why both views conclude that whistleblowing is morally obligatory.

We will not discuss the philosophical cogency of this view here. It will suffice to notice that in the case of whistleblowing other considerations matter for the justification of disclosures. The first of them is that a would-be whistleblower may have other reasons for *not* disclosing information: personal safety is the most important, but also the risk of failure counts. Of course, we concede that if the would-be whistleblower has contributed somehow to the wrongdoing, she might have a over-riding reason to go public to expiate her guilt. This reason however has nothing to do with the aim of blowing the whistle. A would-be whistleblower may seek for-giveness by exposing herself, without contributing effectively to justice.

The second consideration is that the prescription that one ought to blow the whis-tle to avoid complicity is even more problematic when we consider the case of the person who omits to do so when she has not contributed to the wrongdoing. There is a morally significant difference between the person who has somehow contributed or benefited from a wrongdoing, and the person who just comes in possession of the information about a wrongdoing. We find it self-evident that the moral obligation to go public, when one's fundamental interests are at risk and the prospects of success are volatile, is unreasonable in theory and ineffective in practice. To be sure, we are not claiming that the faultless person is not blameworthy when she can act to avoid harm. If she can do it at little cost for herself, she should act and is blameworthy if she does not. However she does not have a moral obligation to do so.

The third consideration concerns the reasons for disclosure. A whistleblower can act upon reasons that are independent of the burdens of complicity: truth-telling and public interest are among them. A whistleblower can also act upon less noble reasons, including self-gain, rancor against a colleague, and even in the pursuit of a reward when the laws permits it. More often, a whistleblower acts upon mixed rea-sons, where the good motives for disclosure are reinforced by personal incentives. When the whistleblower acts upon these reasons, or a mix of them, the burdens of complicity are not the primary reason for action. Discharging those burdens may contribute to the decision, but only as part of a cluster of reasons. Assuming the burdens of complicity as the main criterion of justification for disclosure reflects a poor understanding of the moral psychology of whistleblowers.

2.4.4 Integrity

Any justification of whistleblowing we have reviewed so far insists on the principle of responsibility in one way or another. A whistleblower is responsible to act in the public interest, to avoid harm, or to escape complicity in wrongdoing. However few authors till recently, with the exception of the early Bok, have explored the virtues of whistleblowing. In a more recent proposal, George Brenkert (2010) has called attention to the value of integrity and its significance for professional responsibility. He argues that what a person stands for, the commitments one wants to live by, and what kind of person she wants to be, are integral part of the morality of whistleblow-ing (ibid.: 589). However, integrity does not mean being just faithful to one's own deepest convictions. On the contrary, the integrity of the whistleblowers depends on the positional responsibility they occupy within the organization, that is: 'one's other responsibility to the organization, the possibility of effectively reporting the wrongdoing, and the risks to oneself, one's other responsibilities and projects' (ibid.: 575). To blow a whistle requires considering 'whether one has good moral reasons to blow the whistle but also whether one should, all things considered, blow the whistle given the balance of responsibilities and ideal forms of behavior to which he or she is committed' (ibid.). Since integrity means evaluating responsibilities on the balance, a person is morally obliged to blow the whistle only

> when the wrongdoings are of a significant nature (either individually or collectively), when one has special knowledge due to one's circumstances that others lack, when one has a privileged relationship with the organization through which the wrongdoing is occurring (or has occurred), and when others are not attempting to correct the wrongdoing (ibid.: 582).

There is an important insight here: given her position in the organization, a person may have information that others do not possess. When this is the case, and the information concerns a serious wrongdoing, the person has an obligation to contribute to the process of redress by disclosing the information. The responsibility to disclose depends on the *stringency* of the situation and the weight attached to it based on a reading of the personal situation and abilities (ibid.: 584–85, emphasis in the original). That said, when the circumstances do not oblige to disclose, blowing the whistle is supererogatory, and can only be praised when it occurs (ibid.: 588).

Brenkert, M. Davis, and Jubb seem to be motivated by opposite concerns: professional integrity is accepting one's role as a participant in the organization, not avoiding complicity in wrongdoing. Fair enough, we may say: integrity does not justify evasion from one's responsibility. But, consider again the point of complicity: a person is complicit in wrongdoing even when she omits to act, not only when she has actively contributed to cause it. Can a person maintain her integrity by simply refusing to participate in a wrongdoing instead of blowing the whistle? The question is not marginal: often employees with a strong sense of duty find themselves caught between conflicting loyalties, not only towards their firm but also towards colleagues. It is not rare that a disclosure may lead to lawsuits and financial risks, including loss of jobs for employees who have no responsibility in the wrongdoing. On the balance of reasons, the person may then conclude that the mere refusal to participate in the wrongdoing can save the firm and her colleagues from the disruptive consequences of a disclosure. Cases like this call upon the very definition of integrity and the duties it implies. If non involvement in wrongdoing is sufficient to preserve one's integrity, then the person who decides not to blow the whistle in conflicting circumstances is not blameworthy. Conscientious refusal, a term by which scholars sometimes indicate conscientious objection, is a model for the justification of noninvolvement. However, refusal and noninvolvement are difficult to distinguish from evasion, a practice that in common morality we perceive to be at odds with the virtue of integrity. This tension sheds light on the fact that integrity requires more than conscientious refusal. It refers also to a civic virtue, that is a habit of conduct defined by an ideal of good citizenship involving participation in the public life. Therefore, the employees who conceive of themselves as good citizens, ought to consider their commitments towards their fellow-citizens, and integrity may require prioritising them over the responsibilities towards the firm and fellow-colleagues.

2.4.5 *Whistleblowing as a Civic Duty*

The civic nature of whistleblowing is also crucial for Candice Delmas (2015), who argues that whistleblowing is a form of political vigilantism that challenges the state allocation of power, and—by transgressing the boundaries of state secrets—determines the proper scope of secrecy and the purpose to which institutional resources of the state are deployed. Delmas assumes that the state's allocation of power is never absolute and can be overruled by countervailing considerations. Whistleblowers act legitimately within this contested space, and have a prima facie duty to disclose 'when the state does not constitute a dependable disclosure recipient' (2014: 60):

> When institutions fail to be trustworthy, this general responsibility entails special vigilance or alertness, which is not only an appropriate response to imperfect and less-than-trustworthy institutions, but is also a significant tool to enhancing institutions' trustworthiness, by holding them (and officials in them) accountable (ibid.).

The civic duty of keeping the citizens informed 'enhances the community's epistemic position and promotes its self-determination' (ibid.: 61). Hence, 'graver the wrong, the more important the benefits, the weightier the duty' (ibid.). She presents three conditions that need to be satisfied for a justification of whistleblowing. They are neither necessary nor sufficient but *ceteris paribus* constraints on justifiable government whistleblowing. First is *the subject condition*:

> The moral duty to respect the allocation of state power is overridden—and government whistleblowing may be justified—when the state conceals from the public serious government wrongdoing or programs and policies that ought to be known and deliberated about (ibid.: 96).

Under the subject condition whistleblowing is justified when it exposes severe crisis in political legitimacy due to secrecy, serious wrongdoing, and informational deficits. Policies need not involve genuine wrongdoing to qualify as a candidate for disclosure. Rather, the subject of disclosure can be even those policies that escape public deliberation and scrutiny because of secrecy. Edward Snowden's disclosure on domestic spying program, and disclosures on CIA's black sites would constitute an example of justified whistleblowing under this account. Second is *the act condition*:

> The act (i.e., unlawful acquisition and disclosure of secret information) should generally be undertaken after lawful attempts to make the information public have been attempted, unless there are reasons to think these would be useless (ibid.: 96).

Under the act condition, internal disclosures should be preferred over external revelations. Public disclosures are only justified when attempting internal disclosures is constrained or has proven to be futile in the past. The third one is *minimize the harm* condition:

> The whistleblower should take serious precautions in the disclosure so as to minimize the harms that could potentially ensue, including carefully choosing the leaks' recipients and editing the information (ibid.: 96).

Delmas' is perhaps the most convincing account of whistleblowing in the recent literature. One of her merits is to have shifted the attention from the dominant debate on the morality of corporate disclosures to the political dimension of government whistleblowing. We agree that in contexts of national emergency where the allocation of power is contested, institutions can become less than trustworthy, especially when the power of secrecy is increasingly concentrated in the hands of the executive (and in the agencies depending on it). In such a case, it is reasonable to say that citizens have a civic duty to stay alert (and thus vigilant!) against the arbitrary use of government power. However, it is important to remark that vigilance against the arbitrary use of state power is not a form of political vigilantism, when by this term we mean the practice of undertaking personal justice against a wrong. Vigilantism in this second sense is a narrative apt for rogue contexts characterized by widespread injustice, violence, lack of democracy, violation of rights, sometimes hardly distinguishable from personal revenge. We will come back to vigilantism in Chap. 5.

2.4.6   Good Faith and Loyalty

One of the most debated aspects of whistleblowing concerns the weight we should give to the reasons for disclosure. De George (2014), Bowie and Duska (1990) argue that whistleblowing should be governed by appropriate moral motives: the good faith requirement is meant to rule out malicious intentions and disclosures motivated by personal gain. Any disclosure pursued for personal gain—to score a point over the employer or a fellow employee, to disrepute them, or for mixed motives—would not qualify as legitimate. For this reason, disclosures should be backed by evidence, with the reasonable belief that a wrongdoing has effectively occurred and can be redressed only through a public disclosure.

The good faith requirement is also recognized in many legislations,[36] although recent trends demonstrate a partial change of attitude in the opposite direction.[37] A good faith requirement is demanding, and can also rule out public interest disclosures.

---

[36] Many international conventions require disclosures to be done in good faith for them to be eligible for protection. Some examples are the *United Nations Convention against Corruption, 2003; the OECD Convention on Combating Bribery of Foreign Public Officials in International Business Transactions; the Economic Community of West African States Protocol on the Fight Against Corruption, 2001. The Sapin II law in France enacted in 2016, the Protection of Whistleblowers Act 2013 in Malta, the Dutch House for Whistleblowers Act 2016 in Netherlands, the Integrity and Prevention of Corruption Act in Slovenia, the Complaints and Public Disclosure Act* of 2014 in Hungary also have a good faith requirement for the whistleblowers to qualify for protection, while the Romanian anti-corruption law assumes that whistleblowers are acting in good faith until proven otherwise.

[37] The *UK Public Interest Disclosure Act*, 1998 originally had a provision for good faith which was amended in 2003. Ireland's *Protected Disclosure Act* (2014) also does not have a good faith requirement.

Motives can also be misrepresented to sound as genuine when they are far from it (Jubb 1999: 89). Good faith can also be controversial, often difficult to ascertain given the subjective nature of assessment, and raise concerns of testimonial fairness when the word of the whistleblower is not given credibility. Moreover, motives may also be not transparent to the whistleblower herself, who may act for more than one reason. It seems then that an evaluation of the intent provides only a negative criterion for ruling out malicious motives, rather than establishing good faith.

Along with good faith, another often cited reason against disclosure is the duty of loyalty that employees owe to their organization and their fellow colleagues. Loyalty in whistleblowing is a controversial topic that has evoked multiple responses. For De George an agreement to work for a firm requires not only a sufficient degree of commitment towards her work but also a positive attitude towards the organization and fellow employees (2014: 325). Loyalty can emerge from the gratitude for employment (especially in an economy where unemployment is high), and further because workers have a stake in the firm, which requires a 'positive concern' for the enterprise, 'if not full identification' with it (ibid.). Loyalty however—he argues—cannot be always binding. When the firm or organization requires the employee to engage in wrongdoings and hide a harm from the general public, the role obligation that grounds the duty vanishes (ibid.). In the same vein, Norman Bowie (1982: 140–43) maintains that whistleblowing is a *prima facie* violation of the duty of loyalty towards the employer, which can be overridden by considerations of higher duties in the name of the public good. Sissela Bok also defends a similar position, when she argues that

> the whistleblower hopes to stop the game; but since he is neither referee nor coach, and since he blows the whistle on his own team, his act is seen as a violation of loyalty. In holding his position, he has assumed certain obligations to his colleagues and clients: stepping out of channels to level accusations is regarded as a violation of these obligations. Loyalty to colleagues and to clients comes to be pitted against loyalty to the public interest, to those who may be injured unless the revelation is made (1980: 281).

In addition, whistleblowers face pressures from within the institution where fidelity 'to one's agency, to one's superiors, and to colleagues is stressed in countless ways. It may be supported by a loyalty oath, or a promise of confidentiality' (ibid.). So a whistleblower is someone with divided loyalties and before disclosing should balance their responsibility towards their colleagues and the institution they work for against the correlative responsibility to serve the public interest (ibid.: 277).

Contrary to the prima facie duty of loyalty, Ronald Duska has argued that 'one does not have an obligation of loyalty to a company, even a *prima facie* one, because companies are not the kind of things that are properly objects of loyalty. To make them objects of loyalty gives them a moral status they do not deserve and in raising their status, one lowers the status of the individuals who work for the companies' (1984, 2007: 141–42). Loyalty, for Duska, 'depends on ties that demand self-sacrifice with no expectation of reward'. (ibid.: 144). The relation between the employer and employee is not based on demands of self-sacrifice but on expectations of profit. This relation allows them to part ways when the expectation is not fulfilled on either side (ibid.). For Duska, 'whistle-blowing is not only permissible but expected when a company is harming society' (ibid.: 146).

John Corvino (2002) has replied to this argument arguing that 'business does require some degree of self sacrifice without expectation of a reward' (ibid.: 182).[38] However, loyalty allows for some degree of tolerance, especially when 'serious moral costs are at stake', and can require a public criticism of the company, including blowing the whistle 'under right conditions' (ibid.: 183–184).

Robert Larmer (1992) comes to the same conclusion: there is no conflict between whistleblowing and upholding loyalty to one's employer. He too finds Duska's views on employee loyalty inadequate because loyalty does not entail complete reciprocity, and even though a company cannot be described as a person, loyalty holds towards fellow colleagues or shareholders of the company (ibid.: 126). He presents an interest based account whereby loyalty implies 'acting in accordance with what one has good reason to believe to be in that person's best interests', and this might require working against the actual wishes of the person one is loyal to (ibid.: 127). According to this view, loyalty does not demand refraining from reporting an immoral action because it is not in the best interests of any person to act immorally. For instance, loyalty does not require the duty to report directly to the person (whom one is loyal to) regarding their misconduct.

Wim Vandekerckhove and Ronald Commers argue that the debate on loyalty does not properly take into account the perspective of the organization. Loyalty extends beyond 'the physical aspects of the company—buildings, executives, boards, hierarchies, colleagues' to include the statement of missions and values, the goals, and the code of conduct of the organization (2004: 229). The employee is supposed to be loyal in the rational sense of being bound to the mission and values of the organization as stated, not to its current affairs, even more when these affairs run counter to the company's publicly stated goals and purposes. It follows that whistleblowing is not a violation of loyalty, but it rather upholds 'rational loyalty', and the employees have a duty to blow the whistle to 'prevent harm and further the well being of society' (ibid.: 230).

Finally, Jukka Varelius criticizes the very idea that employee loyalty is compatible with whistleblowing. The conception of loyalty that these authors assume is armchair loyalty, a scholarly and abstract conception that deviates from the standard accepted model of loyalty in the firm (2009: 271). The moral problem of whistleblowing stands because the arguments employed are 'too swift' and lack 'sufficient grounds for our accepting the new conception of loyalty' they propose. He argues that these views do not constitute a 'plausible explication of what we have meant by

---

[38] Corvino argues that the denial of the duty of loyalty relies on two premises: (i) that loyalty is dependent on ties based on self-sacrifice without an expectation of reward; (ii) the employer-employee ties do not demand such self-sacrifice. These premises lead to a dilemma: 'One can interpret "relationships that demand self-sacrifice without expectation of reward" narrowly to include only relationships whose obligations are indissoluble (like the parent/minor-child relationship). But then the first premise is false: loyalty is appropriate in a broader range of relationships than that. Or else one can interpret the phrase more broadly, to include any relationship where one must subordinate one's interest to that of a larger group. But then the second premise is false: the employee-company relationship requires such subordination. Either way, Duska's argument is unsound and must be rejected' (2002: 183).

loyalty all along' and thus 'cannot account for important intuitions about the nature of loyalty.' (ibid: 272) The failure to accommodate the standard accepted accounts of loyalty is symptomatic of the fact that the problem of permissibility of whistle-blowing has not found a solution yet.

In conclusion, loyalty is a core aspect in the debate on the justification of whistle-blowing. We do not discuss this issue further. We only note that those who claim that whistleblowing is compatible with the duty of loyalty, can argue so only at the cost of revising the conception of loyalty as generally understood. On the contrary, if whistleblowing and duty of loyalty are not compatible, then a justification of whis-tleblowing must specify under which conditions a disclosure can trump the claims of employee loyalty. In Chap. 5 we provide an argument to this effect.

2.5   A Definition of Whistleblowing

2.5.1   A Definition

We have not yet provided a proper definition of whistleblowing. Partly the reason is that whistleblowing identifies a collection of practices, and not a single phenomenon. We believe that any attempt to provide a general theory of whistleblowing should also define the proper use of the concept. This effort involves taking into account different aspects of the practical deliberation involved in the decision to blow the whistle: its intent, content, purpose, and the practical circumstances in which it takes place. We propose a definition sufficiently general to encompass the different uses of the term that we find more or less explicitly at work in the current debate:

> Whistleblowing is an *act of public disclosure,* carried out by an *agent having privileged access* to *confidential or classified information* of a *private or public organization*, concern-ing *present or past wrongdoings or an abuse of state power* of immediate or potential harm to the *public interest* (2.1)

The definition is sufficiently general to include both cases of corporate and gov-ernment whistleblowing. Its constitutive elements are five: the public nature of the disclosure, the role of the agent, the confidential nature and content of the disclo-sure, and its significance for the public interest. In what follows we briefly discuss each of them, and eventually draw a further distinction often overlooked by whistle-blowing scholars.

2.5.2   Constitutive Elements

An Act of Public Disclosure   First, whistleblowing is an *act*, not a practice or a pro-cedure. It requires an agent who performs an action and is responsible for the con-sequences that follow from it. Such a characterization is also common in the literature, where whistleblowing is considered a deliberate yet not obligatory act of disclosure (Jubb 1999: 78; see also McConnell 2003; Bok 1983; Elliston 1982). Second, disclosures are of two kinds: internal or external (see Chiasson et al. 1995). Internal whistleblowing involves raising complaints within the organization through established reporting channels. In such a case, disclosures are made to either individual persons or organizations that are able 'to effect action' (Near and Miceli 1985: 4). External whistleblowing, on the other hand, involves disclosing information to bodies outside the institution. The targeted audience for external whistleblowing is either the general public, media outlets, governmental bodies responsible for investigating crimes and corruption, or company stakeholders who can ensure redress.

Third, whistleblowing involves acting *publicly*. The literature has overlooked so far a tension in the very idea of a disclosure. The tension lies in the fact that internal and external whistleblowing exemplify two distinct notions of publicity. Consider the case of internal disclosure in a legal organization. One may argue that since the corporation is a legal entity, disclosing a wrongdoing through its internal channels is public because the procedures of internal disclosures must be set according to valid laws. However, this argument suffers from formalism. Loyalty and considerations of responsibility towards the firm or colleagues may also stop the agent from overstepping internal procedures even when these reveal themselves to be ineffective. Internal disclosures would be public in this minimal sense of being subjected to the public law. We should argue instead that internal disclosures are public only when they are followed by an independent review and proper hearing in front of public officers that are external to the firm.

The case of external disclosure is different: a disclosure is public in this second sense when it addresses a public, independently of the procedures of internal disclosures, and often overstepping them. Public disclosures in this second sense are commonly considered to be justifiable only when they are acts of last resort, that is acts taken after all other alternatives have been excluded. Only external disclosures are public according to the relevant sense of publicity we have examined in this chapter. External disclosures serve in fact as mechanisms of popular control of the government, but they can also contribute to the quality of public deliberation.

The Agent of Disclosure   The second constitutive element of whistleblowing concerns the agent itself. A whistleblower can only be an agent having a privileged access to information. They are generally members of an organization (current or former) 'who lack authority to prevent or stop the organization's wrongdoing, whether or not they choose to remain anonymous…and whether or not they occupy organizational roles which officially prescribed whistleblowing activity when wrongdoing is observed' (Near and Miceli 1985: 2–3). Whistleblowers are generally insiders[39] with access to information regarding wrongdoing, with an expertise to assess the gravity of the information before choosing to disclose it to the general public.[40]

The whistleblower understands the magnitude of the information, is able to edit the relevant parts, and present it in a legible manner to the intended audience. Since whistleblowing often raises serious charges against the perpetrator of a wrongdoing, it must be exercised with due care to avoid false accusation. It follows that any disclosure through gross negligence, mishandling of information, or error does not constitute whistleblowing, and should find no protection under any law that protects confidential disclosures.

The whistleblowers face a conflict between personal and organizational values, and a divided loyalty between the organization and the wider constituency. It is aimed at 'avoiding complicity and maintaining personal integrity', (Jubb 1999: 82) but also to uphold the public interest (Bok 1983, see also McConnell 2003). The disclosure aids the whistleblower to overcome the perceived helplessness of not being able to correct wrongs within institutional settings. Only when such procedures are found limited, absent, or dysfunctional, she may choose to go public.[41] In

---

[39] Bowie and Duska (1990) argue that the whistleblower must be necessarily an insider. See also Farrell and Petersen (1982). Janis and Mann (1977), Miceli and Near (1992) and Near and Miceli (1985) argue that even former members can be whistleblowers. Jubb maintains that 'the term "member" is sufficiently general to capture employees plus the various other relationships just listed and, perhaps, potential whistleblowing candidates among suppliers, customers or clients. The reason for wanting to include them is that all are, like employees, persons whose relationships with the organisation allow them access to information from which they may then learn about organisation related wrongdoing. But "member" is also a problematic term since it suggests a community of purpose between individual members and between members and the organisation itself. That assumption of shared goals may not be warranted' (1999: 86). Contrary to Jubb, Terrance McConnell maintains a whistleblower is often but not necessarily an insider. He discusses the case of Henry Beecher. Beecher, a physician, published an article in *The New England Journal of Medicine* in 1966 that exposed the unethical protocols of many published studies involving human subjects. Beecher is a whistleblower for McConnell, not by virtue of an actual membership, but through a potential identification of membership of a larger scientific community whose practices he exposed (McConnell 2003; see also Beecher 1966). Michael Davis argues instead that whistleblowers are only those individuals who reveal information they are entrusted with. (2003: 543) On this point see also De Maria (1994) and A. Chambers (1995).

[40] For Sissela Bok, whistleblowers 'sound an alarm based on their expertise or inside knowledge, often from within the organization in which they work' (1983: 211). We take no stance here on whether a whistleblower could also be a third-party, someone who is not a member of the organization. No principled argument excludes that an external subject may have access to privileged information that she decides to disclose in the public interest. Sometimes, an insider may pass information to an outsider who decides to make them public. This is the case of Wikileaks, who offers a platform for disclosures.

[41] As Snowden puts it regarding the futility of exposing the wrongs internally: '[W]hen you talk to people about [abuses] in a place like this where this is the normal state of business people tend not to take them very seriously and move on from them. But over time that awareness of wrongdoing sort of builds up and you feel compelled to talk about [them]. And the more you talk about [them] the more you're ignored. The more you're told it's not a problem until eventually you realize that these things need to be determined by the public and not by somebody who was simply hired by

order to disclose, the whistleblower should have sufficient reasons, based on the available evidence, that obtaining internal redress is not a viable option. A whistleblower is someone who believes that mere refusal or abiding by the duty of loyalty under the given circumstances is not an option she could accept (Jubb 1999). Finally, the disclosure must be chosen and intended, not done under duress, and should be an expression of a 'direct' and 'unambiguous form of dissent' (ibid.: 80).

Another feature that characterizes the role of the agent is the mode of disclosure. An agent has fundamentally three modes to blow the whistle: public, anonymous, and partially anonymous. The first kind involves the public release of the information concerning the identity of the whistleblower. In this case, the whistleblower publicly accepts responsibility for the disclosure and provides reasons in support of her act. The identity is also known to the perpetrator. Full anonymity instead is the case when the identity of the whistleblower is unknown to both the receiver of the communication (the media outlet, the internet leaking platform, or the investigative agency) and to the audience. Finally, partial anonymity is the case when the identity is shared with external parties, generally media houses or the investigative agencies, but not with the public at large.

The legitimacy of partial or complete anonymity depends on an assessment of the probability of the risks involved. The inadequacy of protection laws, lack of public support, and a high probability of professional and personal retaliation can influence the decision against public disclosures. When the whistleblower is unwilling to bear the personal cost involved in whistleblowing, anonymous disclosure is preferred over no disclosure. In these circumstances, anonymity allows individuals, who would otherwise remain silent for fear of reprisals, to come forward. In doing so it promotes the *public welfare* which may be subverted by abuses of power of government officials, or the *public safety*, which may be threatened by dangerous practices of the private industry. It may also promote honesty and accountability among managers who find it difficult to conceal their indulgence towards corrupt practices (Elliston 1982: 175).

Confidential or Classified Information   Let's consider now the nature of the information disclosed. We said that public disclosure can be of either confidential or classified information. In general, classified is information whose unauthorized disclosure is necessarily illegal. Confidential is instead the information whose disclosure is not necessary illegal. This distinction needs clarification, and a few caveats.

First, consider classified information. In theory, when information is classified, authorized public agencies operate in the interest of national security. The United

---

the government' (quoted in Ludlow 2013). Similarly the mathematician William Binney, the NSA analyst J. Kirk Wiebe, and the NSA cryptologist Edward Loomis tried to expose the fraud behind the multi-billion contract for 'Trailblazer' which was supposed to revolutionise intelligence. They explored internal channels but not only were their attempts frustrated; they faced deleterious consequences through lawsuits and the revocation of their security clearance (See Shorrock 2013).

States' National Security Classification (Executive Order 13526/2009) lists three categories of classified information: 'Top Secret, 'Secret', 'Confidential':

"Top Secret" shall be applied to information, the unauthorized disclosure of which reasonably could be expected to cause exceptionally grave damage to the national security [...]

"Secret" shall be applied to information, the unauthorized disclosure of which reasonably could be expected to cause serious damage to the national security [...]

"Confidential" shall be applied to information, the unauthorized disclosure of which reasonably could be expected to cause damage to the national security [...]

The classification shows some interesting features: first, the value of the information is a function of the expected damage, not the content of the information per se. Second, the damage must be caused by an unauthorized disclosure. Third, the classification is justified by the inherent interest of national security.

Consider now confidential information. We can distinguish between two kinds of it. The first is the one just reported above. Confidential is the information whose unauthorized disclosure is unlawful. The term is used here in a technical sense, as a label.

The second kind is confidential information whose meaning does not depend on the expectation of damage. Confidential—in this non technical sense—is the information that is in the interest of someone to be kept secret. For instance, doctor-patient relationships are based on confidentiality: it is in the legitimate interest of the patient to keep her health records confidential, unless she decides to the contrary.

However, there are also cases of confidentiality based on illegitimate interests. The paradigmatic case is corruption. It is in the interest of the parties involved in a corrupt exchange to keep their deal away from the public eye, but this interest is obviously illegitimate because it concerns an illicit conduct. Illegitimate confidentiality, as we may call it, is different from all other cases. It concerns information that can be legally disclosed without authorization or damage to any legitimate interest.

The distinction between confidential and classified information is crucial to draw important distinctions between different forms of whistleblowing, and their legal and moral status.

First, whistleblowing is not necessarily illegal. Obviously it is illegal when it is an unauthorized disclosure of classified information concerning national security; but it is not when the disclosure reveals confidential information regarding an illicit conduct. Second, whistleblowing can affect legitimate or illegitimate interests. When whistleblowing is legal, no legitimate interest is harmed. In this case, legal whistleblowing is also morally legitimate.

The difficult case is when whistleblowing is illegal. In some cases whistleblowing is illegal for the right reasons. A disclosure that, among other things, reveals the health records of a patient would be illegitimate in that regard. In this case legality and morality converge again: illegal whistleblowing is also morally illegitimate.

There is an important case however where morality and legality depart. It is when unauthorized disclosures reveal abuses of executive power, such as the violations of civil and constitutional rights. Despite being not authorized, disclosures of this kind serve the legitimate interests of the public.

The Content of Disclosure. The disclosed information should concern a conduct considered illicit and as such sanctioned by the law. As Jubb puts it, the content of such disclosures should concern 'non-trivial illegality or other wrongdoing whether actual, suspected or anticipated' (Jubb 1999: 78). Typically, the information concerns 'a bad news message about misconduct, incompetence, fraud and the like alleged to have been ignored and/or covered up; or it might be about good news concealed for private advantage'(ibid.: 79), and the accusation should single out 'individuals or groups within the organization as *responsible for* the harm being perpetrated'(McConnell 2003: 572 emphasis in the original).[42]

Disclosures include also information about the arbitrary use of power, either by the government or by private agencies working for the government.

We have two cases: the first is the case of shallow secrecy, when an abuse of power is perpetrated in virtue of secret policies that are perfectly legal. In a constitutional democracy a secret policy is a policy passed by representative body, containing provisions that are not accessible to the general public. Although the specific provisions are unknown, oversight committees retain the power of control over information from the government agencies that enact those provisions. In such a case, the abuse of power may happen only within the scope of discretionary power conferred to the executive agencies that enact those provisions, for instance when a personnel of the agency conducts covert operations hidden from the parliamentary oversight. The abuse from hiding information falls within the case of 'wrongdoings' cited in the definition.

A different case is that of deep secrecy, that is when the very existence of a policy, not only specific provisions therein, are unknown to the representative body. Deeply secret policies may have a vestige of legality, for instance when they are approved through executive orders in times of national emergency. Anti-terrorism policies find sometimes justification in the purported necessity of this sort. Deep secrecy is essentially abusive of democratic power, because when a policy is concealed from any representative body, it is impossible in principle to judge whether the imminence and the gravity of the threat justify the policy. Examples of deep secrecy abounded in the post 9/11 scenario, when US courts deferred to the executive the evaluation of the threat.

Harm to the Public Interest Reference to the public interest is common in the political and legal discourse on the morality of whistleblowing. It is often said that

---

[42] In the same vein Elliston argues that whistleblowing is a form of accusation. The accusation is 'directed to people—not just in the sense of warning those who are in danger, but in the sense of locating responsibility for the danger' (1982: 169).

disclosures of wrongdoings, abuses, negligence are justified when they threaten the public interest (Bok 1983: 211; see also McConnell 2003: 572).

However, there is no agreement on what public interest should be, and often public interest is equated to notions such as common interest, national interest, public goods.[43] Our contention is that this is wrong. A justification of whistleblowing depends on public interest in two distinct ways: first, the disclosure is of a presumptive interest for the public, that is it reveals information of possible relevance to the public at large; second, it is an interest concerning the fundamental rights of citizens, not merely the positive or negative effects of a policy. The first aspect of public interest is part of the communicative purpose of informing the *public*; the second aspect concerns the nature of the *interest*, in other words what such an interest consists in. In Chaps. 3 and 5 we analyze these aspects in detail.

2.5.3 Civic and Political Whistleblowing

We need at this point to clarify an important distinction that goes generally unnoticed in the current debate. Although the literature on whistleblowing has largely evolved in the context of business ethics, the most contentious cases of whistleblowing arise in the context of government secrecy. When the distinction is drawn, it is usually framed as 'corporate vs government' whistleblowing.[44] We think that this distinction refers to the context in which whistleblowers operate, but does not do justice to the aims of the disclosure. Our concern is to draw a distinction that cuts across the common split between government whistleblowing and corporate whistleblowing. We distinguish between two forms of whistleblowing: civic, and political.[45]

Civic whistleblowing arises when an individual reveals cases of corruption within an institution, whether private or public. There is no principled distinction between corruption in the private or the public sector: use of public office to further personal interests such as misappropriation or mismanagement of funds, financial cover-ups that exploit loopholes in the legislation, but also unfair practices in hiring, discrimination in the workplace, are examples of wrongdoings that call for civic alert. International financial flows may fall within the scope of civic disclosure: the recent case of the Panama papers, which exposed to the world how rich elites have been

---

[43] See the discussion of the Bok's Moral Choice View above (*infra* 2.4) and Vandekerckhove (2006).

[44] See Delmas (2014, 2015) who speaks of 'government' or 'national security' whistleblowing. Richard De George (2014: 322) also distinguishes 'governmental' whistleblowing from other kinds. His definition is similar to what we call political whistleblowing, except for the fact that it does not account for those forms of political action whose intended subject is the state. Consider for instance disclosures by whistleblowers about subversion of rules by corporations to suit particularistic ends. The Panama Papers are an example in this regard.

[45] As far as we are aware, a similar distinction is only drawn in a recent book by Avishai Margalit (2017: 37), who also refers to 'political whistleblowing' at one point (ibid. 45).

hiding incomes and assets from taxation in fiscal heavens, was made possible by an anonymous leak inside the law firm that consulted, designed, and managed the operations. The transfer of funds is not per se illicit, but the disclosures were received world-wide by the public opinion with the same despise reserved for criminals.

Why should we call it civic? For three reasons: first, it is a civic in the same sense in which we say that a person carries out a civic activity when she contributes some of her time, effort, or financial resources to provide a service to the community or to help a cause without being obliged to do so. Civic, in this first sense, refers to the participation of the person to the public good of a community, a city, or a town. Volunteering few hours a week to keep open a local library is a civic activity. Whistleblowing is civic in this first sense when the disclosures contribute to the common activities of the local or national community affected by the wrongdoing. Notice that, in virtue of the voluntary nature of its contribution to the public life, civic whistleblowing in this first sense is not a moral duty, but only implies praiseworthiness as a supererogatory act.

However, whistleblowing is also civic in the sense of being a civic duty. Voting is a civic duty: it is not legally compulsory, but it is morally expected of good citizens who are active members of their community.[46] Civic whistleblowing in this second sense is a moral duty of the whistleblower as a citizen. We have already discussed what some authors consider to be circumstances that make whistleblowing morally obligatory. Here it suffices to say that there are many ways to justify the civic duty of whistleblowing. One is to argue that when the whistleblower is a full member of a political community—call it a polity—their moral duty stems from their status of citizens of the polity. Another strategy is to appeal to the political allegiance of the whistleblower and the sense of loyalty to their own country. We pursue a different strategy: the civic duty of whistleblowing is not absolute. Its stringency depends rather on how deeply the public interest of a polity is affected by the wrongdoing the whistleblower has the power to unveil and redress. We explore this strategy in the next chapter.

Finally, whistleblowing is civic in the sense that its purpose is to uphold the law of the country by denouncing its violation. Civic whistleblowers who report episodes of corruption face serious conflicts between their loyalty to the firm and the duty to report the crime, but they do not face the further conflict between their duty to report and the duty to obey the law.[47] We may say: a civic whistleblower is a good citizen who acts in the name of the law, within the limits of the law. In virtue of their civic commitment, the legal status of whistleblowers is recognized in an increasing number of countries, protected and sometimes incentivized as an effective strategy to fight corruption.

Political whistleblowing refers to the disclosure of classified information protected by the law. We call it political because its purpose is to reveal the democratic

---

[46] Compulsory voting does indeed exist in some countries. In some it is enforced but legal justifications apply for non-voters; in others it is not enforced at all. Voting is not compulsory in the vast majority of countries.

[47] For various ethical tensions that exist in an act of whistleblowing see Jensen (1987).

deficits that arise from the arbitrary exercise of state power. By arbitrary exercise we refer to those decisions and policies enforced by a government that exceed the constitutional boundaries of its executive power. Hence, by political whistleblowing we mean an act of disclosure against the arbitrary exercise of the executive power that suspends or limits the constitutional rights and democratic procedures in a constitutional democracy. One of the most common exemplifications of an arbitrary exercise of power in a democracy is when a government (or an agency enabled with executive prerogatives) classifies policies and decisions of public interest and yet denies the citizens the right to adequate information about the content and reasons for the classification. The paradigmatic case of such an abuse is the surveillance policies revealed by Edward Snowden, enacted by the US National Security Agency, and which had a considerable impact on the privacy rights of unaware US and foreign citizens.

It should be clear at this point how political whistleblowing differs from civic whistleblowing. Contrary to civic whistleblowing, political whistleblowing is a disclosure of classified information which are themselves protected by the law. The context in which political whistleblowing arises is usually in the sphere of unregulated action enabled by the veil of secrecy. Governmental secrecy creates a state of affairs whereby constitutional controls over abuses of power cannot always be exercised.[48] It is in this context that conscientious insiders seek to safeguard democracy from those abuses. Political whistleblowers stand witness to the fact that institutional and constitutional checks are not always sufficient to mitigate the threats that result from secrecy. Those who are inclined to consider political whistleblowing a form of espionage, a threat to national security, or even betrayal of the country, will deny the good faith of whistleblowers. In reality, what they reject is the more fundamental claim that a critique of the established law can take the form of an act of dissent against the law itself. In Chaps. 5 and 6 we argue that this claim is justified when it addresses concerns of public interest. Matters of public interest override the respect for the established law not only when the law itself is unjust, but also when its provisos preclude the public from paying attention to matters that is in its legitimate interest.

2.5.4   *What Whistleblowing Is Not*

With now a proper definition at hand, we can better understand what whistleblowing is not. Let's clear first that, despite the metaphor, a whistleblower is not an *umpire, referee,* or *a traffic signalman* because whistleblowers do not enforce the rules of the game (Jubb 1999: 79). Whistleblowing obviously involves signaling and

---

[48] We will discuss the problems of state secrecy in Chap. 4. For a debate, see Sagar (2007, 2013), Bok (1983), Warren (1974), Rourke (1960, 1966), and Shils (1996). For a discussion of the relationships between executive privilege and governmental secrecy see Rozell (1994, 2002), and Kitrosser (2007).

warning but with the knowledge that the warning party does not have the authority to enforce the rules they perceive to be violated. Moreover, whistleblowing is an act of dissent against a status quo which seems to emerge within an institution. Whistleblowing goes against such inertia in a way a referee hardly does.

Another confusion is often made between whistleblowing and *acts of leaking*. Whistleblowing is only in a narrow sense an act of leaking: information leaks can be of any sort, while whistleblowing is generally concerned with malpractices, illegal acts or omissions within an organization (Fasterling and Lewis 2014: 72). Moreover, leaking can have many purposes and serve different agendas, including to influence the public opinion in favor of the cause the leaker stands for. In this regard leaking is similar to covert acts of whistleblowing, but the similarities are contingent on the nature of the information and the purpose of disclosure. While the purpose behind leaking can be to manipulate, misguide, or influence public opinion to serve a particular interest, the motivation behind whistleblowing (even through covert forms) is to serve the public interest or to address a grievance that cannot be addressed if not by the disclosure (ibid.). Whistleblowing assumes the form of leaking only when the procedural safeguards for disclosure and redress are absent or ineffective. In these circumstances, individuals are left with no recourse other than undertaking covert disclosures.

Finally, the main confusion comes with the allegation that whistleblowing is just a form of espionage, especially when disclosures pertain to sensitive information protected by secrecy laws. Despite its allure, the allegation is flawed. Generally speaking, a spy is an agent employed by a government or other organization with the task of secretly gathering intelligence on behalf of enemy government or organization. Spies can be embedded in the organization or the country they spy on, but this is not necessary. Their distinctive trait is rather this: they serve the interests of the country or organization they work for, and often they also pay allegiance when their activity is motivated by ideological reasons. On the contrary, a whistleblower by definition does not owe any allegiance or serve the interest of neither foreign governments or competing organizations. Quite the contrary, whistleblowing is sometimes motivated by the concern that the institution the agent works for does not deviate from its publicly avowed purpose. There is, however, another argument underlying the idea that whistleblowers are spies. The argument is that whistleblowers betray their country by leaking information that will be used by the enemy (there is always an enemy!), and it's their betrayal that deserves the same contempt reserved for spies. But, what does it mean to betray one's country or firm?

Avishai Margalit argues that connotations of treason and betrayal are assessments of the agent, not of the act itself. They are evaluations of the morality of whistleblowers. According to Margalit, allegations of betrayal rests on the assumption that whistleblowers entertain a moral relationship with the organizations they work for. Hence the business community 'tends to treat whistleblowers as informers who not only spoil the reputation of the firm but also destroy the firm's sense of hierarchy' (2017: 37). Likewise, 'people who are hostile to political whistle-blowing feel that shaming their government in the eyes of the world is akin to betrayal… It erodes political authority and create a climate of irreverence' (ibid.: 45). Yet, the assumption is flawed, for it conflates thick and thin relationships. Thick relationships are mainly 'our relations with strangers', whereas thick relations are 'modeled on our relations with friends and family' (ibid.: 12). Betrayal is a thick notion that only applies to thick relationships *within* the organization, essentially with the whistleblower's co-workers, not to thin relationships *with* the organization.

Margalit observes that confusing these relationships is symptomatic of a feudal conception of morality, where 'gratitude comes before everything else' (ibid.: 40), and of a paternalistic picture of politics, where the public is considered 'a bunch of unruly children who need a disciplinarian father to set them straight'(ibid.: 45). The same holds for the allegation of espionage against whistleblowers. Allegations of this sort borrows derogatory force from the common tendency to confuse an act of civil dissent with personal betrayal. Treason is the notion often invoked in these discursive contexts to express this moralized contempt for dissent. Whistleblowers are traitors because they are political betrayers; and since treason is the ultimate crime against the state, the state is justified twice, morally and politically, to punish the whistleblowers.

2.6   Concluding Remarks

Our effort in this chapter was to define the concept of whistleblowing and delimit its proper use. We reconstructed the history of the practice and insisted on the idea that by speaking truth to power, whistleblowers reenact the ancient Greek practice of parrhesia, often demonstrating similar features of courage, fearlessness, truthfulness, and the value of upholding the truth at extreme costs for oneself. As part of this classical heritage, whistleblowing is a form of political agency that sits within the same liberal tradition that emphasizes publicity and transparency as the normative principles a constitutional democracy should follow in accommodating conflicts of political legitimacy between citizens and political authorities. We stressed the point that since whistleblowing refers to acts of public disclosure, it also evolves with the changing circumstances of democratic and institutional engagement. Many definitions of the term in the current debate appear too narrow in scope, often relying on the debate within the field of business ethics. Our main concern was to offer a comprehensive definition of whistleblowing and widen its understanding beyond the common use in the literature. To this purpose, we pointed out which features are constitutive of whistleblowing, and insisted on a distinction between two forms of whistleblowing, civic and political, often conflated in the literature. In the next chapter we will focus on the justification of civic whistleblowing and elaborate a conception of the public interest.

References

Alford, C. Fred. 2002. *Whistleblowers: Broken Lives and Organizational Power*. New York: Cornell University Press.

Amoureux, Jack L. 2015. *A Practice of Ethics for Global Politics: Ethical Reflexivity*. New York: Routledge.

Andrade, Julio A. 2015. Reconceptualising whistleblowing in a complex world. *Journal of Business Ethics* 128 (2): 321–335.

Arendt, Hannah. 1972. *Crises of the Republic: Lying in Politics, Civil Disobedience on Violence, Thoughts on Politics, and Revolution*. San Diego/New York/London: Harvest Book, Harcourt Brace & Company.

Barrett, Grant. 2006. *Hatchet Jobs and Hardball: The Oxford Dictionary of American Political Slang*. New York: Oxford University Press.

Beecher, Henry. 1966. Ethics and clinical research. *The New England Journal of Medicine* 274: 1354–1360.

Bentham, Jeremy. 1838. An essay on political tactics. In *The Works of Jeremy Bentham*, ed. John Bowring, vol. 8, 301–374. Edinburgh: William Tait.

Bok, Sissela. 1980. Whistleblowing and professional responsibilities. In *Ethics Teaching in Higher Education*, ed. Daniel Callahan and Sissela Bok, 277–295. New York/London: Plenum Press.

———. 1983. *Secrets. On the Ethics of Concealment and Revelation*. New York: Pantheon.

Bollier, David. 2002. *Silent Theft: The Private Plunder of Our Common Wealth*. New York: Routledge.

Bowie, Norman. 1982. *Business Ethics*. Englewood Cliffs: Prentice Hall.

Bowie, Norman E., and Ronald F. Duska. 1990. *Business Ethics*. 2nd ed. Upper Saddle River: Prentice Hall.

Brenkert, G. George. 2010. Whistle-blowing, moral integrity, and organizational ethics. In *The Oxford Handbook of Business Ethics*, ed. George G. Brenkert and Tom L. Beauchamp, 563–601. Oxford: Oxford University Press.

Chambers, Andrew. 1995. Whistleblowing and the internal auditor. *Business Ethics: A European Review* 4 (4): 192–198.

Chambers, Simone. 2004. Behind closed doors: Publicity, secrecy, and the quality of deliberation. *Journal of Political Philosophy* 12 (4): 389–410.

Chateauraynaud, François. 2013. Lanceur d'alerte. In Dictionnaire critique et interdisciplinaire de la participation, ed. I. Casillo, R. Barbier, L. Blondiaux, F. Chateauraynaud, J-M. Fourniau, R. Lefebvre, C. Neveu, et D. Salles. Paris: GIS Démocratie et Participation. http://www.dicopart.fr/it/dico/lanceur-dalerte. June 2013. Accessed 10 Feb 2018.

Chiasson, Michael, Gene H. Johnson, and J. Ralph Byington. 1995. Blowing the whistle: Accountants in industry. *CPA Journal* 65 (2): 24.

Corvino, John. 2002. Loyalty in business? *Journal of Business Ethics* 41 (1): 179–185.

Council of Europe, Civil Law Convention on Criminal Corruption. https://rm.coe.int/CoERMPublicCommonSearchServices/DisplayDCTMContent?documentId=090000168007f3f5. Accessed 8 Feb 2018.

Dandekar, Natalie. 1991. Can whistleblowing be FULLY legitimated? A theoretical discussion. *Business & Professional Ethics Journal* 10 (1): 89–108.

Davis, Kevin. 1991. Kantian 'publicity' and political justice. *History of Philosophy Quarterly* 8 (4): 409–421.

———. 1992. Kant's different 'publics' in the justice of publicity. *Kant-Studien* 83 (2): 170–184.

Davis, Michael. 1996. Some paradoxes of whistleblowing. *Business & Professional Ethics Journal* 51 (1): 3–19.

———. 2003. Whistleblowing. In *The Oxford Handbook of Practical Ethics*, ed. Hugh LaFollette, 539–563. Oxford: Oxford University Press.

De George, Richard. 1990. *Business Ethics*. London: Macmillan.

————. 2014. Whistleblowing. In *Business Ethics: Readings and Cases in Corporate Morality*, ed. Michael W. Hoffman, Robert E. Frederick, and Mark S. Schwartz, 320–338. Chichester: Wiley.

De Maria, William. 1994. *Unshielding the Shadow Culture*. Department of Social Work and Social Policy, University of Queensland.

Deane, Silas. 1737–1789. *American Eras*. Encyclopedia.com. http://www.encyclopedia.com. Accessed 21 July 2016.

Delmas, Candice. 2014. The civic duty to report crime and corruption. *Les ateliers de l'éthique/ The Ethics Forum* 9 (1): 50–64.

————. 2015. The ethics of government whistleblowing. *Social Theory and Practice* 41 (1): 77–105.

Dickey, Colin. 2013. Dark Pages. *The New Inquiry*. December 13, 2013. http://thenewinquiry.com/ essays/dark-pages/. Accessed 25 July 2016.

Duska, Ronald F. 1984. Whistleblowing and employee loyalty. In *Contemporary Issues in Business Ethics*, eds. Joseph Des Jardins and John McCall, 295–300. Belmont, CA: Wadsworth. This has been henceforth published in Duska, Ronald. F. 2007. *Contemporary Reflections on Business Ethics*. 139–147. Dordrecht: Springer.

Economic Community of West African States Protocol on the Fight Against Corruption and The South African Development Community Protocol Against Corruption. https://www.unodc.org/ documents/corruption/publications_compendium_e.pdf. Accessed 8 Feb 2018.

Elliston, Frederick A. 1982. Anonymity and whistleblowing. *Journal of Business Ethics* 1 (3): 167–177.

Ellsberg, Daniel. 2003. *Secrets: A Memoir of Vietnam and the Pentagon Papers*. New York: Penguin.

Ernest, Walter, and Roger Casement. 1912. *The Putumayo: The Devil's Paradise; Travels in the Peruvian Amazon Region and an Account of the Atrocities Committed Upon the Indians Therein*. London: T. Fisher Unwin.

Ernest, Walter, and Charles Reginald Enock. 1912. *The Putumayo: The Devil's Paradise*. London: T. Fisher Unwin.

Farrell, Dan, and James C. Petersen. 1982. Patterns of political behavior in organization. *Academy of Management Review* 7 (3): 403–412.

Fasterling, Bjorn, and David Lewis. 2014. Leaks, legislation and freedom of speech: How can the law effectively promote public-interest whistleblowing? *International Labour Review* 153 (1): 71–92.

Foucault, Michel. 2001. *Fearless Speech*, ed. Joseph Pearson. Los Angeles: Semiotext(e).

Gallie, Walter B. 1956. Essentially contested concepts. *Proceedings of the Aristotelian Society New Series* 56: 167–198.

Glazer, Myron P., and Penina M. Glazer. 1989. *The Whistleblowers: Exposing Corruption in Government and Industry*. New York: Basic Books.

Gosseries, Axel, and Tom Parr. 2017. Publicity. In *The Stanford Encyclopedia of Philosophy*. (Spring 2018 Edition), ed. Edward N. Zalta. https://plato.stanford.edu/archives/spr2018/ entries/publicity/. Accessed 20 Feb 2018.

Greenwald, Glenn. 2014. *No place to Hide: Edward Snowden, the NSA, and the US Surveillance State*. New York: Macmillan.

Gutmann, Amy, and Dennis Thompson. 1996. *Democracy and Disagreement*. Cambridge, MA: Harvard University Press.

Harding, Luke. 2014. *The Snowden Files: The Inside Story of the World's Most Wanted Man*. London: Guardian Faber Publishing.

Hoffman, W. Michael, and Robert E. McNulty. 2010. A business ethics theory of whistleblowing: Responding to the $1 trillion question. In *Whistleblowing: In Defense of Proper Action*, ed. Marek Arszulowicz and Wojciech W. Gasparski, 45–59. New York: Transaction Publishers.

Hoffman, W. Michael, and Mark S. Schwartz. 2014. In *Business Ethics: Readings and Cases in Corporate Morality*, ed. Michael W. Hoffman, E. Robert Frederick, and Mark S. Schwartz, 338–350. Chichester: Wiley.

Janis, Irving L., and Leon Mann. 1977. *Decision Making: A Psychological Analysis of Conflict, Choice, and Commitment*. New York: Free Press.

Jensen, J. Vernon. 1987. Ethical tension points in whistleblowing. *Journal of Business Ethics* 6 (4): 321–328.

Johnson, Roberta Ann. 2003. *Whistleblowing: When It Works—and Why*. Colorado: Lynne Rienner Publishers.

Jubb, Peter B. 1999. Whistleblowing: A restrictive definition and interpretation. *Journal of Business Ethics* 21 (1): 77–94.

Kant, Immanuel. 1991. Perpetual peace: A philosophical sketch (1795). In *Kant: Political Writings*, ed. H. Reiss, 93–130. Trans. H. Nisbet. Cambridge: Cambridge University Press.

Karfakis, Nikos, and George Kokkinidis. 2011. Rethinking cynicism: Parrhesiastic practices in contemporary workplaces. *Culture and Organization* 17 (4): 329–345.

Kitrosser, Heidi. 2007. Secrecy and separated powers: Executive privilege revisited. *Iowa Law Review* 92 (2): 489.

Kline, A. David. 2006. On complicity theory. *Science and Engineering Ethics* 12 (2): 257–264.

Kohn, Stephen M. 2011. The Whistleblowers of 1777. *The New York Times*. http://www.nytimes.com/2011/06/13/opinion/13kohn.html?_r=0. Accessed 25 July 2016.

Larmer, A. Robert. 1992. Whistleblowing and employee loyalty. *Journal of Business Ethics* 11 (2): 125–128.

Legislation of July 30, 1778. *Journals of the American Congress*. Vol. 2: Jan. 1, 1777 to July 31 1778. Washington, DC: Way and Gideon.

Lewis, David, and Wim Vandekerckhove. 2011. *Whistleblowing and Democratic Values*. London: Open Source eBook: The International Whistleblowing Research Network.

Liddell, Henry G., Robert Scott. 1996. *Greek-English Lexicon*. Ninth Edition with a Revised Supplement, ed. Henry Stuart Jones. Oxford: Clarendon Press. Thesaurus Linguae Graecae® Digital Library. Ed. Maria C. Pantelia. University of California, Irvine. http://stephanus.tlg.uci.edu/lsj/#eid=1&context=lsj. Accessed 10 Feb 2018.

Lozano Ethan, Alan Joyce, Robert Schiemann, Adam Ting, and Dominique Yahyavi. *Wikileaks and whistleblowing*. Digital information leakage and its impact on society. http://cs.stanford.edu/people/eroberts/cs201/projects/2010-11/WikiLeaks/background.html. Accessed 20 July 2016.

Luban, David. 1996. The publicity principle. In *The Theory of Institutional Design*, ed. Robert E. Goodin, 154–198. Cambridge: Cambridge University Press.

Ludlow, Peter. 2013. The banality of systemic evil. *The New York Times*. http://opinionator.blogs.nytimes.com/2013/09/15/the-banality-of-systemic-evil/. Accessed 30 Aug 2016.

Mansbach, Abraham. 2009. Keeping democracy vibrant: Whistleblowing as truth-telling in the workplace. *Constellations* 16 (3): 363–376.

———. 2011. Whistleblowing as fearless speech: The radical democratic effects of late-modern parrhesia. In *Whistleblowing and Democratic Values*, ed. David Lewis and Wim Vandekerckhove, 12–26. London: The International Whistleblowing Research Network.

Margalit, Avishai. 2017. *On Betrayal*. Cambridge, MA: Harvard University Press.

Martin, Brian. 1981. The scientific straightjacket: The power structure of science and the suppression of environmental scholarship. *Ecologist* 11 (1): 33–43.

———. 1996. Critics of pesticides: Whistleblowing or suppression of dissent? *Philosophy and Social Action* 22 (3): 33–55.

———. 2007. Whistleblowers: risks and skills. In *A Web of Prevention: Biological Weapons, Life Sciences and the Governance of Research*, ed. Brian Rappert and Caitriona McLeish, 35–49. London: Earthscan.

Martin, Brian, and Will Rifkin. 2004. The dynamics of employee dissent: Whistleblowers and organizational jiu-jitsu. *Public Administration Review: A Global Journal* 4: 221–238.

McConnell, Terrance. 2003. Whistle-blowing. In *A Companion to Applied Ethics*, ed. Raymond Gillespie Frey and Christopher Heath Wellman, 570–582. Malden, MA: Blackwell.

Miceli, Marcia P., and Janet P. Near. 1992. *Blowing the Whistle: The Organizational and Legal Implications for Companies and Employees*. New York: Lexington Books.

Mill, John Stuart. 1977. Considerations on representative government (1861). In *Essays on Politics and Society*, ed. J. M. Robson, 371–616. In *Collected Works of John Stuart Mill. Vol. XIX*.

Morel, Edmund Dene. 1905. *King Leopold's Rule in Africa*. New York: Funk and Wagnalls.

———. 1907. *Red Rubber: The Story of the Rubber Slave Trade Flourishing on the Congo in the Year of Grace*. London: TF Unwin.

Nayar, Pramod K. 2010. Wikileaks, the new information cultures and digital parrhesia. *Economic and Political Weekly* 45 (52): 27–30.

Near, Janet P., and Marcia P. Miceli. 1985. Organizational dissidence: The case of whistle-blowing. *Journal of Business Ethics* 4 (1): 1–16.

———. 1986. Retaliation against whistle-blowers: Predictors and effects. *Journal of Applied Psychology* 71: 137–145.

Neary, V. 1992. *The Trials of a Whistleblower: Interim Report on Victimization and Harassment for Blowing the Whistle*. Turramurra: NSW.

OECD. *Convention on Combating Bribery of Foreign Public Officials in International Business Transactions*. https://www.oecd.org/daf/antibribery/ConvCombatBribery_ENG.pdf. Accessed 8 Feb 2018.

Paine, Thomas. 1906. *The Writings of Thomas Paine*. New York/London: G. P. Putnam's Sons. Bartleby.com. http://www.bartleby.com/184/122.html. Accessed 3 Aug 2016.

Plato. 1992. *Theaetetus*, ed. Bernard Williams and Myles Burnyeat. Trans. M. J. Levett. UK edition. Hackett Publishing.

Rawls, John. 1955. Two concepts of rules. *The Philosophical Review*, 64 (1): 3–32 (reprinted in John Rawls, *Collected Papers*, 5–46, ed. Samuel Freeman. Cambridge, MA: Harvard University Press).

———. 1999. *A Theory of Justice: Revised edition*. Cambridge, MA: The Belknap Press of Harvard University Press.

———. 2005. *Political Liberalism. Expanded edition*. New York: Columbia University Press.

Rothschild, Joyce, and Terance D. Miethe. 1994. Whistleblowing as resistance in modern work organizations: The politics of revealing organizational deception and abuse. In *Resistance and Power in Organizations*, ed. John M. Jermier, David Knights, and Walter R. Nord, 252–273. London/New York: Routledge.

Rourke, Francis E. 1960. Administrative secrecy: A congressional dilemma. *American Political Science Review* 54 (3): 684–694.

———. 1966. *Secrecy and Publicity: Dilemmas of Democracy*. Baltimore: Johns Hopkins University Press.

Rozell, Mark J. 1994. *Executive Privilege: The Dilemma of Secrecy and Democratic Accountability*. Baltimore: John Hopkins University Press.

———. 2002. Executive privilege revived?: Secrecy and conflict during the Bush Presidency. *Duke Law Journal* 52 (2): 403–421.

Sagar, Rahul. 2007. On combating the abuse of state secrecy. *The Journal of Political Philosophy* 15 (4): 404–427.

———. 2013. *Secrets and Leaks: The Dilemma of State Secrecy*. Princeton: Princeton University Press.

Sebald, Winfried G. 2002. *The Rings of Saturn, 1998*. Trans. Michael Hulse. London: Vintage.

Sen, Amartya. 1980. Famines. *World Development* 8 (9): 613–621.

Sheehan, Neil. 1971. *The Pentagon Papers: As Published by the New York times*. Vol. 3. New York: Quadrangle Book.

Shils, Edward. 1996. *The Torment of Secrecy: The Background and Consequences of American Security Policies*. Chicago: Ivan R. Dee.

Shorrock, Tim. 2013. Obama's crackdown on whistleblowers. *The Nation*. https://www.thenation. com/article/obamas-crackdown-whistleblowers/. Accessed 30 Aug 2016.

Sorensen, Roy. 2016. Vagueness. In *The Stanford Encyclopedia of Philosophy*, ed. Edward N. Zalta. https://plato.stanford.edu/archives/win2016/entries/vagueness/. Accessed 20 Feb 2018.

Stiglitz, Joseph. 2002. Transparency in government. In *The Right to Tell: The Role of Mass Media in Economic Development*, ed. Roumeen Islam et al., 27–44. Washington, DC: The World Bank.

Taussig, Michael. 1984. Culture of terror—Space of death. Roger Casement's Putumayo report and the explanation of torture. *Comparative Studies in Society and History* 26 (03): 467–497.

The African Union Convention on Prevention and Combating Corruption. http://www.eods.eu/ library/AU_Convention%20on%20Combating%20Corruption_2003_EN.pdf. Accessed 8 Feb 2018.

Tully, John. 2011. *The Devil's Milk: A Social History of Rubber*. New York: New York University Press.

United Nations Convention against Corruption. https://www.unodc.org/documents/brussels/UN_ Convention_Against_Corruption.pdf. Accessed 8 Feb 2018.

United States President Executive Order 13526. Classified National Security Information. 29 December 2009. *Information Security Oversight Office (ISOO)*. https://www.archives.gov/ isoo/policy-documents/cnsi-eo.html. Accessed 1 Feb 2018.

Vandekerckhove, Wim. 2006. *Whistleblowing and Organizational Social Responsibility: A Global Assessment*. Farnham: Ashgate Publishing Limited.

Vandekerckhove, Wim, and M.S. Ronald Commers. 2004. Whistle blowing and rational loyalty. *Journal of Business Ethics* 53 (1–2): 225–233.

Varelius, Jukka. 2009. Is whistle-blowing compatible with employee loyalty? *Journal of Business Ethics* 85 (2): 263–275.

Waldron, Jeremy. 2001. Hobbes and the principle of publicity. *Pacific Philosophical Quarterly* 82 (3–4): 447–474.

———. 2002. Is the rule of law an essentially contested concept (in Florida)? *Law and Philosophy* 21 (2): 137–164.

Warren, Earl. 1974. Governmental Secrecy: Corruption's Ally. *American Bar Association Journal* 60 (5): 550–552.

Weiskopf, Richard, and Yvonne Tobias-Miersch. 2016. Whistleblowing, Parrhesia and the Contestation of Truth in the Workplace. *Organization Studies* 37 (11): 1621–1640.

Weiskopf, Richard, and Hugh Willmott. 2013. Ethics as critical practice: The "Pentagon Papers", deciding responsibly, truth-telling, and the unsettling of organizational morality. *Organization Studies* 34 (4): 469–493.

Williamson, Timothy. 1994. *Vagueness*. London: Routledge.

Winter, Larry C.L. 2010. Thomas Paine First American Whistleblower. http://lwinter.blogs.red-ding.com/2010/12/thomas_paine_fi/. Accessed 20 July 2016.

Winton, Dave. 2007. *Whistleblower*. Wordorigins.com. http://www.wordorigins.org/index.php/ site/comments/whistleblower/. Accessed 20 Feb 2018.

Chapter 3
Public Interest and the Threat of Corruption: A Case for Civic Whistleblowing

Abstract Political corruption is a fraudulent exchange for the mutual advantage between parties entrusted with public power, and whose costs bear on third parties who do not enjoy the benefit of that transaction. A defining feature of political corruption is that it affects the public interest of constituencies by diverting public funds for personal advantages, dumping the costs of diversion on the polity at large. In this chapter, we argue that the role of civic whistleblowing in the fight against corruption should be properly understood within a conception of public interest. In this chapter, we argue that whistleblowing contributes to the public interest when it exposes crimes that cause an unfair allocation of the burdens of cooperation.

Keywords Accountability · All-purposive rights · The public · Political corruption · Public interest

Corruption is a fraudulent transaction among two or more agents who exchange information, services, or money for their mutual profit, and whose costs are borne by third parties who do not enjoy the benefit of that transaction. The Transparency International Corruption Index, a standard reference on the perception of transparency worldwide, shows discomforting data about the magnitude of corruption.[1] The 2017 Report, which measures the perceived levels of corruption in the public sector worldwide, confirms for this year too that none of the countries among the 180 considered gets a perfect score, and two-thirds score below 50, on a scale of 0 (highly corrupt) to 100 (very clean). Transparency International reminds that, population-wise, as of 2015 six billion people live in countries with endemic forms of corruption, often times at the cost of social trust, the rule of law, the stability of institutions, the civil and economic rights of citizens, and socio-economic inequality. Political corruption, which represents a specific form of corruption, occurs when one of the parties involved in the fraudulent transaction is a public official who abuses their power to exact a personal profit. In short, it is an abuse of power by persons entrusted

---

[1] The Index is released annually. See Transparency International Corruption Perceptions Index 2017.

© Springer International Publishing AG, part of Springer Nature 2018
D. Santoro, M. Kumar, *Speaking Truth to Power – A Theory of Whistleblowing*,
Philosophy and Politics - Critical Explorations 6,
https://doi.org/10.1007/978-3-319-90723-9_3

with a political authority for their private gain.[2] A defining feature of political corruption is that it affects the public interest of constituencies by diverting public funds for personal advantages, ultimately dumping the costs of diversion on the polity at large.

In this chapter, we defend the role of what we call *civic* whistleblowing (to distinguish it from political whistleblowing) in the fight against political corruption. The chapter is divided into three parts. First, we will review some conceptions of political corruption and provide a working definition that in turn will be useful for the second part, where we distinguish between two broad characterizations of public interest. The first is based on the aggregation of non-competing individual interests, while the second will be cast in terms of all-purposive rights. In the third and final part, we will argue that the right-based view of public interest captures an important feature of the injustice of political corruption, namely that it affects citizens' capacity to enjoy their rights. We suggest that the injustice of corruption does not primarily consist in disrupting the demands of accountability and the value of equality of citizens in their social relationships, but in interfering with legitimate entitlements citizens have in virtue of their citizenship status.

3.1 Political Corruption

The literature on political corruption is vast, and yet political philosophers have only recently started to address the injustice of political systems affected by pervasive phenomena of corruption. Political scientists and economists have approached political corruption as a multi-faceted phenomenon, identifying social instability and governance accountability as key aspects of corrupt phenomena. Much attention has been given to *bribery*, often hard to detect given that suspected parties are usually uncooperative with authorities. Moreover, in many countries current legal systems prescribe symmetric liability for both the bribe-giver and receiver, making it hard to blow the whistle on corrupt officials because the bribe-giver has also broken the law and will often face the same consequences of the corrupted official.

A defining feature of political corruption is that it undermines the interests of constituencies that officials represent by diverting public funds for personal advantages, dumping the costs of diversion on the polity at large. Mark Philp has provided a tentative definition of political corruption as a triadic relationship occurring when a public official A violates the rules and/or norms of office to the detriment of the interests of the public B (or some subsection thereof) who is the designated beneficiary of that office, to benefit themselves and a third party C who rewards or incentivises A to gain access to goods or services they would not otherwise obtain (2015: 22).

---

[2] Cf. the definition by Transparency International has now become standard: 'Corruption is the abuse of entrusted power for private gain. It hurts everyone who depends on the integrity of people in a position of authority. This can mean not only financial gain but also non-financial advantages.'

Taking Philp's as a working definition, we can identify two features of individual behavior that identify an act of corruption. Political corruption is

1. a purposeful violation of law motivated by an incentive,
2. at the detriment of 'the interests of the public.'[3]

Usually issues concerning the injustice of corruption insist on the first of these two features, for an act of corruption is a blameworthy (and also culpable) *quid pro quo* that harms third parties without their knowledge or consent.

Along with these features of personal morality, political corruption is also a morally relevant phenomenon that affects the framework of public rules, because of two other consequences it brings about:

3. The distributive problem: political corruption deprives local and national constituencies of funds that could be used for services, infrastructure, education, etc. thus leading to uncontrolled rises in public expenditure;
4. Abuse of power: political corruption secures the privilege of elite powers that have the financial capacity to bribe public officials in order to manipulate and privatize resources for their private benefit.

The distributive problem and the abuse of power cases are instances of politically corrupt practices that fall within the second feature highlighted by Philp's working definition because of how they affect the interests of the public as a collective body, and are somewhat independent of moral judgments we may entertain about the behavior of the corrupted officials. Along with these features, political corruption induces issues of trust:

5. The trust problem: political corruption prompts a generalized distrust in public institutions, their accountability and their capacity to enforce fair rules.

Recent attempts have emphasized the normative dimension of this problem: the distinctive political wrong of corruption consists in the abuse of public power when its agendas are 'surreptitious', that is when they cannot be publicly vindicated because they violate fundamental liberal-democratic principles such as impartiality and equality of opportunity (Ceva and Ferretti 2017: introduction).[4]

Philp's definition encompasses the individual aspect of culpable intent (and moral blameworthiness) for voluntary acts of corruption, and the institutional consequences that follow from the act. Yet, his definition falls within an *individualistic* understanding of corruption. Collective phenomena of corruption are the result of a sum of individual acts of corruption. Yet, this use of the term may hardly explain the claim that corruption is also a feature of institutions, not of individuals.

---

[3] For an analysis of the perverse effect of political corruption, see Dalla Porta and Vannucci (1997).

[4] They add: 'the corrupt behaviour of public officials should not only be considered either as a breach of personal morality or only in view of the implications it may have for the trustworthiness and efficacy of public institutions. It is itself inherently problematic in politically relevant terms.' (Ibid.: Conclusion)

Lawrence Lessig (2011) has provided a further analysis of this point, criticizing the reduction of the variegated phenomenon of political corruption to individual transactions. In particular, he distinguishes between two conceptions of political corruption. One is the ordinary conception of corruption as *bribery* that is taking money in exchange for favors or privileges from the government, *quid pro quo*. The other is *dependence corruption*, which occurs when a political institution becomes dependent on private interests. This second form of corruption—according to Lessig—does not directly concern individuals 'who are corrupted within a well-functioning institution'. Instead, it refers to 'an institution that has been corrupted, because the pattern of influence operating upon individuals within that institution draws them away from the influence intended' (2011: 231). According to Lessig, dependence corruption is not the aggregate of many smaller cases of quid pro quo corruption. The two may overlap, but they are not coextensive... [and] to regulate one is certainly not to regulate the other (ibid.).

Lessig's dependence argument is an instance of a more general *institutionalist* view according to which corruption occurs when one or more actors (whether public officials or not) have the capacity to exercise systemic and strategic influence which may even be legal, yet which 'undermines the institution's effectiveness by diverting it from its purpose or weakening its ability to achieve its purpose...' (Lessig 2013: 553).[5] The dependence view can explain important features of political corruption, in particular why the abuse of power can be stable over time as a consequence of the generalized expectation that in a corrupt system individuals will not defect. Such expectation reiterated over time establishes a path where the abuse of power becomes a standard practice. This way, abuse of power does not need to manifest in overt threat or blackmailing, for it is not usually necessary to exercise one's power when potential defectors have no incentives to blow the whistle in the context of a corrupted institution.

Whether a proper definition of corruption should be provided in terms of methodological individualism or as a feature of institution is not an issue we will discuss here. For the purpose of this chapter, it is instead crucial to highlight that both views conceive of political corruption as promoting the private interests of those involved. What is plundered by the pursuit of private interests? Our answer is: the public interest of polities.

---

[5] Along the same lines, Dennis Thompson (2013) stresses that a clear distinction must be drawn between individual and institutional corruption, but—unlike Philp—he insists on the fact that institutional corruption can damage the legislature and the democratic process.

3.2 The Public Interest

A defining feature of political corruption is that it necessarily involves plundering goods that are of public interest.[6] This is quite explicit in Philp's working definition, but it is also quite common to find reference to public interest in the legal, political, and moral discourse. For instance, reference to the public interest is ubiquitous in political life and in the legal terminology, such as the UK Public Interest Disclosure Act (1998), whose preamble declares to protect individuals who make disclosures of information in the public interest and to allow such individuals to bring action in respect of victimization. Likewise, in the recent debate on the protection of whistle-blowers, the EU Parliament deplored 'that whistleblowers, who provide national authorities, in the public interest, with crucial information about misconduct, wrongdoing, fraud or illegal activities or practices, can be subject to legal prosecution, as well as to personal and economic repercussions…' (§19).[7]

Although the appeal to the public interest is pervasive in political discourse, governments and opposition groups refer to public interest in ways that often appear to be inconsistent. For instance, sometimes public interest is used in reference to matters of national interest, and other times in reference to the distribution of public and common goods. Despite the common usage of term, there is hardly a precise understanding of the notion of public interest. This complaint was already voiced by Souraf (1962: 186), for whom 'conceptual muddle' and 'semantic chaos' surrounded the term, while for others (Downs 1962: 1–2) public interest, 'plunges the inquirer into a welter of platitudes, generalities, and philosophical arguments' (*sic.*). Oskar Kurer is among those who have in recent years insisted on the importance of a definition or conceptualization of public interest, especially in relation to corruption in democracy (Kurer 2015: 34). He refers to the idea that public interest is defined by a betrayal of—or damage to—the 'democratic transcript', that is when politicians and public officials prevent the exercise of accountability. He also agrees on the difficulty of finding a common account, 'something which is unlikely to be forthcoming' (Kurer 2015: 39). With few exceptions, political philosophers have instead been scarcely interested in defining the concept and distinguish it from other cognate notions, often leaving the job of attempting a definition to empirically oriented political scientists and scholars of the public administration.[8] Yet, the claim

---

[6] Not all forms of corruption affect the public interest. Corporate corruption may damage the company's stakeholders, but not the interests of a community at large, at least insofar as public money is not used to repair the losses incurred from the corrupt practice.

[7] For further details, see the European Parliament resolution of 25 November 2015 on tax rulings and other measures similar in nature or effect (2015/2066 (INI)).

[8] For some, public interest reflects the fiduciary role public administration has in administering common goods (see King et al. 2010), while for others public interest has a regulative function, serving as a barometer for citizens to judge public decisions (Downs 1962). King et al. (2010) offer an interesting definition of public interest based on three criteria: '(a) the fiduciary duties to the commons as defined and constrained by constitutional principles, (b) policies that are congruent with our democratic values, and (c) the practice of non-idiosyncratic and universalized ethical administrative leadership and decision making' (2010: 961). The constraint posed by constitu-

that corruption affects public interest does not seem to be a merely rhetorical appeal. In what follows, we will review some attempts to define public interest and ask what exactly 'public interest' is and how or if it is damaged or plundered by corrupt practices. We will then propose a definition of public interest and argue that anticorruption whistleblowing is a justified instance of public interest disclosures.

We can identify two characterizations of the notion of public interest. The first characterization is what we will call the non-competing interest view. The second we will call the all-purposive rights view.

3.2.1 Non-competing Interests

According to the non-competing interest view, public interest is an interest that every member of a society shares.[9] For instance, John Rawls refers to this characterization when—in *A Theory of Justice*—he spells out the principle of the common interest. According to this principle, 'institutions are ranked by how effectively they guarantee the conditions necessary for all equally to further their aims, or by how efficiently they advance shared ends that will similarly benefit everyone' (Rawls 1999: 83). Rawls' notion of common interest encompasses both the conditions for the attainment of private ends, and those shared ends that are for everybody's benefit. For this reason, he includes within the common interest the regulations for public order and security, public health and safety, and also what he calls the 'collective efforts' of a country in times of emergency (ibid.).[10]

Brian Barry argued that the public interest is an interest in which everyone in society shares in his or her capacity as a member of the public. As he writes: 'the definition of the meaning of the "public interest" which I propose makes it equivalent to those interests which people have in common *qua* members of the public' (Barry 1965: 190). Barry's extensive and detailed discussion of public interest is

---

tional principles is also crucial to our own understanding of public interest. Given the scope of the work, here we only focus on the debate among authors mostly interested in defining 'public interest' as a political theoretical concept.

[9] As Goodin notices (1996: 333), this idea can be already found in Locke's *First Treatise on Government* (1988: section 92).

[10] Perhaps not coincidentally, virtually all major works on public interest have appeared in the 1960s, before the first publication of *A Theory of Justice* in 1971. See Friedrich (1962), Souraf (1962), Downs (1962), Flathman (1966), Held (1970). One explanation of this poor attention might invoke the fact that, once the debate is rephrased within the Rawlsian assumptions, the notion of public interest as an interest opposed to private interests disappears, for a theory of justice under ideal conditions assumes that the parties in the contract attend to the fair terms of cooperation. Another explanation may instead refer to the later Rawlsian paradigm of Public Reason (see Rawls 1993) and interprets the notion of public interest as the subject matter of Public Reason. However, except for the obvious semantic vicinity, it does not seem that the notion of public interest shares any substantive similarity. In *Political Liberalism* the term 'public interest' does not occur even once.

perhaps the best attempt to define the concept of public interest in Anglo-American philosophical debate.

Two points deserve attention here. First, the definition of 'public' that Barry takes from George Carnevall Lewis. According to this definition 'public', as opposed to 'private', is something that has no immediate relation to any specified person or persons, but may directly concern any member or members of the community, without distinction' (Lewis 1832, cited in Barry 1965: 190). Following this distinction, 'the public' will refer to an 'indefinite number of non-assignable individuals' (Barry 1965: 192). What about the interest? Here Barry argues at length to provide a precise characterization. He claims that, at first approximation, 'an action or policy is in a man's interests if it increases his opportunities to get what he wants' (1965: 176).[11]

The second important point raised by Barry is that there is a distinction between a negative and positive connotation of the use of public interest. The first is the case when the expression 'in the public interest' is used to prevent 'someone from doing something which will have adverse effects on an indefinite group of people' (ibid.: 208). The positive connotation instead refers to the provision of services to an indefinite group of persons identified as the public.

In sum, Barry subscribes to the view that the public interest is the sum of the interests which every member of an indefinite group identified as the public has in common *qua* member of that public, and which increases every member's opportunity to obtain a desirable result, either by preventing someone from acting against those interests, or by means of provisions that will contribute to those interests. Barry's understanding of the public interest is, according to his own terminology, an aggregative concept, and thus defines public interest as the aggregate of the individual overlapping interests of the public. It is perhaps important to note that since statements of common interest are dubious for Barry, this characterization of public interest is not identical to that of 'common interest' (ibid.: 192). Barry argues convincingly that common interests are always contingent on the available policies: 'to say that two or more people have a common interest is to say that there are two policies x and y such that each of them prefers x to y from the point of view of his own interest' (ibid.: 195). Common interests are defined as standards of choice in given circumstances, and can change according to the context: 'common interests are ubiquitous even among enemies and so are divergent interests among allies' (ibid.). On the contrary, something being in the interest of someone—and thus possibly in the public interest of a polity—is a criterion of choice that is invariant across contexts. The best way to speak of common or divergent interests, or of interests that coincide or conflict, is with respect to choices among different policy options (ibid.: 196). It follows that, even when a policy that acts against the public interest

---

[11] Barry distinguishes between four different ways 'x being in someone's interest' does not equate to 'A wants x' (1965: 178–183). However, he does subscribe to the view that, although an action being in someone's interest does not imply that the action must satisfy her immediate wants, it should nonetheless put the person in a better position to satisfy those wants. In other words, something cannot be in someone's interests, unless that person wants the results of x (ibid.: 183).

is introduced, there is a conflict over that policy between two kinds of interests: the interest of the person or group promoting, say lobbying, the policy, and the interests of all those affected by that policy who belong to an indefinite group identified as the public.

With this characterization in hand, we can now proceed to examine the nature of the aggregative concept of public interest. According to this view, public interest consists of the largest set of the non-competing private interests of the members of a given polity or community. In order to provide a framework for public interest as a set of non-competing interests, we can draw on the analysis of public interest set out by Virginia Held (1970: chapter 2). We can say that:

A policy or action x is in the public interest when x is in the interest of every individual in a set $I_i \dots I_n$, constituting a group G; (3.1)

The formula says that public interest is a set of individual interests that are consistent across a social set. Such set can be a group belonging to a community or society defined by certain criteria of membership, including self-ascription. For instance, trade unions or political party members are groups whose membership is formally defined, while being a practitioner of a religious community is usually self-ascriptive. The group can otherwise be a polity at large, whose belonging is defined by the terms regulating the membership of a political constituency, such as citizenship, nationality, or other legal or political entitlements. The interesting aspect of the consistency requirement expressed by this view is that public interest is the interest in common to all members of a given group. Public interest, in this first formulation, is after all a form of group interest given by convergent preferences (or wants).

However, (3.1) is vulnerable to three objections. First, the claim that public interest is given by convergent preferences or wants confines the discussion about the nature of the public interest to an aggregative framework where interests are necessarily self-regarding. We argue that this is not always the case. First we may conceive of other-regarding interests that cannot be explained by self-regarding interests.[12] Second, when individual interests are interpreted as wants or preferences, they will conflict in every distributive circumstance that makes someone worse off. A policy of increasing taxation on tobacco may benefit people through the additional funds made available for social services, and act against my present preferences as a smoker, but it might be in my future best interest as a means to disincentivize smoking. But since the policy could be in my future interest, it would also be in my interest now to promote it, even if it affects my present preferences.

---

[12] An indirect argument that bypasses the distinction is that people can have self-regarding altruistic interests. The idea is that although interests are necessarily subjective preferences, their satisfaction may depend on someone's preference being satisfied at the same time. If it is in my interest that a football team wins because I have made a bet on it, it is in both the football club's and in my interest that it wins, and my preference depends on the satisfaction of the club's interest. But this is not always the case: for instance, a terminally ill patient who would prefer to end her life to escape excruciating pain, may still not go ahead if she believes that her beloved ones would suffer a great deal from her suicide.

We may then have circumstances where a certain policy may lead to a conflict between preferences and interests. Conflicts of this nature are well known, especially when the objective interests of a person (those based on welfare or capabilities) conflict with her desires when the person is not aware of those interests. Interests encompass also possible future preferences and possibly objective conditions for the fulfillment of human goals.

The third—most important—objection is that public interest may not be in the interest of every member of a given social set. After all, the appeal to public interest is—in some crucial cases—adversarial. It is an appeal against private or corporate interests. But, how can something in the public interest not be in the interest of every member of the public? One way to answer this question is by appealing to a *majoritarian* view:

> A policy or action x is in the public interest when x is in the interest of the largest subset of individuals $I_i... I_n$, belonging to a group G. (3.2)

This formulation is unsatisfying in many ways.[13] What distinguishes a public interest from the interest of the majority is that public interest may not be in the interest of the majority of members of a given social set. In fact, collective decisions distribute both costs and responsibilities among the social members. In a democracy, where the majority rule usually applies, minorities bear also the costs of collective decisions they oppose.[14] The fundamental issue concerning the legitimacy of democratic regimes is to justify why people should accept the costs of decisions they oppose and be subjected to the political obligation of complying with those rules. This is the majoritarian interpretation of public interest. Something in the public interest can certainly be an interest of the majority, but not necessarily so. A public interest can be an interest that protects minorities, disadvantaged groups, groups which are affected by those decisions but do not belong to the advantaged social set, or even future members that do not yet have a way of expressing their interests or preferences, as in the case of future generations.

Another refinement of (3.1) is what Held calls the view of *common interest*, that is the idea that public interest coincides with the interests that *all* members of a polity have *in common* (ibid.: 44). The principle of common interest should not be confused with the aggregative views of utilitarian guise, for the view of the common interest insists on the unanimity and compatibility of the public interest.

---

[13] The majoritarian view can be interpreted as an instance of what Held calls *preponderance theories* (1970: 42–43; 49–98). Preponderance theories claim that 'public interest… cannot be in conflict with the *preponderance* or *sum* of individual interests' (ibid.: 43).

[14] Sometimes, even the contrary is true: majorities bear the costs of minorities who enjoy more power or special privileges; and while this is true of authoritarian regimes, even modern capitalist democracies suffer the same condition.

3.2.2   The Common Good

In a recent discussion on the topic, Philip Pettit (2012) provides a criticism along the same lines and defends a view of the public interest as a common good. He argues that the conception of public interest as 'nothing more than the intersection of people's private interests' is not satisfactory since private interests, those a person has independently of social life, only partially overlap, and even when the overlap is larger, it is still unstable (2012: 244). Pettit argues that a conception of the public interest should assume that people living in society have no option but to live together. Thus, we should all have—as a minimal normative presumption—a post-social interest to the common sharing of certain goods on an equal footing:

> [t]he public interest, conceived in this way, is composed of those goods that anyone who accepts the necessity of living on equal terms with others is likely to want to have collectively guaranteed or promoted. It consists in the interests that people are going to share insofar as they have equal status as members of a polity.

A formulation of the public interest that captures this normative injunction can be expressed as follows:

> A policy or action x is in the public interest when x is a set of shared goods guaranteed to the set of individuals $I_i \ldots I_n$, having an equal status as member of a given polity. (3.3)

The distinction between (3.2) and (3.3) lies in the nature of the goods that are the object of public interest. While the preponderant interests of a majority are the aggregation of private pre-social interests—to use Pettit's expression—whose satisfaction implies that other less preponderant interests will not be attended to, common interests are interests that cannot be satisfied unless everyone within a polity can equally enjoy their provision. Pettit insists that this view is radically different from the idea of 'the good of the nation or people, considered as a corporate entity' (2012: 245), since, while a nation can survive and prosper, its good 'may have little to do with the good of the individuals who make it up at any time' (ibid.).

What could be a conception of the public interest as a non-corporate form of common good? The obvious candidate is the notion of public goods: the provision of public services such as health care and public pensions (at least where universalist systems are in place), as well as public order and personal safety, national security and defense are all examples of public goods, that is goods which are neither excludable nor conflicting, and in which everyone has an equal interest in. Political corruption affects public interest in this sense when it diverts the provisions of public funds in order to secure these non-competing interests. This is also what Rawls has in mind in his principle of common interest.

However, public goods cannot be the only component of public interest: if we consider public goods of the sort just mentioned, the pro-quota allocation of the costs needed to provide those goods through a system of taxation make them costlier for some members of the polity than for others. Public goods allocate the burdens of provision unequally, thus leading to competing individual interests. The advocate of the common good may of course accept this consequence and argue that there is nothing wrong with a distributive scheme that taxes some people more than others, even more so if the system is designed according to progressive taxation. But there is another case in which the public interest, understood as a set of public goods, has perverse effects on the equal status of citizens. This is the case where the cost of public order and national security is unevenly distributed because of the targeting and profiling of specific social groups to ensure the enjoyment of the good. When people of certain religions or nationalities are prevented from entering a country, and are subjected to extreme vetting, searches, profiling, and questioning in the name of preventing acts of terrorism, national security becomes a cost only for those groups. When in the US African-American people experience a disproportionate amount of police scrutiny or when the number of inmates of color is two-thirds that of whites, the common interest of public order and penal justice does not come at a common cost.

Common goods, that is, goods that are both non-excludabe and rivalrous, is another way to understand the public interest. Often, the case in point concerns the provision of natural resources, social services, schools, health, and public safety when financial resources are limited. In all of these cases, the public interest does not include securing non-competitive interests, because the legitimate interests of the members of a polity will come into conflict as resources are depleted. Crucially, this is also the case for fundamental rights set forth by constitutions, which have priority over trade-offs with other kinds of interests. Freedom of speech and movement, as well as the right to privacy are cases in point. For instance, a growing trend in the post 9/11 scenario (which is now re-emerging in response to the November 2015 Paris attacks) calls for a balance between fundamental liberties and national security, often invoking public interest arguments. We will discuss the shortcomings of striking a balance in the next chapter. It suffices to say here that the very nature of that contention provides evidence of the widespread use of public interest arguments that assume uncritically the rivalrous nature of rights and liberties against the competing interest of security, thus leading to the conclusion that the distributive effects of imposing uneven burdens on specific minorities, religious or political groups, is after all justified. The view of public interest as a set of common goods does not seem to account for these distributive effects, but it does contribute to understand what public interest cannot be.[15]

---

[15] Pettit's conception of the public interest is part of a complex conception of democratic control that he calls 'dual-aspect model of democracy'. The two aspects are the popular influence of individuals who intentionally force the government to promote policies in the public interest; and the market-like functioning of such influence, which does not impose a general will, but rather leads to collective decisions through a process akin to an invisible hand (2012: 309). We will not enter into the details of such a conception. It suffices to say though that Pettit's proposal does not address the question of what criterion (of public interest) should decide which interests of which people prevail in cases of conflict.

3.2.3   *Deliberative Accounts*

Before we move to argue for our proposal, it is worth mentioning the *idealist* under-standing of the public interest. According to this view, public interest is the object of an ideally *justifiable* political or distributive principle. According to Virginia Held (1970: 45, 135–162, who refers to this family of conceptions as *unitary* views), this conception excludes that there could even be a justifiable conflict between indi-vidual interests and the public interest.[16] The idealist conception of the public inter-est is common to all those theories of political legitimacy that are an outcome of ideal circumstances of agreement. We have already seen this view at work in Rawls' principle of the common interest, which is justified by the two principles of justice as fairness in the original position under a veil of ignorance. Another important view in this family is the deliberative interpretation of public interest, the family of theo-ries—inspired by the Habermasian paradigm—which associate the public interest with the outcome of a universally acceptable democratic deliberation under rational constraints. The requirement of a 'rational' constraint is essential in this context, for otherwise the public interest would collapse into a form of unstable negotiation among private interests. On the contrary—as Ian O'Flynn puts it in a recent contri-bution to the topic—public interest is fundamentally a moral idea about 'the proper ways of making collectively binding political decisions' (2014: 300).[17] What these proper ways are, however, is a matter of debate among deliberativists. One way in which public interest can be conceptualized within the deliberativist paradigm is by defining public interest as an outcome of a rationally constrained deliberation. But this view exposes the deliberativists to the objection that, in the absence of an inde-pendent criterion of judgment, the outcomes could potentially be contrary to justice and even poorly informed. Discursive ethicists offer a rejoinder to this challenge arguing that a deliberation where individual claims are sincere, truthful, and norma-tively sound, would represent a favorable (if not quasi-ideal) speech situation to scrutinize the public validity of those claims and curb the excess of individual inter-ests. Some epistemic democrats have, however, objected to this view that the out-comes of deliberation do not necessarily track the truth, no matter how informed and dedicated to the public cause the participants might be. For instance, a local or even national community may decide to have an informed debate on whether the construction of a new bridge is in their public interest. Yet, there is still a risk that even the most inclusive form of participatory architecture could deliberate some-thing that may prove to be the wrong decision with respect to environmental and financial constraints. Engineers may advise against a project for valid reasons based on their expertise, and yet their opinion might not count in such a deliberative scenario.

Some deliberativists might actually bite the bullet, admitting that 'we can only deliberate about the public interest if the public interest is, at least in principle,

---

[16] She includes Plato and Aristotle among the unitary conceptions (Held 1970: 135–162).

[17] See also O'Flynn (2010) on the same point.

identifiable independently of our deliberations' (O'Flynn 2014: 302). In fact, the norms and rules by which deliberations are conducted cannot be subject to deliberation themselves, but must rather hold as a rational foundation of discourse ethics. The rights associated with the free and equal exchange of reasons are—in this very narrow sense—a common interest of all the members of a polity.[18] But the appeal to the shared interest in having common rules of the democratic game does not answer the objection we are facing: who can be in the position to judge by an independent criterion when the outcome of a decision is not acceptable? One answer to this question is that, in virtue of the common participation in the game of reasons, anyone who is a legitimate holder of a claim should have such a power of judgement, or of criticism at least. But normative ideals of this sort fall short of explaining how common rules can be manipulated by political schemes, or by factional pressures within the context of real-word constitutional democracies.

3.2.4 Proceduralist Accounts

The same issue holds for a contrary strand of democratic theorists known as proceduralists. Harold D. Lasswell (1962) provides an early proceduralist view of public interest. According to Lasswell, public interest is a common interest that has inclusive value effects, as ascertained by state procedures of inquiry. Value effects refer here—in Lasswell's jargon—to the inclusive ideal of human dignity that takes the entire body politic into consideration (1962: 60). Thus, a proceduralist view of the public interest refers to those policies that are 'sufficiently great to warrant the use of inclusive procedures of choice' (1962: 64).

Proceduralists in the post-Rawlsian era have preserved, to some extent, the idea of value-laden procedures, but have substantially shifted their focus from human dignity to a normative understanding of the requirements of justice. According to contemporary proceduralists, the legitimacy of democratic authority stems from the justice of the procedures by which laws are passed. Justice, in one version of proceduralism, is procedural justice, that is a political ideal that respects the equal value of persons through procedures suitably designed to embed equal respect. In other words, the features of the procedure, and not the quality of the outcome, are what makes an outcome just. The procedural ideal of equal respect demands that decisions concerning matters of public interest should be justifiable to every participant in social cooperation in virtue of the benefits they enjoy from it. But the ideal of public justification conflicts with historical constitutional systems governed by democratic decision-making. When procedures are designed to reflect the will of the majority, a minority may suffer the consequences of those decisions in a manner that may not be acceptable to all. Sometimes the interests of a minority may just be factional, in which case the procedural justification of the legitimacy of democracy

---

[18] The same holds for proceduralists (see section below), since the requirement of public justification to every member of a polity can only be obtained if those procedures apply to all.

should be sufficient to offset the disavowal. But in other cases the minority may appeal to reasons that overcome the argument derived from the procedural correctness of a democratic majority. One such case is when Supreme Courts strike down laws passed through democratic procedures and yet affect fundamental rights and interests that are protected by the Constitution. Proceduralists accommodate this conflict by arguing that constitutional principles incorporate the idea of equal respect. This is a reasonable accommodation, and we do not contest it. However, the conflict that arises in the adjudication between rights and interests constitutionally protected highlights a difficulty for proceduralists, since they reject the idea that justice is defined by an independent criterion (the same difficulty—we argued—faced also by the deliberativists). Transposing the debate from justice to public interest presents the same difficulty: if a decision in the public interest depends only on the features of deliberation or procedures, we do not need an independent criterion of public interest to judge whether the decision is correct. Conversely, if there is such a criterion, then procedures and deliberations should be subjected to an independent scrutiny, which may conflict with democratic ruling when verified by experts or non-elected judges.

3.2.5 Epistemic Objections

A different answer to the question of who should be able to appeal to the public interest of common rules arises from the debate on the role of judicial review in democratic theory (Waldron2006; Dworkin 2011; Christiano 2008, 2011; Brettschneider 2007, 2011). A system of law based on the separation of powers is made possible by the balance between those powers. Within such a system the job of the Courts is to adjudicate between conflicting demands. Courts of justice play a pivotal role in reviewing decisions of the executive when it exceeds its constitutional mandate. For example, the recent decisions of several US Federal Courts to overturn the travel ban issued by the newly elected Trump Administration is a textbook example of judicial review. While many believe that Trump's election is an absolute setback for the country and a threat to democracy—a position hard to debate—it is true that this anti-immigrant policy of the current US administration has at least met firm opposition from the judiciary, reaffirming once again the stability of the American constitutional system. And yet, as we said, courts are not elected by the electorate. Although the powers of Supreme (or Constitutional) Courts derive from the presidency—or, as in other countries, from a mixed appointment of the President and the Parliament—the democratic investiture they receive is only indirect, and sometimes their makeup does not reflect the current political majority within the country. Is their power then legitimate when they exercise judicial review? For some, the role of Constitutional judges is marred by a fundamental suspicion towards the capacity of democratic self-control (see Waldron 2006). For others, the resort to judicial review is justifiable when Courts live up to certain democratic values (see Brettschneider 2007). In either case, Courts have a privilege of review whose justification requires an independent criterion of public interest to judge if such role is justified.[19]

We can now sum up the argument and move on to discuss the role that whistleblowers play in public interest disclosures. To recall: the objection is that deliberativists and proceduralists offer an ideal conception of public interest based on rational constraints and rational deliberation, or on a shared framework of procedures that incorporate the ideal of equal respect. However, within the context of real-world democracies, such a framework is only a normative ideal, unattainable in most, if not all cases, and corrective measures must be deployed in order to guarantee that common rules of discussion, deliberation, and outcomes of procedures are not thwarted.

Two problems arise in this context: first the requirement of an independent criterion of public interest; second, that those who can appeal or decide on such criterion may not have the required democratic legitimacy, but only the expertise deriving from their role. This is the case of the judiciary. The problem posed by the role of expertise and their discretion to judge according to an independent criterion of justice is similar, in many respects, to the riddle posed by the role of whistleblowers in public interest disclosures. Here too, none of the proposed conceptions (or characterizations) of the public interest seem to account for the role whistleblowers play in constitutional democracies. The reasons are straightforward: first, whistleblowers appeal to public interest often against the interests of a majority (at least within the government or organization they work for). Second, whistleblowers may also act against the presumed shared interests of a polity, and assume the responsibility of deciding when the disclosure is in the public interest. Third—and most importantly—by doing so they act by disclosing classified information in virtue of the privilege deriving from their epistemic advantage. However, contrary to judges, whose privilege is protected by constitutional guarantees, whistleblowers often act outside the confines of the law, or against the corporate rules of the institutions they work for. The question is then: what justifies the role of whistleblowers when they decide to act in the public interest? What account of public interest may fit the role whistleblowers play in both political and corporate contexts?

In the following, we will spell out an account of public interest that cuts across the characterizations we have so far discussed. The account we provide comes in two steps. In the next section we will defend a view of public interest that justifies disclosures in corporate and administrative contexts, or when the whistle is blown in order to denounce episodes or practices of political corruption. We have defined such a form of whistleblowing *civic* in order to stress its goal of contributing to the re-establishment of the common rules of the polity. In the next chapter we offer a justification of *political* whistleblowing, which we refer to as disclosures of government secrecy. We will argue that these disclosures are in the public interest when they reveal both wrongs perpetrated against constitutional rights, and in response to the lack of governmental accountability.

---

[19] A version of this argument is defended in Santoro and Liveriero (2017).

3.3   A Presumptive Interest for All-Purposive Rights

The definition of public interest faces a trilemma. It is either a sum or an aggregation of individual non-competing interests; or an interest of the prevalent majority of a polity at one point in time; or a common good that can be enjoyed only collectively. We have discussed different objections to these views. All of them—in different ways—try to explain away the 'public' in terms of some other concept: individuals, majorities, or collective entities.

How can we then qualify the 'public' in a way that it does not fall prey to any of the horns of this trilemma? Our proposal is to define public interest by dissecting two components of the notion: the nature of the 'public' addressed by claims of public interest, and the nature of the 'interest', i.e. the content or object of the public interest.

3.3.1   The Public

What does it mean for an interest to be public? At first approximation, an interest is public when it is *in the interest of the public*. The distinction is not self-evident, for while in the expression 'public interest' *public* is used as an adjective, in the second occurrence it figures as a noun. As we mention above, Brian Barry already remarked on this distinction (1965: 190–192): if we read 'public' as an adjective, its definition is opposite to 'private', that is something that stands in no direct or immediate relation to any specific person, but concerns all members of a polity without distinction (see G.C. Lewis 1832: 233–234, quoted in Barry). Barry notices that the semantic opposition also holds for Bentham who defines 'private offences' as '[t]hose which are injurious to such or such assignable individuals. An *assignable* individual is such or such an individual in particular, to the exclusion of every other' (1894: 240). Barry argues that non-assignability is also what defines the use of public as a noun, for the emphasis should be on 'an indefinite number of non-assignable individuals' (1965: 192). Non-assignability has two components: first, it conveys the idea of impartiality on the part of the members who are potential beneficiaries of a public interest policy; second, it implies that the provision of public interest policies are made under a veil of ignorance, otherwise the distribution of those provisions would not be impartial.

This is unconvincing though. Barry is right when he distinguishes the two uses of the term public, but he jumps too quickly to the conclusion of interpreting 'public' as an adjective. First, something can be in the public interest of a polity even if not every individual has an interest in the matter. In other words, something can be in the public interest in the sense that it does not address a specific individual, and yet in every distributive circumstance address a specific subset of the public, thus requiring information about the identity of specific individuals. Affirmative action policies articulate this point well, for they are in the public interest of polities that host disenfranchised groups, and yet they target only those identifiable groups. The provision of goods and services in national emergencies are in the public interest of every member of that society and yet address only specific local populations.

Non-assignability instead pertains to the communicative aspects of a policy, not to its content. It requires the public interest to address every member of the public, independently of how the public interest is distributed. We can express this idea by saying that something is in the public interest when there is the *presumption* that its content can be of a common concern for the members of a polity.

> A policy or action x is in the public interest when there is the presumption that x is in the interest for every individual $I_1...I_n$ who is member of a polity. (3.4)

The statement above represents a *sufficient* condition for a claim of public interest. In other words, it is sufficient to presume that a policy may affect the interests of (the members of) a polity to conclude that it is in the public interest. Earlier we said that a policy may affect persons in different ways, benefitting some more than the others. When a policy is in the public interest, its distributional effects are of common concern independently of who benefits from the policy. We can express this clause by adding the following to (3.4):

> A policy or action x is in the public interest when there is the presumption that x is in the interest of every individual $I_1...I_n$ who is member of a polity, independent of whether the outcomes of x directly benefit every member.[20] (3.5)

The last formulation clarifies that an interest is public when the policy in question affects every member of a polity, although it is not necessary that the outcomes of the policy in question directly benefit every member. It is important to stress here again the distinction between 'public' in the adjectival sense of 'public relevance' in discussions and debates, and 'public' in the substantival sense of the particular policy promoted in the public interest, which may only benefit a selected group.

To elaborate on this point, we may draw from two authors of the pre-Rawlsian era. Richard Flathman (1966) contributed to the definition of public interest as a constraint on policy, requiring public officials and administrators to take into account the effects of a decision on all affected persons. In a similar vein, David Braybrooke presents another interesting idea about the nature of public interest. According to Braybrooke, the concept of public interest should be limited to the following cases:

> ...first [when] a person or firm or relatively small group of people with special interests is arrayed against "the public"—a body open in membership to anyone who does not belong to the social group, and ... which therefore varies in identity as the special group changes

---

[20] Pettit (2004: 153) distinguishes between *ex ante and ex post* interests in the context of Barry's argument for the public interest. The distinction is between policies that, before distribution, are expected to benefit everybody, but due to the effects of luck end up after distribution to be worse for some individuals. Pettit argues that it would be counter-intuitive to say that since the state does not serve the persons' ex-post interests, then it allows an arbitrary presence of luck in their life. What counts is that the state serves people's ex-ante interests non-arbitrarily. We agree on this point. However, our emphasis is not on the ex-ante distribution, but on the presumption that members of a public are interested in policies affecting the polity.

from case to case. Second the question whether the government shall act or not act will be raised if other measures for assisting the public should fail. The existence of the government is therefore presupposed. Third, the issues debated in the cases are approached as issues of domestic and internal concern (1962: 130–131).

Braybrooke claims that his view provides a set of minimal conditions to identify instances of public interest.[21] He makes two compelling points: first, that 'public interest' is identified by the private interests of the person, group or firm[22]; second, that the composition of the public is defined by how private interests affect the public. Braybrooke proposes to identify instances of public interest by looking at the prevalent special interests. Thus the public interest is the interest of the public harmed by special interests.[23] The other feature of Braybrooke's account requires the existence of a government as ultimately accountable for addressing wrongdoings caused by the pursuit of illegitimate interests. A full-fledged conception of the public interest must presuppose an institutional setting which regulates the allocation of benefits and burdens according to the interests involved.[24] We can model these features of Braybrooke's account by formulating the following conditions to (3.5):

For any policy x: x is in the public interest when:
    there is a private interest y of a person, group, or firm opposed to x that may harm the interests of the public (where public is identified by the set of members of the polity affected by y);
    the government is responsible for addressing wrongdoings perpetrated in the pursuit of illegitimate interests (3.6)

---

[21] Braybrooke calls it the 'deflated' view, meaning that it is not a comprehensive consideration 'for there are obviously many possible disputes over policy from which one or more of these features are missing' (1962: 131).

[22] Defining public interest by what public interest is not recalls Barry's distinction between negative and positive connotations of public interest (1965: 208). Clearly Braybrooke's is a 'negative' characterization. Notice that Barry does not define public interest as being opposite to private illegitimate interests.

[23] The idea that public interest is an interest arrayed against factionalism can be traced back to a debate on the American Constitution. Robert Goodin (1996) argues that the problem for the American founders was to find an appropriate balance of power between the different branches of the government, due to the worry of a deadlock in the government for to the excessive measures of check and balances. Goodin provides a defense of the deadlock based on Madison's *Federalist* n. 10, where Madison defines a faction as a group of citizens united by an interest 'adverse to the rights of other citizens, or to the permanent and aggregate interests of the community' (Madison et al. 1987: 57). Thus, the kind of interest that rests in opposition with the factional interest is a general proviso of 'general welfare' – the terms appearing in the Preamble to the American Constitution – which he interprets as a "least-common-denominator" definition of public interest. Also Mark Warren has noticed that James Madison was the first to appreciate the fact that 'the interests of public officials could be aligned with public good by designing institutions that divide and share decision-making powers, thus providing officials with the motives and capacities to check and expose conspiracies against the public interest' (Warren 2015: 45, referring to Madison et al. 1987, no. 51).

[24] Lessig's institutionalist view also insists on the path-dependence of corruption as a response to an expected behavior widespread within an institution.

The last formulation presents a disjunctive case for public interest. It says that the a claim of public interest concerns a private interest that may potentially affect the public or a group thereof. An institutional structure must exist for addressing issues or complaints of public interest. The formulation does not state that a policy is in the public interest only when it satisfies the individual interests of every member of the polity. It just says that there must be a presumptive interest every member of the public has to be informed about a specific policy or action. This is only a presumptive interest, since the public may after all dismiss the information as irrelevant. Still, the presumption holds that the information may potentially be valuable.

3.3.2 The Nature of the Interest

Let's now move to the second question: what is the nature of the 'interest' involved in public interest arguments? We have already discussed Barry's interpretation of an interest as something that increases someone's opportunity to satisfy a want. We argued that this is not always the case: public interest cannot be a preference or a want, because while interests may coincide with wants or preferences, they are not identical. Within the scope of our discussion here, our emphasis is on what kind of interest is a public interest. The next step is to clarify whether public interest is a shared or common interest of some kind. We have already argued in the previous section that it is neither: for any characterization of the public interest in terms of shared or common interest there is an open question: is a shared interest x in the public interest? Is a common interest x in the public interest? We argued that a feature of public interest arguments, including cases involving whistleblowing disclosures, is that they oppose other interests (whether majoritarian, or the special interests of a particular group) whose political, social, and economic influence may warp democratic decision-making.

We propose that matters that fall within the scope of public interests (policies or disclosures) should be judged according to an independent standard of justice. By standard of justice we do not refer to a specific normative conception. The Rawlsian framework of justice as fairness can be one such standard, but our focus is not on ideal-theory. We instead pay attention to standards able to decide cases of conflicts of interest, especially when—in whistleblowing disclosures—there is a presumption in favour of the interest of the public.

To this purpose, we need to supplement the interest-based view of public interest with an account of the institutional design that governs the distribution of social goods. Our proposal is that an independent standard of public interest consists of the set of rights that are 'all-purposive' for the attainment of any social benefit. Public interest in this sense does not include any specific distribution of social benefits, but it is defined by the set of rights that supervise the arrangement of those benefits. Such a set of rights enables the enjoyment and fair distribution of particular social benefits. The socio-economic rights to education, employment, health-care, etc. are all rights that figure in this set. We can sum up the two aspects of public interest as follows:

For any policy or action *x:* *x* is in the public interest when:

(i)   there is a presumption *x* may affect the members of a polity (...); *or:*
(ii) *x* affects the all-purposive rights of the members of a polity that supervise the distribution of social benefits; *or:*
(iii) a private interest *y* opposed to *x* harms the all-purposive rights of those members;
(iv) there is an institutional authority accountable for addressing wrongdoings incurred by the pursuit of illegitimate interests. (3.7)

We may call (3.7) a characterization of the public interest. We derived it from the idea of presumptive interest (see 3.5) and by the idea of all-purposive rights (see 3.7). This characterization states the set of sufficient conditions that define a policy 'in the public interest'. It is not a definition of public interest since it does not say *what* the public interest is, but only in which circumstances a policy is *in* the public interest. The first three conditions are all disjunctions: any of them, provided (iv), is sufficient to determine when a policy is in the public interest. Notice that (3.7) is also neutral with respect to cases of harm or benefit to the public interest. It only specifies which conditions are relevant from the point of view of the public interest. Of course, a policy that favours the public interest will *positively* affect the set of all-purposive rights, and no private interest is opposed to the policy. Conversely, a policy that is against the public interest will *negatively* affect the all-purposive rights, or there is a private interest that leads to harm those rights. The fourth condition is the only strictly necessary: it is meant to express the idea that a policy can be in the public interest only within an institutional framework where demands of accountability can be publicly vindicated. Of course, we do not mean to say that there is no such a thing as the public interest where an institutional authority of this kind does not exist, but only that it is not possible to determine whether 'a policy is in the public interest' or not unless there is an institution that can adjudicate an appeal to the public interest.

It follows from (3.7) that illegitimate interests whose pursuit undermines certain all-purposive rights and their corresponding goods are against the public interest. If we know that a certain policy is likely to harm a certain group more than others, we know in advance that it is against the public interest *qua* the interest of that subject or group.

The public interest is therefore not an *ur-interest*, i.e. an interest that overrides the particular interests of those affected by a distribution, nor it is an interest of more general scope that comprises the interests of everybody involved. It is a standard of evaluation for the legitimacy of the interests involved in a given distribution. In some cases, the public interest may coincide with the particular interests of all members or groups involved in a given distribution. Public goods are goods in the public interests because they are supposed to be shared by all members of a given polity. In other cases the public interest will coincide with the particular interests of some members against others, namely of those who are more vulnerable to certain distributive policies.

The view of public interest we defend has some important advantages over other theories, and captures important *desiderata* of several views that we have discussed so far.

First, it is not an account set in terms of non-competing aggregate interests. Insofar as it is based on rights of distribution, and not just allocation of social benefits, it is a view based on a common core of equal rights.

Second, our view characterizes the public interest as an interest of the polity even if it is not in the actual or present interest of a particular person or social group. We have already touched upon this argument in discussing the preference-based view. What is most important is that the trade-offs between present and future interests in collective decision-making carry similarities with the trade-offs of individuals over time. A person may have a future interest that is not a present interest, and upon reflection develop a present interest for the satisfaction of a future interest. She may also have a presumptive interest in a policy that will affect them negatively now but nonetheless be in her future interest to adopt. The notion of public interest is governed by the same rational constraints on the discount of time of the concept of interest in general. Thus, a policy adopted in the interest of a public should be evaluated not only by the immediate consequences that it will bring about to the polity, but in terms of the future expectations of positive consequences that its adoption can yield to every member of the polity. Not discounting time in public policy decisions explains a feature of the public interest we have defined as being adversarial so far. Public interest is adversarial when it is arrayed—to use Braybrooke's expression— against special interests of different sorts (corporate and individual). An adversarial interest can also be a policy that favors certain underrepresented or disenfranchised groups at the cost of other members of the polity. Whereas public interest decisions may require trade-offs of resources that may negatively affect a part of the population, the return of the trade-off should be possibly beneficial to all. The fact that policies that are beneficial to all in the long term are in the public interest is a reason for the argument that rights governing those policies should also be in the public interest. Every member of a polity is entitled to the same constitutional rights that regulate the distribution of goods or resources, but this does not imply an equal distribution of those goods or resources.[25] What follows instead is that those rights can be exacted in due time by those who benefited less, or even suffered a cost from the implementation of the given policy.

The third advantage of the characterization of public interest we defend is that it accounts for some important aspects of the proceduralist conception of justice. Mechanisms of public accountability, appeal and amendment of the legislation should be part of a comprehensive view of the public interest because such procedures guarantee the enactment of and the appeal to rights in the case of wrongdoings. Our view also encompasses what Lasswell terms the inclusive procedures of public civic interest, which employs mild actions to exact taxation and fines; and of the public order interest, by which he refers to procedures employing severe

---

[25] The Rawlsian two principles of justice are exemplary of how this view can be justified within an egalitarian conception of justice (see Rawls 1971, 1999).

sanctions, such as punishment (1962: 67). Lasswell includes also the criteria of 'regulatory interest' in his view of public interest, that is those constraints on permissible policies that 'limit the degree of permissible inequality'(1962: 74). These procedures fall within condition (iv) of our characterization.

However, there is a caveat. We do not claim that these procedures are all what public interest is about. Quite the contrary, we maintain that an independent criterion for adjudicating matters of public interest must be available not only to institutions, but also to the public at large. In non-ideal settings where policies and procedures are posited by legislatures, we would fall into the positivist trap that identifies policies in the public interest with those public authorities promote (Bodenheimer 1962: 209). Our claim is that public interest is a standard for evaluation in public discussion that should be correlative to existing governmental procedures (see Cassinelli 1962: 46–47). Given the interdependence among the 'public' and the 'public institutions' in the life of a polity, the lack of efficient procedures of adjudication and redress does not affect the validity of the standard.

Who then can decide what the standard is? The view we have defended is that there is a deliberative aspect of public interest. Decisions over matter of public interest should be open to the largest possible public of a polity, in other words,to all those interested in discussions on all-affecting policies. We defend the idea that the disclosure of information regarding the effects of distributive policies on rights and duties, and of private interests that may conflict with those policies, is always in the presumptive interest of a public. Since information improves the capacity of the public to deliberate more effectively, and more democratically, the disclosure of information to the public is justified in the public interest even when individual whistleblowers take up this commitment. We call this form of engagement *civic* whistleblowing.

3.4   The Role of Civic Whistleblowers

At the beginning of this chapter we distinguished between two forms of political corruption: Philp's interactive account, and Lessig's institutionalist view of corruption, characterized by the manipulation of the public rules and procedures that govern a polity. Our account of public interest identifies two corresponding forms of injustice for each form of corruption. First, corrupt interactions preclude the fulfillment of social benefits by drawing from public resources or favoring one party over another. Second, when the rules that govern the distribution of those benefits are designed to allocate the burdens of social cooperation in ways that favor one party over another, not only the benefits, but the very system of rights is bent under a corrupt system of government.

How can whistleblowing contribute to fighting these forms of corruption? The characterization of the public interest we defend states that whistleblowing creates opportunity for *civic* forms of engagement. As we argued in Chap. 2, civic is a form of whistleblowing that occurs mostly in cases of disclosures of corrupt practices. Civic whistleblowers act within the confines of the established law, often against the current trend of the practice they are part of. When civic whistleblowers report cases of corruption, they do not face retaliation from government, departments of states, or secret agencies, but fear exclusion, demotion, stalking, if not even dismissal from their workplace. Moreover, there is a presumption in favor of civic whistleblowers that their disclosures are in the public interest of a polity in virtue of a clear identification of the illegitimate private interests pursued or perpetrated by corrupt criminals. When safe channels of disclosures are absent, it is generally agreed that this is a failure of public duty to fulfill the conditions for an effective right to protection. When whistleblowers reveal cases of corruption, they thus contribute to both redress injustices and wrongdoings with respect to the harm caused by corruption; at the same time, they uphold the procedural values of public accountability. Thus, public interest is not just a rhetorical device whistleblowers appeal to, but what defines the scope of interests that justify disclosures. If we consider the characterization of the public interest defined at (3.7), we can say that:

> Civic whistleblowing is in the public interest when it satisfies at least one of the following conditions:
>
> (a) it discloses information of presumptive interest for a polity or a group thereof;
> (b) it discloses a wrongdoing affecting the all-purposive rights;
> (c) it discloses a private interest that potentially or actually harms the all-purposive rights;
> (d) it exposes deficits of procedures within those institutions that are accountable for addressing wrongdoings incurred by the pursuit of illegitimate interests. (3.8)

Whistleblowing is in the public interest when the disclosures made in the process protect the interests of the public. Disclosures undermine the forms of corruption discussed in Philp and Lessig's accounts. Whistleblowing serves a civic role in both respects: as a form of professional engagement directed at a specific crime against the public interest; and as a form of civic testimony against corrupt practices which upholds the more general principle of the rule of law.

Once made public to the press, the disclosures turns out in legal prosecutions, although more often than not whistleblowers have no legal protection against retaliation in the workplace. Cases such as this occur in domestic contexts where the risk of exposure and sanctioning is low and the expectation is that corrupt officials and their counterparts will not defect. Countries which hold these expectations tend to be marked by a higher perception index of corruption[26] and have weaker public institutions; and, although not always, the magnitude of corruption will accurately mirror the perception index of corruption.[27]

---

[26] See the Transparency International's 2017 Corruption Index for details on the rankings and research methodology.

[27] For details on illicit financial flows, check the work done by Global Financial Integrity. Transparency International even dubs some Northern European countries as 'dodgy' when it comes to corruption overseas, although they perform well domestically for their clean public sector (see Transparency International 2015 Corruptions Index front page).

The denunciatory aspect of whistleblowing serves the public by exposing abuses of power committed by domestic and foreign financial elites who are able to privatize resources by corrupting public officials. However, whistleblowers are not always successful in this regard, especially in countries where public institutions bend the knee to private interests. Land grabbing in Africa is a telling example of this kind of corruption (see Liberti 2014).

Finally, whistleblowers contribute to the restoration of trust towards public institutions by holding public officials accountable. We must then ask whether there is a right to civic whistleblowing, or whether its protection should rather be a duty of the state. The idea that citizens should have a right to blow the whistle is vague. Under which condition should such a right should be granted? What would it exactly consist of? Our replies to these questions follow from the argument defended in this chapter. Civic whistleblowers should have a right to robust legal protection in virtue of the public interest role they play in a democratic polity.

In the last decade, governments have recognized acts of civic whistleblowing and have started to provide channels of disclosure, especially when the information concerns grave matters such as mismanagement of funds, abuse of authority, or hazard to public safety and health.[28] Many international conventions[29] have also recognized the need to protect whistleblowers when disclosures are done with a reasonable belief of a wrongdoing that has occurred. The conventions also require governments to provide adequate channels of disclosure, proper protection against retaliation, and to ensure a proper investigative and advisory authority. Measures of protection include also legal justifications for breach of confidentiality; procedures for the reinstatement in office of dismissed employees, or remedial mechanisms when reinstatement is not mandatory. However, despite the near universal acknowledgement of the beneficial role played by whistleblowers in exposing corruption, public perception is divided among those who consider them to be moral heroes and those who believe them to be guilty of treason. Accusations of treason arise because of the perception that information which should have remained within the confines of an institution has been allowed to go public, betraying the bonds of allegiance and to the detriment of the institution. Whistleblowers often face backlash by superiors and

---

[28] Prominent among whistleblowing legislations are the Public Interest Disclosure Act (1998) in the UK, the Protected Disclosures Act (2014) in Ireland, The Dutch House for Whistleblowers Act (2016) in Netherlands; the Whistleblower Protection Act (1989) and Whistleblower Protection Enhancement Act (2013), the Sarbanes–Oxley Act of 2002, the Dodd–Frank Wall Street Reform and Consumer Protection Act (2010), Foreign Corrupt Practices Act of 1977 (FCPA) in USA.

[29] Some international conventions invite governments to take action against corruption and provide protection for whistleblowers. A partial list includes the United Nations Convention Against Corruption (2003), the OECD Convention on Combating Bribery of Foreign Public Officials in International Business Transactions (1997), the Inter-American Convention against Corruption (1996), the African Union Convention on Prevention and Combating Corruption (2003), the Economic Community of West African States Protocol on the Fight Against Corruption (2001), the Council of Europe Civil Law Convention on Criminal Corruption (1999), the Twenty Guiding Principles for the Fight Against Corruption (1997), and the Committee of Ministers to Member States on Codes of Conduct for Public Officials (2000).

fellow employees who are afraid that their complicity in the crime will be exposed. (De George 2014: 324).

Given these burdens, the protection of whistleblowers has important incentive functions: protected employees are more inclined to report illicit conduct, and civic testimony also helps to break the habit of tolerating corrupt practices. Recent legislative proposals to incentivize disclosures are now being discussed in several Parliaments. Some legislative solutions look at practices already adopted in the United States, where monetary rewards are adopted at the federal level. Others insist on even more contentious legal devices, such as the inversion of the burden of proof. The inversion of the burden requires that the employer who fires a whistleblower must prove that the measure was not adopted in retaliation to the disclosure. However, effective protection is still imperfect or lacking in many European countries and other parts of the world.[30]

3.5   Concluding Remarks

Civic whistleblowing is the disclosure of information concerning corrupt practices taking place in either the public or the private sector. In this chapter we argued that its justification rests on a conception of public interest. We distinguished two broad characterizations of it, arguing that whistleblowing contributes to the public interest when disclosures reveal crimes that cause an unfair allocation of the burdens of social cooperation and whistleblowers who fight corruption should find protection in the law against retaliation. However, despite the increasing attention by Parliaments and organizations of the civil society, more work needs to be done to ensure whistleblowers receive effective protection. In this chapter we articulated a proposal for a public interest protection of civic whistleblowers.

References

Barry, Brian. 1965. *Political Argument*. New York: Harvester Wheatsheaf.
Bentham, Jeremy. 1894. Principles of penal code. In Id. *Theory of Legislation*, 239–472. London: Kegan Paul, Trench Trübner.
Bodenheimer, Edgar. 1962. Prolegomena to a theory of the public interest. In *The Public Interest*, ed. Carl J. Friedrich, 205–217. New York: Atherton Press.
Braybrooke, David. 1962. The public interest: The present and the future of the concept. In *The Public Interest*, ed. Carl J. Friedrich, 129–154. New York: Atherton Press.
Brettschneider, Corey. 2007. *Democratic Rights and the Substance of Self-Government*. Princeton: Princeton University Press.

---

[30] Ireland (in 2014), France (in 2016), and Italy (in 2017) are the most recent EU state members to have passed a law.

————. 2011. Judicial review and democratic authority: Absolute v. balancing conceptions. *Journal of Ethics & Social Philosophy*. Symposium I. August 2011: 1–9.

Cassinelli, C.W. 1962. The public interest in political ethics. In *The Public Interest*, ed. Carl J. Friedrich, 44–53. New York: Atherton Press.

Ceva, Emanuela, and Maria Paola Ferretti. 2017. Political corruption, individual behaviour and the quality of institutions. *Politics, Philosophy & Economics*. https://doi.org/10.1177/14705 94X17732067.

————. 2018. Political Corruption. *Philosophy Compass*.

Christiano, Thomas. 2008. *The Constitution of Equality. Democratic Authority and Its Limits*. New York: Oxford University Press.

————. 2011. Reply to critics of the constitution of equality. *Journal of Ethics & Social Philosophy*. Symposium I. August 2011: 1–14.

Dalla Porta, Donatella, and Alberto Vannucci. 1997. The 'perverse effects' of political corruption. *Political Studies* XLV: 516–538.

De George, Richard. 2014. Whistleblowing. In *Business Ethics: Readings and Cases in Corporate Morality*, ed. Michael W. Hoffman, Robert E. Frederick, and Mark S. Schwartz, 320–338. Chichester: Wiley.

Downs, Anthony. 1962. The public interest: Its meaning in a democracy. *Social Research* 29 (1): 1–36.

Dworkin, Ronald. 2011. *Justice for Hedgehogs*. Cambridge, MA: Belknap Press of Harvard University Press.

Flathman, Richard J. 1966. *The Public Interest: An Essay Concerning the Normative Discourse of Politics*. New York: Wiley.

Friedrich Carl J. 1962. *The Public Interest*. New York: Atherton Press.

Global Financial Integrity. 2006–2018. *Issues: Illicit Financial Flows*. http://www.gfintegrity.org/issue/illicit-financial-flows/. Accessed 10 Feb 2018.

Goodin, Robert E. 1996. Institutionalizing the public interest: The defense of deadlock and beyond. *The American Political Science Review* 90 (2): 331–343.

Held, Virginia. 1970. *The Public Interest and Individual Interests*. New York: Basic Books.

King, Stephen M., Bradley S. Chilton, and Gary E. Roberts. 2010. Reflections on defining the public Interest. *Administration & Society* 41 (8): 954–978.

Kurer, Oscar. 2015. Definitions of corruption. In *Handbook of Political Corruption*, ed. Paul M. Heywood, 30–41. London/New York: Routledge.

Lasswell, Harold D. 1962. The public interest: Proposing principles of content and procedure. In *The Public Interest*, ed. Carl J. Friedrich, 54–79. New York: Atherton Press.

Lessig, Lawrence. 2011. *Republic, Lost: How Money Corrupts Congress—and a Plan to Stop It*. New York/Boston: Twelve, Hachette Book Group.

————. 2013. 'Institutional corruption' defined. *Journal of Law, Medicine and Ethics* 41 (3): 553–555.

Lewis, George C. 1832. *Remarks on the Use and Abuse of Some Political Terms*. University of Missouri Press (reprinted 1970).

Liberti, Stefano. 2014. *Land Grabbing: Journeys in the New Colonialism*. New York: Verso Books.

Locke, John. 1988. *Two Treatises of Government*. London (1689), ed. Peter Laslett. Cambridge: Cambridge University Press.

Madison, James, Alexander Hamilton, and John Jay. 1987. *The Federalist Papers*. London: Penguin.

O'Flynn, Ian. 2010. Deliberative democracy, the public interest and the Consociational model. *Political Studies* 58: 572–589.

————. 2014. Deliberating about the public interest. *Res Publica* 16 (3): 299–315.

Pettit, Philip. 2004. The common good. In *Justice and Democracy. Essays for Brian Barry*, ed. Keith Dowding, Robert E. Goodin, and Carole Pateman, 150–169. Cambridge: Cambridge University Press.

————. 2012. *On the People's Terms. A Republican Theory and Model of Democracy*. Cambridge: Cambridge University Press.

Philp, Mark. 2015. The definition of political corruption. In *The Routledge Handbook of Political Corruption*, ed. Paul M. Heywood, 17–29. London/New York: Routledge.

Rawls, John. 1993. *Political Liberalism*. New York: Columbia University Press.

———. 1999. *A Theory of Justice* (Rev. ed.). Cambridge, MA: Harvard University Press.

Santoro Daniele, and Federica Liveriero. 2017. Proceduralism and the epistemic dilemma of supreme courts. *Social Epistemology* 31 (3): 310–323. https://doi.org/10.1080/02691728.2017.1317872.

Souraf, Frank J. 1962. The conceptual muddle. In *The Public Interest*, ed. Carl J. Friedrich, 183–190. New York: Atherton Press.

Thompson, Dennis F. 2013. *Two Conceptions of Corruption*. Edmond J. Safra Working Papers, No. 16. http://www.ethics.harvard.edu/lab. Accessed 15 Mar 2017.

Transparency International. 2016. *Corruption Perceptions Index 2015*. https://www.transparency.org/cpi2015. Accessed 10 Mar 2018.

———. *What Is Corruption?*. http://www.transparency.org/what-is-corruption/. Accessed 15 Mar 2017.

———. 2018. *Corruption Perceptions Index 2017*. https://www.transparency.org/news/feature/corruption_perceptions_index_2017. Accessed 10 Mar 2018.

Waldron, Jeremy. 2006. The core of the case against judicial review. *Yale Law Journal* 115 (6): 1346–1406.

Warren, Mark E. 2015. The meaning of corruption in democracies. In *Handbook of Political Corruption*, ed. Paul M. Heywood, 42–55. London/New York: Routledge.

Chapter 4
The Threat of Secrecy

Abstract National security and strategic interests of the modern state require a certain amount of secrecy. However, state secrecy poses a dilemma for constitutional democracies, whose legitimacy depends on the transparency of democratic decision-making. In this chapter, we defend the argument that citizens' right to know limits the prerogatives of state secrecy. We start from the debate on the balance between liberty and security and provide some criticisms of the idea that striking a balance is always justified in a democracy. We pay particular attention to the role secrecy plays in matters of national security and the effects of unrestrained secrecy on the enjoyment of rights. We then introduce the notion of epistemic entitlement of rights and argue that secrecy is legitimate within a constitutional democracy only when citizens enjoy a specific right to know in which circumstances their rights can be legitimately limited or restricted. We call this the right of assessment.

Keywords Balance model · Epistemic entitlement · Liberty · Right of assessment · Rights · State secrecy · Security

In Chap. 2 we presented a historical account of whistleblowing by placing it within the liberal quest for publicity and transparency. We described whistleblowing as a practical mode of engagement that challenges the boundaries around institutionalized practices of corruption through covert or overt means. These practices are often protected by the veil of secrecy that precludes any form of accountability. By lifting this veil, advocates of whistleblowing argue that disclosures ensure the detection of practices escaping democratic scrutiny. In this chapter, we want to explore the boundaries of state secrecy, the factors that give rise to it, its justification within a democratic context, and how unrestrained secrecy bears on rights and the democratic processes of accountability.

© Springer International Publishing AG, part of Springer Nature 2018   83
D. Santoro, M. Kumar, *Speaking Truth to Power – A Theory of Whistleblowing*,
Philosophy and Politics - Critical Explorations 6,
https://doi.org/10.1007/978-3-319-90723-9_4

4.1   Liberty and Security: Lessons from the Classics

In the immediate aftermath of September 11, a new political agenda was set to limit
civil liberties to an extent previously inconceivable, a shift primarily induced by the
fear that found acknowledgment in the public opinion. This shift was primarily
enacted through anti-terrorism legislation, such as the US Patriot and Homeland
Security Acts, and a legal foundation of this view can also be found in the European
Convention on Human Rights.[1] Admittedly, this turn in political agenda of many
Western countries seemed to be the only viable option for democratic societies in
times of unforeseeable emergencies. It was not surprising that security was accorded
high priority and scholars urged the need to find a framework to justify it. Criticisms
against the shift focused on the danger of targeting specific individuals through
profiling techniques and the corporate control of peacekeeping operations in Iraq
and Afghanistan. The doubt was that the Muslim terror gold-rush was ineffective for
the most part and lucrative only to some political factions and private contractors.[2]
Yet, political opposition in Congress and in the streets did not find credence insofar
as the public opinion continued to be ruled by fear.

The situation changed as the dust of the war on terror began to settle. The question at this point became whether the shift towards more security at the cost of some
liberties had to be extended even to normal circumstances, where existential threats
against national security were not, or at least did not seem to be, immediate anymore. As Jeremy Waldron has noticed, the political discourse had already assumed
at that point that 'the change in the scale and nature of the harms that threaten us'
was sufficient to explain and justify a concurrent change 'in the scheme of civil
liberties,' a process that was best understood in terms of 'striking a new balance
between liberty and security'(Waldron 2003: 192). However, was this statement
true, Waldron asked. A consequentialist argument has since been invoked to justify
it. According to this argument, a balance is *always* necessary, even in normal circumstances, because of society's need for protection against the harm that may
follow from individual liberties themselves (ibid.: 191–92). Therefore, a security
policy should be evaluated for how well it maximizes the balance between liberty
and security. This way, practices such as data mining and limitation of privacy rights
are justifiable to protect personal security against the potential misuse of liberty.

---

[1] The European Convention protects the fundamental freedoms of thought, conscience, and association as well as the right to privacy with no restrictions on their exercise 'other than such as are
prescribed by law and are necessary in a democratic society in the interests of national security or
public safety, for the prevention of disorder or crime, for the protection of health or morals or for
the protection of the rights and freedoms of others' (Articles 8, 10, and 11). In addition to such
exceptions, the freedom of expression is restricted for 'the disclosure of information received in
confidence' (article 9).

[2] The expression 'Muslim terror gold-rush' is a quote from the 2009 thriller *State of Play*, but there
is some truth to it: 'It is estimated that the US security market generated $29.1 billion in revenue
in 2006 from "the threat of terror", of which about 70 percent came from federal, state, and local
government contracts, and current estimates suggest that this will double by 2010' (Zedner 2009:
102).

These practices did not override but were instead functional to the protection of the political and civil rights of citizens.

Is this a good argument? If we pay attention to the debate following the heyday of the 'war on terror,' it does not seem that political philosophers have embarked on a serious reflection on the consequences of this view for our conception of civil liberties. Theorization has instead come from think-tanks, scholars, or from the legal consultants of the executives, who tried to devise solutions to specific instances, without yet being able to provide a normative framework to tackle the problem in its generality. Yet, the issue is too important to forego philosophical reflection, and a principled solution is needed, even more in these days.

In this chapter, we explore the scope and the limits of the consequentialist argument underpinning the balance model. In the first part we argue that, for a consequentialist justification to hold, it must be assumed that more security is instrumental to the protection of personal liberties. However, this is far from certain. Citizens have typically no control or access to that sensitive information that would justify the particular balance between liberty and security that the executive has set for them. In the second part, we provide an alternative account of civil liberties based on the constraints that restrictions of liberty must fit to be legitimate.

To start with, we need to investigate an issue concerning the very nature of the relationship between liberty and security: whether security is, in general, a necessary element for a theory of constitutional liberties. The history of liberal political thought can be read as an attempt to provide a general answer to this question. Thomas Hobbes is a strong advocate of the view that no liberties are possible outside a strongly secured state. For Hobbes, since 'the end of [the institution of sovereignty] is the peace and defence', it is a prerogative of the sovereign to do 'whatsoever he shall think necessary to be done, both beforehand, for the preserving of peace and security, by prevention of discord at home, and hostility from abroad; and when peace and security are lost, for the recovery of the same' (1996: 124). In the Hobbesian picture, security and peace are the primary goals of government, the pursuit of which confers legitimacy to it. Insofar as the liberty necessary for the industry and commerce is granted, it is also constrained by the demands of security.[3] Such a prerogative is limited even for Hobbes: 'it belonged of right to whatsoever man or assembly that hath the sovereignty to be judge both of the means of peace and defense, and also of the hindrances and disturbances of the same' (ibid.). In other words, although the sovereign retains the power of enforcing the means to ensure peace and security, he is nonetheless subjected to the judgment over the appropriateness of those means.

John Locke's views extend in a way this last proviso but depart from the general Hobbesian picture. Security—for Locke—serves the purpose of preserving liberty and property, for the great end of man's entering into society is the enjoyment of

---

[3] As Hobbes wrote, in a time of war 'there is no place for industry because the fruit thereof is uncertain: and consequently no culture of the earth; no navigation, nor use of the commodities that may be imported by sea;... no arts; no letters; no society; and which is worst of all, continual fear, and danger of violent death; and the life of man, solitary, poor, nasty, brutish, and short' (1996: 89).

those goods in peace and safety. The preservation of society is 'the first and fundamental natural law, which is to govern even the legislative itself' (1980, section 134: 69). Transgression of this law by the legislative through 'an absolute power over the lives, liberties, and estates of the people' is a breach of trust that forfeits 'the power the people had put into their hands for quite contrary ends' such that this power devolves back to them 'who have a right to resume their original liberty, and, by the establishment of a new legislative... provide for their own safety and security.' (ibid. section 222: 111).

Partly on the same line, John Stuart Mill argued that self-protection and prevention of harm to others is 'the sole end for which mankind are warranted, individually or collectively, in interfering with the liberty of action of any of their number' (Mill 1863: 23). It must be noticed though that, while for Locke security is functional to the preservation of liberties (primarily those associated with property rights), for Mill security is a fundamental interest the possession of which, society ought to protect.[4] It is indeed the most vital interest such that 'no human being can possibly do without' since on it—Mill writes—'we depend for all our immunity from evil, and for the whole value of all and every good, beyond the passing moment' (1879: 81). It must be noticed that this view is not strictly consequentialist, but rather a prudential view stemming from the consideration that 'since nothing but the gratification of the instant could be of any worth to us, if we could be deprived of anything the next instant by whoever was momentarily stronger than ourselves' (ibid.).

The rationale behind the prudential view is expressed by Bentham, for whom security is needed to ensure against future harms. Security guarantees in fact the 'expectation of the future' such that 'the successive moments which compose the duration of life are not like insulated and independent points but become parts of a continuous whole' (1838: 308). Bentham's prudentialism carries a stronger conclusion than what we may find in Mill. For him liberty is, in fact, a branch of security, but in a very particular sense: 'personal liberty is security against a certain species of injury which affects the person; whilst, as to political liberty, it is another branch of security—security against the injustice of the members of the Government.'[5] Thus, while Bentham is usually considered to hold a consequentialist view of security, it does not seem that his consequentialism would satisfy the contemporary advocates of the balance model.

John Rawls makes a significant departure from the prudential understanding of the primacy of security in *A Theory of Justice*. Rawls holds that public order and security are necessary to the exercise of individual liberties when the disruption of public order and security is 'a danger for the liberty of all.' This stance is a

---

[4] According to Zedner (2009), Mill argues that security is a precondition for the enjoyment of liberty; but a closer reading shows that this view is not correct because for Mill security is rather a substantive right that falls within a constitutional system of liberties, not the other way round.

[5] Ibid. Ch. 2. In the same vein, Bentham writes that '[i]n legislation, the most important object is security. If no direct laws are made respecting subsistence, this object will be neglected by no one. [...] Security, we have observed, has many branches: it is necessary that one branch of security should give way to another. For example, liberty, which is one branch of security, ought to yield to general security, since it is not possible to make any laws but at the expense of liberty' (1838: 303).

consequence of the argument in favor of the first principle laid out in the original position. Liberty—he claims—can be restricted only 'for the sake of liberty itself,' i.e. when its limitation strengthens the total system of liberties and is 'acceptable to those citizens with the lesser liberty'.[6] Therefore, when the government restricts a liberty 'by reference to the common interest in public order and security,' it must do so in accordance with that very principle[7] (ibid: 187).

From this brief overview of the liberal tradition, one can discern a general agreement in the idea that liberty and security depend on each other, though they seem to differ on the direction of this dependence. In particular, three different kinds of views arise: one that endorses the view that security is the paramount good that state must protect and justifies the limits of individual liberty in the name of that good. This is precisely the Hobbesian conception that strictly privileges security over liberty. The second istead takes liberty as the basic good and security as a means to ensure its protection. Unsurprisingly, Locke and Rawls are advocates of this view in requiring that any constraint on liberty can only be justified if it contributes to enhancing the whole system of liberties. The third one conceptualizes security as a prudential requirement for enjoyment of liberty.

If one takes the lessons of the classics as a guide to chart the map of the contemporary debate on liberty and security, one can see a marked-shift from the principled standpoint of the classical conceptions. This view, which gained increasing consensus partly because of the pressure triggered by the events of 9/11, prioritizes considerations of efficiency over any foundational claims in negotiating the relative weight of liberty and security. Its origins can be traced back to the economic analysis of law. By largely ignoring the lesson from the classics, they offer a metric of balance in response to a question of principle. The view underlying this understanding appears then as a rather unstated consequentialist view that hardly fits even the prudential arguments that one can find in the writings of Mill and Bentham. In the following section, we analyze this conception in detail, showing that its implications for a conception of civil liberties are far more reaching than what the model apparently suggests.

4.2   Striking the Balance?

Although the dominant view in the post 9/11 era conceives of liberty and security as a mutual adjustment, often represented in the form of a balance, the exact idea behind this image and the nature of the relationship are often unspecified. In

---

[6] 'Rawls (1999: 222). Rawls suggests that the fundamental interests in liberty may require certain social conditions sometimes leading to the restriction of basic liberties: 'But once the required social conditions and level of satisfaction of needs and material wants is attained... the higher-order interests are regulative from then on' (Rawls 1999: 476).

[7] Interestingly enough, the justification of security includes the case of conscription, when it is enforced to the end of protecting the defense of liberty itself, domestically, and abroad (ibid.: 334).

particular, it is not clear which standards fix the right point of the supposed balance. This is the case of Richard Posner, who has provided a robust defense of this view. For Posner, terrorist threats require the need to 'restrike the balance between the interest in liberty from government restraint or interference and the interest in public safety.' The ideal way of striking the balance is to calibrate the scope of the right 'by reference to the interests that support and oppose it.' Thus, the balance is the point 'at which a slight expansion in the scope of the right would subtract more from public safety than it would add to personal liberty' or vice-versa. This way, the point of equilibrium keeps shifting depending on the intensity of the threat (Posner 2006: 31).

In a series of works from the last decade, Eric Posner and Adrian Vermeule have articulated the image of balance as a straightforward trade-off between liberty and security. The trade-off can be represented akin to a Pareto production-possibility frontier, representing liberty and security as variables on the axes of a diagram that identifies all the possible points of trade-off. The efficient trade-off is realized, in analogy with the Pareto frontier, on a security-liberty frontier where any increase in the level of security requires a decrease in the level of liberty. A rational and well-functioning government will maximize the outcomes of a particular security policy by aligning itself to the requirements of this frontier when the emergency strikes, and will adjust its policies over time as emergencies come and go. If increases in security are worth more than the corresponding losses in liberty, the government will increase security; but if reductions in security will produce greater gains from increased liberty, the government will relax its security measures (Posner and Vermeule 2007: 12, 21–41. See also Lazar 2009, especially chapter 1) (Fig. 4.1).

The diagram shows that for any policy P below the frontier (for instance, P1), 'either security and liberty can be increased without sacrificing any of the other, and indeed both can be improved simultaneously.' Points beyond the frontier (such as P4) are policies that cannot be attained (Vermeule 2014: 32). Therefore, in this model, the balance between liberty and security is subjected to an efficiency constraint, depending on the available resources of the state. Achieving efficiency constitutes the maximizing goal in this consequentialist view.

One of the crucial points is that the level and shape of the frontier can change over time, depending on the nature of the threat, or to a shift of resources towards or away from security policies. This way, it may happen that policies 'that were previously on the frontier (or beyond it, and thus infeasible) might fall below the frontier, and conversely.' In any case, 'the trade-off thesis is unaffected by such changes; whatever the level and shape of the frontier at any given time, there will still be some such constraint on feasible security policies'(ibid.).

The 'trade-off' method has been criticized in recent years.[8] There are three major strands of criticism. According to the first one, a consequence of the trade-off in times of crises is the deference the legislative and especially the judiciary branch show towards the executive. Posner and Vermeule subscribe candidly to the deference view:

---

[8] See Vermeule (2014) for a discussion and defense of the model.

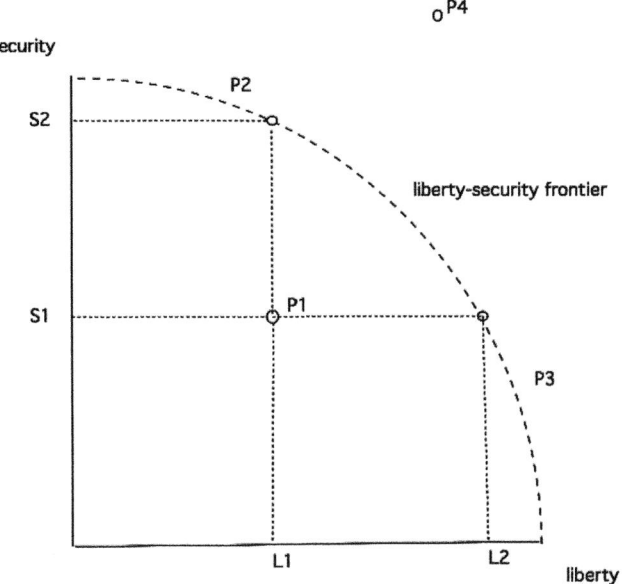

Fig. 4.1 The Pareto-optimality frontier for liberty and security: 'at any point on the frontier, security cannot be increased without corresponding decreases in liberty, and vice versa' (Vermeule 2014: 32). Original diagram modified by the authors

> The deference thesis holds that the executive branch, not Congress or the judicial branch, should make the trade-off between security and liberty. [...] The deference thesis does not hold that courts and legislators have no role at all. The view is that courts and legislators should be more deferential than they are during normal times; how much more deferential is always a hard question and depends on the scale and type of the emergency (Posner and Vermeule 2007: 5–6).

However, when the judiciary is prone to accept the emergency measures of the executive, it is often caused by the lack of due reflection on the proper balance during peacetime.[9] In other words, deference appears to be a consequence of the absence of prior constraints on the acts of the executive. The search for balance may contribute to undermining liberty without enhancing security, with unpredictable consequences on the system of check and balances (Waldron 2003: 198, 209). A case of this sort is the behavior of certain US Federal Courts—particularly those working under the Foreign Intelligence Surveillance Act (FISA)—who authorized top-secret government programs without adequate controls. As revealed in the early revelations of Edward Snowden on the Prism scandal, the US intelligence had access to the servers of several internet companies and telecom corporations for a wide range of digital data and phone records.[10]

---

[9] See Sagar (2009: 168) quoting Justice Brennan (1988).

[10] A problem arising in connection with deference is that courts support unwise expenditures of resources. So, for instance, 'random searches in a subway system of over four million riders a day

A second strand of criticism comes from Jeremy Waldron (2003, 2006). According to him, the problem with the balance model consists in its consequentialist mindset: when the consequence of enjoying a certain degree of liberty is an enhanced level of risk, the model requires taking this risk into account in evaluating whether that degree of liberty should be maintained(Waldron 2003: 208). This way, the balance model makes liberty a function of our perception of fear and security in a misleading way: a necessary element of the model should—but does not—include a 'well-informed belief that the modification will make a difference to the prospects that we fear' (ibid.: 198). However, it is not clear that a diminution of liberty will increase the net-sum of security. If we cannot know whether it is worth giving up some liberties, 'we cannot talk with any confidence about an adjustment in the balance.' On the contrary, 'immediate effects on suspects and dissidents are quite clear'(ibid.: 209). Waldron highlights a crucial weakness in this conception of the balance, namely the uncertainty intrinsic in the assessment of the threats: that diminishing the extent of certain civil liberties *will* increase security, an argument which is yet unproven. An enhanced ability to combat terrorism does not imply an actual diminution in terrorist threat (ibid.: 210). What is rather certain is that, by doing so, we are giving up our commitment to civil liberties. Thus, despite the proclaimed goal of ensuring security, the balance model undermines the reasonable prospect of enjoying our fundamental rights.

Informational uncertainty has far-reaching consequences also for the conception of justice that grounds those rights. The consequentialist reasoning of the balance licenses policy arrangements where the security-gains of most can justify the liberty-losses of a few (ethnic, racial or religious minorities, and political dissidents). Waldron contends that the few/most distinction is a concern of justice that cannot be addressed from the point of view of the liberty/security distinction: 'simply adding something to the "most" side of the balance'—he claims—'is insufficient to justify taking something away from the "few"' (ibid.: 203). What the balance model does not provide is an account of principles of distribution in gains and losses that would justify a particular configuration of the few/most distinction.

In his criticism of the Patriot Act, also Ronald Dworkin highlights the problem of the distributive implications of the violation of equality. He argues that security decisions which are a product of the balance argument will affect perhaps only a tiny number of American citizens, but the impact of such policies will be high for 'those resident and foreign aliens who might very well be ensnared in the less protective and more dangerous legal system' (Dworkin 2002: §§16–17). The trade-off does not pass the test of fairness because it violates equal concern and respect of persons by unjustly targeting a minority in order to make the majority feel secure: 'whenever we deny to one class of suspects rights that we treat as essential for others, we act unfairly, particularly when that class is politically vulnerable, as of course aliens are, or is identifiable racially or by religious or ethnic distinction' (ibid.: § 20). Fairness requires that we extend fundamental rights to everyone

---

deems more symbolic than effective because the odds of the police finding the terrorist with a bomb are very low' (Solove 2008: 348).

affected by the legal system they live in, whether citizens or aliens. In conclusion 'we must reject the balancing argument—it is confused and false' (ibid.).

Although Vermeule has recently replied to some of these criticisms, yet these criticalities cannot be met by more or less extensive adjustments in the specifics of the model, for they stem from the assumptions underlying the balance (see Vermeule 2014). The first of these assumptions concerns the nature of the variables involved, namely the idea that liberty and security are goods whose preference (or utility) can be compared on the same scale, in analogy with the comparison among commodities. The model treats liberty and security as goods whose particular configurations are indifferent to the agent, insofar as they are efficiently allocated. However, people are not indifferent towards these goods. Limitations of civil liberties call for a special justification under constitutional rules that cannot be provided by the trade-off model because the model simply replaces criteria of justification with considerations of efficiency. Absent countervailing considerations against efficiency, the model appears to be too coarse-grained to make room for constitutional constraints on trade-offs particularly unfavorable to the protection of fundamental rights and liberties.

The second assumption concerns the control of information. To serve as an effective policy tool, the model must assume that the executive can make timely adjustments in the balance. Posner and Vermeule assert that 'during emergencies, the institutional advantages of the executive are enhanced' because 'courts, which are slow, open, and rigid have less to contribute to the formulation of national policy than they do during normal times' (Posner and Vermeule 2007: 5). Democratic procedures would fail to provide a quick and efficient response of this sort. However, the prompt readjustment required by the model is possible only under the exclusive control of information, which allows the executive to exercise undue influence in security policies.

The control of information determines as well the distributive framework that allocates the burdens of security among the population. Consider the Dworkin-Waldron criticism again. The general idea is that the trade-off reading of the balance is a consequentialist mode of reasoning in which individual and even group rights can be potentially limited for the sake of security of the majority. Given the sensitive nature of the rights involved, any limitation of rights should be known to everybody affected and a justification provided for those special burdens. The balance model does not make room for a justification of this sort, rather it offers considerations of factual efficiency in response to a normative request. Nor does the model make room for any ex-post act of transparency, such that those people whose rights have been restricted are at least entitled to be informed of the interference in their liberties after states of emergency have ceased. Paramount cases of hidden interferences that last beyond the recall of emergency are those legislations that in the post 9/11 era enhanced surveillance as a precautionary measure against people considered potentially suspect in virtue of their political, ethnic, or religious belonging. The fact that regulatory procedures are given no space in the balance model should not be surprising within this mode of reasoning. Once the idea that government should have the prerogative of exclusive control of information is assumed to be a necessary premise for any effective security planning, the constitutional mechanisms of checks and balances cease to have a regulatory function anymore. As a consequence, people potentially affected by the shifts in the trade-off are deprived of their right to assess their position with regards to a security policy.

A sphere in which the consequences of the executive control of information are particularly revealing is that of secrecy. Generally defined, secrecy consists in the intentional act or practice, performed by an individual or a collective body, of withholding information from being accessible to others. In democratic societies governed by the rule of law, information of public interest are assumed to be available to all, and every citizen has an equal right to be informed of the actions and policies that the government enacts in their name. It is true though that full transparency may, in fact, threaten the existence of the state by divulging important information to potential enemies. This way, the government prerogatives over information seem to be justifiable in the light of the constitutional mandate of ensuring public safety.[11] In what follows, we will explore this line of thought in detail and focus on secrecy as a specific instance of national security. We will look at the debate from a normative standpoint and pay attention to the epistemic dimension of rights; an aspect largely neglected in the ongoing debate. We argue that the limitations imposed on rights by informational asymmetry, and particularly by secrecy measures, can be better understood within this perspective.

4.3   The Threat from Secrecy

The problem of secrecy has been subject to close attention in the past years. The general argument is that for democracy to function properly it needs to protect itself from external and internal threats. Thus, security requires that sensitive information be not open to the public, lest it spill over to the enemy. Stationing of troops, sites of military nuclear power, or intelligence gathering by the secret services are examples of this kind. For this reason, the functioning of the secret services is constitutionally mandated, and their informational resources are exempted from sunshine laws that require functioning of the executive to be open for public scrutiny. Thus, state secrecy privileges, especially executive privilege, are enshrined in the constitutions.[12] Post 9/11—with the discourse on securitization going rampant—the

---

[11] 'The Privilege of the Writ of Habeas Corpus shall not be suspended, unless when in Cases of Rebellion or Invasion the public Safety may require it.'—*American Constitution*, article 1, section 9. On this point, see also Ackerman's proposal of an emergency constitution. (Ackerman 2004)

[12] It is a mistake to assume that the executive privilege, and the secrecy privilege that comes with it, are a product of the constitution. As Mark J Rozell suggests, 'executive privilege is an implied power derived from Article II. It is most easily defined as the right of the president and high-level executive branch officers to withhold information from those who have compulsory power—Congress and the courts (and therefore, ultimately, the public). This right is not absolute, as the executive privilege is often subject to the compulsory powers of the other branches'(2002: 404).

exemptions sought by the executive grew exponentially, due to the portrayal of an invisible enemy with the potential of striking at any time.[13] The response to the threat has resulted in a spate of new laws in the US and other countries.[14] Surveillance operations, data mining, etc. have been on the rise on an unprecedented scale. Thus, it is imperative to look at the implications of the discourse of security on the functioning of democracy, since security is one of the fundamental grounds used by secret agencies for classifying state documents. With the number of such classification on the rise, we should get a better grasp of what security entails in terms of increased secrecy for the democratic functioning of institutions, and its impact on the liberty of citizens.[15] In this chapter, we limit our analysis to the cases of executive secrecy. By executive, we mean that branch of the state which deals with the day to day functioning of the state apparatus. This branch is responsible for the execution and enforcement of the laws, as mandated by the legislature or as interpreted by the judiciary. It is the executive branch that is responsible for maintaining public order.

4.3.1 Secrecy: A Conceptual Analysis

Let's start with a tentative definition of secrecy. A piece of information i is a secret if and only if an agent A (or a group acting as a collective or corporate agent) having information i intentionally withholds it from being revealed to others.[16] Secrecy is, therefore, a particular circumstance of asymmetric information in strategic circumstances. Holding a secret requires three conditions:

(a) agent A disposes of i;
(b) i is not in possession of anyone else other than A;
(c) i is intentionally hidden from others by A.

'Dispose' and 'possess' are employed here to refer to information that the agent possesses, whether or not she knows that the information is veridical.[17] In other

---

[13] A study done by Washington Post shows that there has been an exponential rise in exemptions under state secrecy privileges. See Priest and Arkin (2016).

[14] The attacks of 9/11 followed a spiteful of anti-terrorism legislation all across the world. The Homeland Security Act (2002), the Patriot Act and following amendments in the National Defense Authorization Act in the USA, the Anti-terrorism, Crime and Security Act of 2001, the Terrorism Act (2008) in UK, the Australian Anti-terrorism Act (2005), the Unlawful Activities (Prevention) Amendment Act (2004, 2008, and 2012) in India.

[15] Before embarking on this argument, some qualifications need to be made. The concept of secrecy will be understood in relation to the democratic functioning of the state. We leave out cases of secrecy that concern individuals (for whom secrecy might be a way to preserve their privacy), secret societies, and groups. For a comprehensive analysis of individual and group secrecy see Simmel (1906). For the need for individual secrecy see Bok (1983).

[16] The intentional aspect of secrecy has also been highlighted by Bok (1983).

[17] The predicate 'knowing' will be treated here as *justified true belief*, according to the classical tripartite definition of knowledge Plato already formulated in the Theaetetus. Although there are

words, the information can be kept secret even if A is uncertain about the veridical-ity of the information. The relevant aspect of the secreted information is not its truth, but its disposition to be used (as true) in decision-making contexts, unbe-known to others. What is unknown to others is not the truth-value of the informa-tion, but that someone possesses that information. Whether the agent is able to ascertain the truth of the information is a different matter. In the context of asym-metric information, who disposes of the information will usually be at the advan-tage of being able to check the truth of the information, but this circumstance is not necessary to define secrecy.

The crucial aspect of the informational asymmetry of secrecy is that it is a situa-tion dictated by intentional strategic behavior. It is intentional in the sense that the agent must know that she is in possession of the information and that others do not have access to the same information.[18] The strategic aspect of secrecy consists in the behavior of the agent who must ensure that the information remains undisclosed to others. Secrecy, in this sense, allows the agent who disposes of the information to perform a range of actions whose goal would be unattainable had the information been available in the public domain.Troop movements in a war scenario, or surveil-lance operations designed to capture a fugitive are a case in point. Were this infor-mation accessible to the public, it would defeat the very purpose of the action.

Along with intentionality and strategic behavior, another critical aspect of secrecy is the capacity of agents who dispose of information to control the rational decisions of others in virtue of the control over information. If the information were in the public domain, the behavior of the other parties would differ from what they actually do, for their responses would adapt to the strategic environment. Informational asymmetry confers then an advantage to the informed agent that can be employed to exercise forms of power. Such power is legitimate when the secrecy privileges of executives and dependent agencies are kept in check by independent parliamentary committees. Moreover, such forms of power are not immediately dis-positive, for the activity of gathering information does not usually equate with the executive power of intervention. While this last case is usually most evident, as in the case of bureaus like the CIA, others are designed just to collect, not to act upon information. The US National Security Agency is one such a case. Thus, the sole fact of possessing classified information does not imply *per se* the exercise of exec-utive power. It does, however, constitute a favorable condition for subtler forms of manipulation, for the agency in possession of information can lead others—citizens, or even other agencies within the government—to conclusions contrary to the facts (for instance, by providing them with insufficient or inaccurate information). Manipulation alters the opportunity set in the choice of agents, thus hampering the

---

several counterexamples to the tripartite definitions after Gettier's seminal paper (1963), the scope of our discussion falls outside these aspects.

[18] A might be mistaken in the belief that others are not aware of the secret, but in her knowledge, she is the only one who knows about the secret. Sometimes A herself can be the origin of the secret and would be the only one knowing about it.

very capacity of an agent to act autonomously. This phenomenon, also known as 'framing effect' (Julius 2003), occurs as a result of presenting opportunities and alternatives in a way that affects individual choice and judgments. It is a form of strategic behavior by means of which the framer leads another person to believe and act in ways that advance the interests of the framer. Secrecy can be used in manipulative contexts to elicit a framing effect where the agent believes her choices are informed, whereas they are manipulated instead.

Cases of manipulative framing due to secrecy abound on the geopolitical scene. The notorious argument of an unwilling US Defense Secretary Colin Powell at the UN Security Council in February 2003 is a test case. Powell argued that Iraq was hiding Weapons of Mass Destruction (WMD) from the international inspectors, and harboring al-Qaeda terrorists, among which was Abu Musab al-Zarqawi. The argument was preparatory for the invasion of the country, which happened later that year under the flag of the so-called 'coalition of the willing.' After the invasion and the removal of Saddam Hussein, no WMD were found, as many—including some European countries—had urged given the poor amount of evidence that had been gathered by the intelligence. Although Powell later declared that the US administration—and even the Congress—believed that Iraq had WMD, he recently admitted, in an interview for Frontline, that the speech 'was a great intelligence failure'.[19] Multiple scenarios explain what turned out later to be a disastrous invasion. One is that the US Administration believed in good faith in lousy intelligence. Many factors run against this face-value explanation: other countries did not take too seriously the intelligence the US had shared despite the fact that the US repeated that they had more information confirming the presence of WMD on Iraqi territory. More importantly, the inspector general appointed by the UN, Richard Blix, had repeatedly stated that the Iraqi regime was collaborating with the inspections and nothing had been found by the team before the situation got worse. Finally, in the same interview for Frontline, Powell admitted that President George W. Bush had already made his decision to invade Iraq by the time the Security Council Meeting was taking place. The second scenario is that the US intelligence received insufficient information about the presence of WMD, but the Administration deliberately chose to mislead the public by insisting on the weak evidence.[20] The third scenario is that the Administration had received false information which they took to be accurate and tried to work on it. In the fog of a rampaging consent for pre-emptive war, information carried out by the media outlets suggested in fact that the sources were reliable, but never went on to specify who those sources were in the first place.

None of the three scenarios described above justify the decision of invasion, but out of those three, two invoke an explanation that refers to manipulation (direct or indirect), while one refers to blatant failure and incompetence. Even on the assumption that the US administration had been misled into believing the existence of WMD, it still possessed the power to act upon that conviction. Whatever the

---

[19] Colin Powell made such statement during an interview with Jason M. Breslow (2016).

[20] Fresh evidence claims that the Iraqi foreign ministry told MI6 and CIA before the war about the absence of active weapons of mass destruction. See Norton-Taylor (2013).

reason was for the US administration to believe bad intelligence, those reasons fall outside the nature of information itself. In each of these three cases, the secretive nature of the intelligence accorded an epistemic privilege to the executive to use manipulatively—if not recklessly—the information they possessed. The unchecked privilege of secrecy enhances executive's power to act without any recourse to public fact-checking and the truth-content of the information.

4.3.2   Individual and Institutional Secrecy

The WMD case is instructive of a dimension of secrecy that exceeds the case of individual secrecy. In many cases, institutional secrecy cannot be reduced to privileges accorded to single individuals, for the reasons why specific information are classified can only be explained by reference to the institutional role of the agents having clearance privileges. Moreover, because of their complex structure, the administrative state[21] and modern corporations often partition classified information among multiple sets of agents working on different designated tasks, where only a handful of individuals have full access to the whole picture. Thus, even within corporate or state agencies, information is not common knowledge, and it is often used by some members to gain an advantage within those very agencies.[22] The secretive nature of information is—in other words—defined the institutional structure.

Thus, institutional secrecy cannot be properly understood within the paradigm of methodological individualism, although it carries an informational value (sometimes even financial value) that can confer an advantage for individual use. In either case, institutional secrecy grants freedom to corporate and individual agents to act upon information unknown to external actors, and any abuse resulting from the institutional protection of such privilege depends on how the institution itself functions.

Different institutions have different models to deal with classified information. For instance, industrial secrets are bound by patent laws and internal regulations of non-disclosure usually stated in employment contracts. Public institutions, however, work differently. Within the context of constitutional democracies, the rules and regulations governing the access to classified information are constrained by public interest clauses. External and internal systems of checks are designed for this

---

[21] The expression 'administrative state' refers to that conception of the modern bureaucratic apparatus, which acts as a separate power, quite independent of the constitutional hierarchy of power. Eric Posner and Adrian Vermeule have recently argued that the complexity of the modern administrative state is an impediment in principle to the idea that governments have full executive powers. See Posner and Vermeule (2011).

[22] A case of such non-collaborative division of informational labor was the lack of collaboration between CIA and the FBI in the events leading to the 9/11 attacks. The CIA did not share intelligence gathered on some of the terrorists, which could have been used by FBI to thwart the terrorist attacks. See 9/11 commission report for more details on this point.

purpose. While the external checks may be absent in countries where the independence of the press is weak, internal checks are—or should be—part of the very system of procedures that regulate access to information. The possibility for corporate and institutional agencies to act upon classified information, as well as the privileged access for individual actors within those agencies, opens up a space of incentives, opportunities, and advantages that might run contrary to the law or specific duties. Corporate agencies may keep secrets they are entitled to by patent laws for innovation they conduct in their research labs, although their technological advance can also be used to serve unlawful or even criminal goals, as in the recently revealed history of the IBM-Nazi relationships during the Second World War.[23] Likewise, state agencies may classify information for justifiable reasons of national security, but may also abuse their power for political purposes that would shake the stability of executives and political majorities. The Pentagon Papers affair is a case in point.[24]

Along with corporate and state agencies, individuals might also want to trade information for a variety of reasons: for their personal benefits with enemies, as in the case of insider trading, or espionage toward foreign countries, a case where ideological creed may also play an important role. However, individuals, unlike corporate or state agencies, may also act out of reasons of conscience. Acts of this nature are usually forms of dissent that involve an element of (conscientious) objection or outward disobedience against the rule and policies protected under the privilege of secrecy, which the agent judges to be contrary to the stated objectives of the institution and harmful to the public. In such cases, agents receive no incentives or rewards, instead they act upon a moral interpretation of their duty of office—for instance when the agent judges that her actions thwart her legal duty towards the public interest—or upon concern over the democratic institutions of the country. We will consider these cases more in detail in next chapters where we discuss the case of political whistleblowing.

---

[23] During WWII, IBM Corporation sealed a strategic alliance with the Nazi regime, helping the Third Reich to create software technology for cataloging programs and identification of people. Edwin Black tells this secret story of corporate collusion with the Third Reich in *IBM and the Holocaust* (2012). The secret deal, made by the home corporation in the US (led by its CEO Thomas J. Watson) through its subsidiary in Germany Dehomag (led by Willy Heidinger, a fervent Nazi supporter), allowed IBM to provide punch card machine-read technologies to the new regime for its 1933 census survey. The technology helped the new regime to identify ethnic groups—above all Jews—in Germany and later in the occupied territories, as well as organizing the concentration camp slave labor, often anticipating the Reich's needs (2012: chapter 3).

[24] For the story and details of this case, see Ellsberg (2002) and Herring (1993).

4.4 A Democratic Justification of Secrecy?

The discussion in the last section highlighted some features of the concept of secrecy, specifying how those features should be treated in institutional and corporate settings. Our concern in this section is whether secrecy can be justified within a democracy. Since democracy is thought to be—at least in ideal theory—a system of government governed by public laws, the question we should ask is whether a democratic government should always be open for public review and criticisms. What is often called the paradox of democracy (see Bobbio 1987) is the conflict between two principles that hold *prima facie*. One is the principle of transparency in the decision-making of elected governments whose legitimacy rests upon the consent of the governed; the other is the principle that secrecy is a democratic instrument necessary to protect democracies against its enemies, even more in the face of existential threats, whether these threats are from external or internal enemies. However, here is the paradox, the democratic quality of decision-making depends on the possibility of scrutinizing the activities of the elected representatives, and thus any form of secrecy that preventing the governed from performing this role would be in violation of the very principle of democracy that secrecy is supposed to protect. The realist response to this paradox lies in the perceived difference between 'democracy as it should be' and 'democracy as it is' and contends that an ideal-theoretic conception of democracy cannot establish rules of government for real-world democracies.[25] The ideal of democracy may convey normative commitments of openness and transparency, but the actual practices require negotiation and secrecy. The realist challenge does not take the paradox too seriously, partly because it does not insist on the legitimacy requirements of democratic states. Realists read legitimacy as state authority, and therefore an authority that imposes secrets on sensitive matters of national interest exercises its power just within the limit of its function. However, the democratic ruling is not just a blank cheque, and even the justification of historical democracies cannot but refer to the constitutional process by means of which laws are passed, and to how the executive enacts them. Secrecy policies are no exception, even more when their function is necessary—as the realists claim—to the functioning of the democratic process (see Sagar 2007 on this point). 'The conflict—as Dennis Thompson says—'is not primarily between secrecy and democracy but arises within the idea of the democratic process itself. Some of the best reasons for secrecy rest on the very same democratic values that argue against secrecy' (1999: 182).

The argument is that some level of secrecy can justifiably coexist with the normative requirements of transparency in a democratic government (Sagar 2007). However, which levels of secrecy would be compatible with democracy? When shall we say that a secret is justified? The answer lies in policies that might not be

---

[25] See Bobbio (1987: chapter 1) for a discussion of the paradox. In this section, we analyze the legitimate practice of secrecy in a democracy, and do not take into account *realist* account of state secrecy. For a discussion on the realist account of state secrecy see Mark Neocleous (2002). On state secrecy as a form of executive power see also Max Weber (1978), Neocleous (2008).

carried out effectively without their being kept secret, at least to some extent. Policies requiring discretion can still be in the public interest. They are policies

> …citizens would consent to if they had an opportunity. The most familiar examples are in foreign policy and law enforcement. If the Dayton negotiations on Bosnia had been open to the press and all the terms of the final agreement fully disclosed, the leaders would almost certainly not have been able to reach an agreement. Or, if the plans for a sting operation to catch drug dealers were revealed even after it took place, the safety of informers and future operations of a similar kind would be jeopardized (Thompson 1999: 182).[26]

We see in the above statement three strands of justifications emerging for secrecy. One is the standard justification based on security. The second is based on what we may term as 'deliberation enhancing reasons.' The last one is based on effectiveness. These arguments do not stand alone, but rather reinforce each other. So a security policy might need to be secretive for it to be effective. Similarly, a closed chamber discussion might be required on certain policy matters for policymakers to approach the best possible solution. The argument of effectiveness runs through the other two justifications as well: it is because the information about the Dayton agreements was kept confidential that made it feasible in the first place. Let us run through these arguments in detail.

The first justification for secrecy stems from necessity and effectiveness. We have already discussed above how the arguments in favor of striking the balance are justified by the incumbent threats of emergency. If the democratic institutions are to be protected, they should be secure (Bok 1983). Paraphrasing what he calls a moderate version of Machiavelli, Bernard Williams provides a reason generally cited in favor of maintaining governmental secrecy:

> The responsibilities of government are sufficiently different from those of private individuals to make governmental virtue a rather different matter from that of individuals—or rather (and this is very much the point) from that of individuals who are being protected by a government. In particular, any government is charged with the security of its citizens, a responsibility which cannot be discharged without secrecy, and which it will be lucky if it can discharge without force and fraud (Williams 1996: 607).

This is precisely the kind of argument that lays ground to what Williams calls the 'anti-tyranny' argument famously advocated by liberals; the argument casts suspicion on the acts of state endowed with enormous power. Excessive power needs to be controlled lest it violates the very rights and liberties for which the state has been created. In order to enjoy life and liberties, citizens have to be assured that the basic institutions of democracy are protected, that their life is secured from both external and internal threats. This existential requirement requires vigilant institutions of defense and internal security that guard against potential threats. Secrecy is required for a state to act against criminals, mafias, drug cartels, etc. or track the movements of the terrorists; publicity will endanger the effectiveness of such policy. Therefore,

---

[26] Similar kinds of reasons were invoked in the Reagan memorandum when it argued for the case of executive privilege regarding secrecy in some of its affairs. It allowed for secrecy in the cases where information might impair national security, the deliberations of the executive branch, or some of the functions of the executive as mandated in the constitution (Rozell 2002).

governmental agencies that gather and use classified information (not only the secret services but also the police and investigative bureaus) are not an exception; they are instead necessary for the very functioning of democracies.[27]

Executive secrecy is derived from the prerogative and the function constitutionally designated to the executive. The idea is an old one: according to Locke, the executive can 'act according to discretion, for the public good, without the prescription of the law, and sometimes even against it' (Locke 1980: 84). The prerogative is required

> ...for since in some governments the lawmaking power is not always in being, and is usually too numerous, and so too slow, for the dispatch requisite to execution; and because also it is impossible to foresee, and so by laws to provide for, all accidents and necessities that may concern the public, or to make such laws as will do no harm, if they are executed with an inflexible rigour, on all occasions, and upon all persons that may come in their way; therefore there is a latitude left to the executive power, to do many things of choice which the laws do not prescribe (ibid.).

Executive prerogative thus enables the executive to assess and respond promptly in circumstances of emergency, sometimes even in extra-legal ways insofar as these actions are performed for the public good.[28] We can sum up the argument in favor of governmental secrecy as follows:

1. National security is a fundamental public good that states ought to provide to their citizens;
2. The executive is the branch of constitutional states whose function—among others—is to grant order and national security;
3. National security—especially in times of emergency—requires certain acts of the executives to be secretive for their successful enactment.

However, the argument as such contains a further implication that is often concealed in the debates over the justification of secrecy. Security matters require an expert review of sensitive information to handle emergencies effectively. Effective fulfillment of a security policy requires secrecy for operations that cannot be made public without informing the enemy at the same time. Moreover, the expertise argument requires that judgments on matters of national security be taken by people who have the requisite knowledge on the matter. Only the executives are in such a position to decide upon the actual existing nature of the threat (see Posner and Vermeule 2007). Given these circumstances, public judgments in conditions of partial or no information are often deferred to the executive, for citizens neither have sufficient information nor the expertise to provide meaningful inputs. They ought, instead, to surrender their judgment to the executive.

---

[27] See Sunstein (1986), Solove (2008), Sagar (2009), Moore (2011), and Article 8 of the European Convention on Human Rights.

[28] It is not clear where Locke would stand on governmental secrecy, but one may speculate that his support for executive prerogatives would justify a certain amount of it.

Another argument that favors secrecy over publicity resorts to the impact that secrecy has—in some instances—in enhancing the quality of deliberation.[29] The idea was already outlined by Sissela Bok, who argued that

> [Publicity] tempts participants to rigidity and to posturing, increasing the chances either of a stalemate in which no compromise is possible, or alternatively, of a short-circuited and hasty agreement. To pull back from an opening offer, often made for bargaining purposes only, might be interpreted, if done in full public view, as giving in' (Bok 1983: 184).

In the same vein, Simone Chambers contends that 'the public nature of the debate forces speakers to make general appeals, but there is little or no critical accountability to ensure that those appeals are well reasoned' (Chambers 2004: 398). The reasons presented in public would be shallow or pertain to narrow interests of the representatives' own constituencies, thus resorting to demagoguery. At the same time, interest groups can influence the way decisions are taken. In circumstances where the public eye exercises such conditioning, the decision makers might not be interested in upholding the virtue of truth but will strive to gain support for their cause, manipulation and pandering being their means (ibid.). Thus, the quality of deliberation would improve when the officials deliberate in secret, for they can fearlessly play out their reasons, revise their positions and better appreciate others' reasons; avoiding being stuck in ideological oppositions (Gutmann and Thompson 1996).Widely different and contrasting positions can thus be resolved and reconciled. Similarly, if the representatives have to carry on deliberations in private, they have to be assured that their tentative proposals are not made public (Bok 1983). Doing otherwise will compromise their fundamental freedoms and also restrict their participation.

4.5 Pitfalls of State Secrecy Justifications

A democratic government cannot rely upon secrecy prerogatives unless they are justifiable in the light of democracy itself. The arguments in favor of state secrecy we have reviewed so far justify secrecy by pointing out that a stable democracy requires security, effectiveness in decision-making, and informed decisions, especially in times of crisis. When state secrecy contributes to fulfilling the conditions of stability, secrecy is instrumentally justified. However, stability is just one among the many aims of democracies. Publicity, transparency, participation, and respect for individual rights are also other vital aims of democratic government. When these values clash with secrecy, does secrecy override the respect for these values or it holds only *pro tanto*? In this section, we will review some of the arguments against secrecy. The general problem with state secrecy is that it opens up the space for arbitrary power. When information is classified, individuals and agencies in

---

[29] For a debate on the enhancing role of secrecy in deliberation see Elster (1995), Gutmann and Thompson (1996), Chambers (2004), Sunstein (1986), Dryzek, (2000).

possession of this information are significantly empowered with unchecked power. The arbitrariness of decision under conditions of secrecy privilege has significant implications for the balance of power in constitutional democracies. In fact, under such conditions, the executive branch is the only institution which may hold power to access secret information and preclude others from having control over the use of information. 'An indication of power', suggests Adam Moore 'is the ability to forcibly demand access to information about others while keeping one's own information secret' (Moore 2011: 141). This executive privilege compromises the balance of power between the different branches of the state, and tilts it in the favor of the executive. Access to information puts the executive in the position to decide on the potential harms of disclosing the content of the information. The internal checks are missing or reinforce the existing trends in maintaining secrecy (see Fuchs 2006). In the following, we discuss the main arguments against the idea that secrecy is always justified in the name of national security.

4.5.1   Abuse of Information

Secrecy privileges confer a competitive advantage to the knower with respect to the non-knower, especially when the informational good in question is rivalrous or the information might impact the non-knower's life in adverse ways. This is the case of secret trades, such as the recent and now abandoned attempts to pass TTIP (the Transatlantic Trade and Investment Partnership) between the US and the European Union. As trade agreements were underway, citizens and civil society organizations were denied access to the terms of the agreement.[30] The arbitrary power of secret information is enhanced when corporations and government agencies have the power to gather information over counterparts, unbeknown to them. Data mining and surveillance exemplify such phenomenon (see Moore 2011 on this point).

4.5.2   Deception

As we mentioned earlier, asymmetric relation generated by secrecy also provides a fertile ground for deception, since the one who possesses information can selectively decide to leak or withdraw certain information from others, in order to tell a coherent story that the deceiver wants the hearer to believe. Being the sole arbiter, the executive often denies the legislature and the policy-makers important

---

[30] This is not only the case of state secrecy. Any person who intentionally hides information potentially relevant for a counterpart, exercises an arbitrary power that may inflict harm on the other person. Take the example of an individual who suffers from a communicable disease, and intentionally hides the information from all those who might potentially get infected. See Simmel (1906) for an analysis of this aspect of personal secrecy.

information and influences them in matters of public policy. The Iran-Contra affair is a case from the Reagan Administration that hit the front pages of newspapers for quite some time in the late 1980s. The administration had secretly authorized the selling of weapons to Iran despite an embargo in order to finance in return the support of a right-wing paramilitary opposition to the Socialist regime in Nicaragua.[31] The Congress had been pushed to support the Contras, a move which was initially thwarted by the legislative branch. The hope was that, by keeping the support to the Contras secret, the Congress would have been left with no other options than to agree to support them at a later stage. The idea was to manipulate the public opinion and the opinion of the Congress in this direction.

The executive can also resort to selective leaks from time to time, in order to orient public support in their desired policy direction (see Fuchs 2006; Berman 2009). An example from a 2011 ACLU report on the war in Afghanistan corroborates this point of view:

> In September 2009, Bob Woodward of the Washington Post obtained a leaked copy of a confidential military assessment of the war in Afghanistan that included General Stanley McChrystal's opinion that more troops were necessary to avoid mission failure. The purpose of this leak was to manipulate the policy debate by putting public pressure on President Obama to comply with the commanding general's preferred strategy (German and Stanley 2011: 13).

The obfuscation due to secrecy allows the executive to watch and control the behavior of the public (through the existence of surveillance technologies), and wield power over them.[32] When secrecy is employed as a tool for social control, informational resources are manipulated with the goal of shielding the excesses of the executive from being known to the public.[33] Secrecy privileges often involve not only the content of the information but also the very existence of classified content. In these circumstances, citizens can be largely unaware that such excess is occurring in the first place, for they lack not only information about secret acts, but also the knowledge that such acts take place. They are thus doubly disadvantaged: firstly, as citizens who are unaware of what the state does in their name; and secondly they are unaware of how secrecy meddles with their own rights. This phenomenon can also affect the legal standards of due process, as in the denial of the request made by

---

[31] For more on the Iran-contra see Shenon and Engelberg (1987). See also the Report of the Congressional Committees Investigating the Iran-Contra Affair (S. Rep. No. 216, H.R. Rep. No. 433, 100th Cong., 1st Sess.). United States Government Printing Office, November 11, 1987. See also Parry and Kornbluh (1988).

[32] Cf. Bobbio on this point: 'If we take the pair command/obedience as the epitome of the asymmetrical power relationship, the more hidden from sight the person who commands, the more terrible he is (the subject knows that there is someone looking at him but does not know exactly where he is)' (1987: 90).

[33] 'Privileged access to the sources of relevant knowledge makes possible an inconspicuous domination over the colonized public of citizens cut off from these sources and placated with symbolic politics.' Habermas, cited in footnote 28 by Chinen (2009: 8).

lawyers and families to provide information on the names of Guantanamo prisoners, de facto denying *habeas corpus* to them.[34]

Notice that the usurpation of secrecy privileges may also lead some officials to act not just out of considerations of national interest (a justification often used by past US adminitrations in their meddling with South-American elected governments), but also to use their office to further personal or sectarian interests that conflict with the public good.[35] As we saw in the previous chapter, this is also the case with corruption, when a certain group or individual is favored over another by granting private benefits to the public employee. Information, in the absence of proper check or review, might be withdrawn or not revealed to shield public officials from critical scrutiny or prosecutions.[36]

4.5.3   Quality of Deliberation

Finally, secrecy can even affect the capacity of judgment of those very subjects who enjoy secrecy privileges. As Sissela Bok points out:

> Secrecy can harm those who make use of it in several ways. It can debilitate judgment, first of all, whenever it shuts out criticism and feedback, leading people to become mired down in their own stereotyped, unexamined, often erroneous beliefs and ways of thinking. Neither their perception of a problem nor their reasoning about it then receives the benefit of challenge and exposure. Scientists working under conditions of intense secrecy have testified to its stifling effect on their judgment as journalists, police agents, and spies, or about living incognito for political reasons, have described similar effects of prolonged concealment on their capacity to plan and to choose, at times on their own sense of identity (Bok 1983: 25).

This point needs to be highlighted: secrecy privileges may shield their possessors from criticism, but in doing so, they also confine the deliberators behind closed doors, increasing the likelihood of reinforcing bias and self-deception, even more when the selection process of the pool of agents is not sufficiently variegated. A telling example, epitomized by Sidney Lumet's movie *Twelve Angry Men,* is that of all-white juries called to express a verdict over African-American defendants. There is plenty of evidence that when the jury selection process does not reflect racial diversity, verdicts of guilt are much more common. Contrary to what deliberativists maintain, behind doors deliberation can also lead to intentional or even unconscious

---

[34] Similar cases involve extraordinary rendition, where suspects were kidnapped in foreign territories and taken to secret CIA prisons outside the US (the so-called 'black sites') and submitted to waterboarding practices.

[35] Interestingly, Cass Sunstein shows that at times the justification for secrecy in deliberations might be required so that a particular group having 'intense preferences' might want to orient the policy in their preferred direction (See Sunstein 1986).

[36] See Stiglitz (1999), Moynihan (1998), Fuchs (2006). In the Reynolds case the judiciary was refused any insight into the case citing crucial national security information, but in the end when the information was revealed it was found that the secrecy around the affair was to shield some neglect on the part of some officials. For more analysis see Fisher (2007).

neglect of information that would improve the quality of deliberation. This may happen for several reasons: (i) there is no warrant that all the given positions and interest groups have been represented; (ii) it is not possible to ascertain whether the participants in the discussions were not swayed by sectarian interests (Sunstein 1986); (iii) secret deliberations might prove counterproductive, and might betray their own ends.[37]

4.5.4   Deference to the Executive

Secrecy privileges generate situations of asymmetric information where no counterpart can check whether the devised strategies are effective and well planned. This is the case of weak oversight bodies that show deference to executive decisions in times of emergency. The post 9/11 situation is exemplary of this situation since the FISA courts called to pass the requests of the government to spy in bulk on American citizens, almost always granted the requests due to the purported emergency of the situation. Admittedly, certain decisions are justified by the need of taking immediate action, but when the decision over fundamental constitutional rights is systematically deferred to government experts, an entire spectrum of ethical, political, and epistemic conundrums opens up, calling into question the assumption that when national security is at stake, the consent of the citizens is implicitly assumed. A similar case is the increased employment of drones in war, which increased under the Obama Administration. Despite their use was systematically classified, their impact on the civilian population and enemy combatants has been leaked to the news media. The use of drones as an official policy was not assented till recently.[38]

It can then be asked whether the American public would have assented to this policy, had the policy been made public. When consent is not sought openly, are citizens responsible for the actions of their government? On one reading of this problem, ignorance of the affairs of the state does not reduce the culpability of the citizens, at least when systems of democratic control are in place. The authority of the state to act on their behalf is justified by the scheme of social cooperation that citizens benefit from. When political obligations are justified through the system of democratic legitimation,[39] it is the duty of the citizens to actively refuse to be part of

---

[37] One of the examples of fallouts of secret deliberations was the Bay of Pigs fiasco: 'The Bay of Pigs debacle was caused, in part, by the fact that the government of the United States had entered into negotiations with exiles from Cuba in secret, and had planned the invasion without allowing the American Public to participate in the decisions regarding such a venture. The temptation is strong to negotiate in secret with a faction within a foreign country: perhaps a junta that is about to take over or to be toppled, or a political party one hopes will be more friendly than others to one's position. The indignation that follows upon the discovery of such secret talks, both at home and abroad, bespeaks the sense of unfairness that they arouse' (Bok 1983: 186).

[38] For an informed analysis of the US drones agenda, see Calhoun (2015).

[39] For a review of the main theories of political obligation in contemporary political theory, see Horton (2010).

the harms caused in their name.[40] The conundrum of legitimacy arises when a necessary condition for active duties of civic opposition is not met, and the information is only shared within the expert circle of government agencies.

Deference to the judgment of experts[41] opens up a 'democratic deficit.' However, the judgment of the expert does not betray democracy by belittling citizens' rational abilities; on the contrary, it supposedly celebrates it (Bobbio 1987: 92). In fact, the argument in favor of expertise is not that the citizens do not have the critical faculties in order to judge the circumstances for themselves. The justification is rather that the experts have better epistemic grounds to assess facts. They possess the required skill, technical know-how, resources and the crafts of the trade in order to make better judgments. The courts have continuously shown this tendency to defer to the judgment of executive when it comes to the matter of national security, and one of the reasons cited by courts is the lack of expertise to correctly assess the matter at hand. This is the deference thesis. As Posner and Vermeule argue

> … the executive branch, not Congress or the judicial branch, should make the tradeoff between security and liberty. During emergencies, the institutional advantages of the executive are enhanced. Because of the importance of secrecy, speed, and flexibility, courts, which are slow, open, and rigid, have less to contribute to the formulation of national policy than they do during normal times. The deference thesis does not hold that courts and legislators have no role at all. The view is that courts and legislators should be more deferential than they are during normal times; how much more deferential is always a hard question and depends on the scale and type of the emergency (2007: 5–6).

The core of the deference argument is that judges often do defer to executive judgments in matters of security, especially when it comes to circumstances of emergency. This is because

> judges are at sea, even more so than are executive officials. The novelty of the threats and of the necessary responses makes judicial routines and evolved legal rules seem inapposite, even obstructive. There is a premium on the executive's capacities for swift, vigorous, and secretive action. Of course, the judges know that executive action may rest on irrational assumptions, or evil motivations, or may otherwise be misguided. However, this knowledge is mostly useless to the judges, because they cannot sort good executive action from bad, and they know that the delay produced by judicial review is costly in itself. In emergencies, the judges have no sensible alternative but to defer heavily to executive action, and the judges know this (ibid.: 18).

---

[40] According to Mill, 'A person may cause harm to others not only by his actions but by his inaction, and either way he is justly accountable to them for the harm' (1863: 26). In case of secrecy, though, it can be assumed that this inaction is due to the lack of information. See also Pogge (2008a) for why it is a duty of the citizens to refrain from harm being done in their name.

[41] This deference to the experts stems not from 'the traditional contempt for the common people as an irrational crowd, incapable of making rational decisions even in its own interest, unable to raise its eyes so that instead of staring at the ground of its own daily necessities it might contemplate the blazing sun of the common good. Rather it stems from an objective recognition of its ignorance, or rather its lack of scientific know-how, of the unbridgeable gulf which separates the expert from the layman, the competent from the incompetent, the technician's or scientist's laboratory from the high street' (Bobbio 1987: 92).

Is the deference argument correct? We find it flawed in many ways. First, it assumes that decision-making in a democracy can be at times messy when numerous stakeholders have to be integrated into the process. However, at the time of emergency the executive might not have enough time to deliberate and reach out to wider audiences; thus classification of information can be sought to speed up the process; executives are therefore to be trusted.[42] While we agree that during emergencies decisions cannot be made in a perfectly sound deliberative manner and that not all concerns can be taken into account, those emergency decisions should nonetheless be open for retrospective evaluation or deliberations. The problem is that deference to executive becomes a consolidated practice even in non-emergency circumstances, halting due time evaluation in the post emergency. We are left with outright paternalism, if not just disregard for democratic procedures (cf. Sagar 2007). The problem, in essence, is not whether the experts can be trusted to design fair laws and take just decisions, but whether the procedures are fair and just.

The availability of epistemic resources in democracies contributes to the quality of its outcomes because it grants that decisions will be fairer in virtue of being largely inclusive, and also that informed democratic processes better track truth claims.[43] Achieving truth is not necessarily the criterion which binds those decisions, though truth can be a normative benchmark on which decisions can be judged in some cases. In either case, no matter whether fairness or truth is the criterion of democratic decisions, secrecy prevents the circulation and scrutiny necessary for an informed decision.[44] Moreover, citizens are deprived of sufficient epistemic warrant to trust the judgment of the executive. Writing on the Pentagon Papers case, Hannah Arendt argued that it was a closed group of individuals, who were supposed to be the ones deciding on the security policy. These individuals had enough confidence in their own built technocratic models to allow any fact to interfere with or to correct their judgments. So even when the facts necessarily pointed to the opposite direction, they were unwilling to use them. This was one of the reasons for the disasters in the Vietnam campaign, where the war was carried on just to live up to the image of a superpower, without paying due notice to the basic facts on the ground (Arendt 1972). The example suggests two things about the aspect of secrecy which are deeply troubling: first, secrecy can distort the judgment of individuals or even groups, and executives are not averse to this kind of failures; second, judgment formation in important policy matters will sooner or later be impaired in the process.

---

[42] Citing the case of the affidavits filed by the FBI officials and the Department of Justice on disclosures of the information on the detainees held post 9/11, Mark Fenster suggests that executive agencies working on national security matters often think the sunshine laws and the openness required under them to be 'at best a burden and, at worst, a threat to their work' (2005: 892).

[43] With regard to the so-called 'epistemic' strand of democratic theory, see Cohen (1986), Estlund (2009). Cf. also Anderson (2006).

[44] Sunstein (2002) convincingly shows that those decisions are generally efficient where people from different stand points and dissenting voices are allowed to contest and put forward their claims. The possibility is not allowed, especially in closed groups where like-minded people generally echo each others' ideas. Secrecy allows for such a like-minded group to be formed who generally disregard any sense of dissenting opinion.

The disturbing aspect is that errors creep in because dissenting opinions are not allowed while making decisions, leading closed expert circles to keep holding their own firmly held convictions (see Sunstein 2002; Pozen 2010).

4.6   Secrecy and Civil Liberties

Perhaps the most significant consequence of security policies shielded by secrecy privileges is that they can severely limit the enjoyment of basic liberties of individuals, and in some cases of whole groups, without them being aware of it. Let us illustrate with some examples. The Guantanamo prison is a paradigmatic case of an extra-territorial prison run by the US military in which non-American enemy combatants and suspected terrorists captured from different parts of the world were often kept in solitary confinement for most part of the day. Until 2017, despite Obama's promise to close the prison, 41 (out of almost 800 since 2002) were incarcerated as 'indefinite detainees' without trial. The justification for such practice under the Bush Administration was that, since the prison is not part of the United States territory, courts have a limited role in reviewing military decisions, and thus they should defer to the military's decision. Those still detained were declared too dangerous to be released but ineligible for trial due to either lack or insufficiency of evidence. As a consequence, prisoners were not produced before a court of law, and torture and extra-legal means were used to extract confessions and information.[45]

A number of basic civil liberties crucial for the very idea of constitutional democracy have been violated at Guantanamo: the right to appear before a court and be notified with accusations (*habeas corpus);* the basic right to due process and fair trial; the right of appeal to a court's decision. This is a secret violation of a right, for these policies were kept secret from the citizens at large, another case of the failure of the United States' government to inform its citizens of policies enacted on their behalf.

Even if the state has noble objectives,[46] acts of secrecy arouse legitimate suspicion. As Pogge suggests

---

[45] Citing various sources, Pogge describes the ordeal of these prison inmates. 'Labelled "unprivileged combatants," "unlawful enemy combatants" or "security detainees," these people have been routinely humiliated and degraded at will by coalition personnel: stripped naked, forced to masturbate and to simulate sex acts, abused with dogs, shackled in stressful positions, kicked and beaten with electric cables, and tortured with electric shocks, drugs, sleep deprivation, induced hypothermia and "waterboarding" (simulated drowning)'(2008b: 16).

[46] Citizens should beware of their threat to liberty even when the objectives of the state are well meaning. As Louis Brandeis points out in Olmstead vs. the United States: 'Experience should teach us to be most on our guard to protect liberty when the Government's purposes are beneficent. Men born to freedom are naturally alert to repel an invasion of their liberty by evil-minded rulers. The greatest dangers to liberty lurk in insidious encroachment by men of zeal, well-meaning but without understanding' (277 U.S. 479, 1928).

At these "black sites" our governments are imprisoning so-called ghost detainees—
unknown numbers of unknown persons for unknown reasons under unknown conditions.
Our governments are telling us that nothing untoward is going on at such sites. However, it
would be irrational and irresponsible to trust that basic human rights are being respected
in locations no one else has access to when such rights are not being respected in locations
from which a fair amount of information is leaking out. Common sense suggests that, once
persons have been caught in the secret prison system, their captors are reluctant to release
them even when they become convinced of their innocence: Wholly unaccountable for their
actions, these captors prefer innocent persons to remain missing indefinitely over their
resurfacing with information about conditions in the secret facilities and possibly with
knowledge that might be used to identify particular torturers, interrogators, or collaborating
doctors (Pogge 2008b: 19).

The Guantanamo case is revelatory of the extent of illiberal policies even for citizens at home who might be under threat of future attacks as a response to wrongful—call it imperialist—policies.[47] Moreover, the threat to civil liberties can also
from the state itself. Given the record of civil liberties violation outside the country,
it can be legitimately asked: can a state which tramples liberties abroad be trusted to
maintain liberties at home? The answer is no. The history of civil liberties testifies
to the spillover of emergency legislation into domestic constituencies. For this reason, the lack of transparency in dealing with the liberty of others should be worri-
some for citizens protected under constitutional rights, since under the uncertain
conditions of suspended legal procedures, no assurance can be given that similar
policies will not be conducted towards suspected citizens at home. David Cole
anticipates this threat by reflecting on the history of civil liberties. The illegal
internment of Japanese American citizens famously exposed in Korematsu case,
and the retaliation against citizens holding communist views during the McCarthy
period are some of the many examples that testify to the spillover of emergency
security provisions on the rights of citizens and dissidents. He argues:

History reveals that the distinction between citizen and alien has often been resorted to as a
justification for liberty-infringing measures in times of crisis. In the short term, the fact that
measures are limited to noncitizens appears to make them easier for the majority to accept-
citizens are not asked to sacrifice their own liberty. However, the same history suggests that
citizens should be wary about relying on this distinction because it has often been breached
before. What we are willing to do to noncitizens ultimately affects what we are willing to
do to citizens. In the long run, all of our rights are at stake in the war against terrorism (Cole
2003: 309–10).

Also Lucia Zedner, reflecting on the history of the criminal justice system, warns
that citizens should indeed be wary of emergency security provisions because emergency measures affect the criminal justice system in its daily practices, primarily as

---

[47] One reason provided by terrorists is the injustice of the policies of the US government against
their own people. They generally resort to providing evidence of the death of civilians and innocent
persons in the war against terror launched by the US and its allies. In fact, the death of innocent
civilians allows the terrorists in some cases to find recruits who are willing to avenge the death of
their fellows.

the policing discourse shifts towards a preventive 'pre-crime' model.[48] She argues that

> [t]he conclusion that 'people like us' have nothing to fear from security measures may thus be born of a naive failure of imagination. To posit our loved ones or ourselves as possible subjects of security measures is no abstract act of jurisprudential conjecture. Instead, it is the stark, self-interested recognition that where measures are defined so as to capture every instance of political protest, we too might find ourselves subject to the very provisions whose introduction we approved (2005: 515).

These historical reflections do indeed paint a grim picture of what holds for the present. In fact, this has already happened. The killing of two US citizens—Anwar al-Awlaki and his son—in two different drone strikes in Yemen in late 2011 is a case in point of outright denial of due process. Although suspected of being a top Al-Qaeda recruiter, Awlaki had never been arrested nor prosecuted but the Obama Administration put him on the CIA's top list of targets to be eliminated due to their terrorist activities. Despite that, his guilt was assumed and he was executed along with his innocent son.[49] Some new important laws have also empowered the US government since 2001 to run covert military action. The Authorization for the Use of Military Force (AUMF), signed by Bush in the immediate aftermath of 9/11, authorizes the use of US Army against the terrorists responsible for terrorist attacks, and any of their associated forces with 'necessary and appropriate force.' AUMF was cited as a justification in a US Department of Justice memorandum on the Al-Awlaki's assassination: 'We believe that'—the memorandum says—'the AUMF's authority to use lethal force abroad also may apply in appropriate circumstances to a United States citizen who is part of the forces of an enemy authorization within the scope of the force authorization'(Ackerman 2014).[50] The Patriot Act also provides powerful tools to the executive to collect information, which may involve the use of data mining and surveillance devices. More recently, the National Defense Authorization Act (NDAA) 2012 has legalized indefinite detention without trial of supposed enemy combatants. These laws added to the fallouts of the Espionage act (Van Buren 2012) suggesting that the Administration can use considerable force not only against individuals who represent security threats but also against dissident voices, both at home and abroad (see Waldron 2003). Three cases

---

[48] Zedner argues that criminal justice system has increasingly shifted towards a 'pre-crime' preventive model: 'we are moving from a 'post-crime' society in which crime is thought about primarily as harm or wrong done and in which dominant ordering practices arise post-hoc, to a 'pre-crime' society in which the perspective is shifting to anticipate and forestall that which has yet to occur. Under the post-crime model, the dominant mechanisms of crime control are the police, the criminal process, trial, and punishment. Dedicated to detecting offenses, ascribing responsibility, determining guilt, they impose penal burdens either proportionate to the wrong done or consistent with consequentialist aims of punishment. The precrime model has a different, prospective orientation, concerned rather with the calculation of risk and the prevention of future harms in the name of security' (2007: 259).

[49] For further details see Greenwald (2017).

[50] The AUMF (Public Law 107–40) signed on September 18, 2001, by President George W. Bush, has been expanded by President Obama last year. See Savage et al. (2016).

of whistleblowers have especially hit the front pages of the media in the last few years: the former CIA officer John Kiriakou (alleged to have disclosed to the media about the waterboarding and torturing of Al-Qaeda suspects); Chelsea Manning (charged with handing over the information which led to revelations by Wikileaks). She was recently pardoned by Barack Obama before he left the White House, for reasons widely believed to be due to her poor psychological conditions, rather than as an act of contrition for the revelations she made about the recordings of assassinations of innocent Iraqi civilians by the US Army during the occupation. Finally, Edward Snowden, whose revelations on the NSA surveillance programs has since then led to a global debate on the invasive powers of the US government. All have been charged under Espionage Act and stealing of government material. Under a plea deal, only the charges on count of Espionage Act was dropped against Kiriakou.

The treatment of dissenters is symptomatic of the way states handle dissent in general. When dissent tries to challenge the official line of reasoning, it is termed dangerous. Individuals with access to information might resort to playing safe if revealing information comes at a high cost to their personal interests; public officials bend rather than risk being in the wrong books of higher authorities. This has severe implications for basic liberties, which cannot be enjoyed in peace if possibilities to challenge such limitations are restricted, or worse criminalized. In the next section, we offer a principled argument in defense of the right to civil liberties against the excess of governmental secrecy.

4.7   An Epistemic Framework for Liberty and Security

As argued in the previous section, the whistleblowing affairs that afflicted the US administration in the last decade—especially in the Snowden case—testifies to the impact of government surveillance programs to access and monitor private data. This, we said, might be justified for reasons of security as it is the duty of secret agencies to gather and classify information under control of the legislative and the judiciary branches. But given that secrecy provides an unlimited domain of action for the executive, measures of public accountability are often limited in their scope. Such limitation constitutes a severe violation of the democratic process because it limits the citizens' assessment of the restrictions imposed on their rights and of the circumstances that justify such restrictions. Secrecy practices thus allow for an unrestrained sphere of executive action that has the potential of limiting rights.

To understand the threat posed to rights by secrecy practices we first need to address the nature of rights. The contemporary debate over rights comprises two families of theories (Steiner 1994; Raz 1986; Jones 1994; Wenar 2011; Kramer et al. 1998): will theories (sometimes called 'choice' theories), and interest theories (sometimes also called 'benefit' theories). According to will theorists, rights protect the freedom of will of agents over their choices. Since rights are correlative of duties imposed on others not to interfere with the sphere of free action of the right-holder, the ultimate authority of the right-holder lies in enforcing these duties of non-interference, or waive them if she wishes. Property rights are usually a conventional example of waiving rights, for instance when a person forgives a credit she may have towards a debtor. Perhaps, more interesting is the case of the waiver of the right to appeal a decision made by a court or a public official. The so-called ESTA program, which allows foreign nationals of certain countries to visit the United States on a Visa waiver program, waive—along with the Visa—also their right to appeal the Border Control Patrol decision in front of a court if the officer—for whatever reason—decides that the visitor should not be admitted.

Interest theories conceive of rights as protecting some specific human interests and justify the imposition of correlative duties on other agents to fulfill that right. According to Joseph Raz, interests are aspects of the well-being of a person, such that a person has a right if and only if her interest is a sufficient reason to impose a duty on some other person (1986: 166).

According to Peter Jones, a third view is of rights as 'entitlements,' that is as marks of possession of a title (Jones 1994: 38). For Jones, the conferral of a right by a legal or a moral system on a person means that the possessor becomes 'the locus' of legal or moral status: 'If his title concerns his own actions (as in the case of liberty-rights), it justifies or legitimates those actions. If it concerns the actions of others (as in the case of claim-rights), it provides the ground for others' being required to act in ways that the title requires' (ibid.). According to Jones, the 'entitlement' theory of rights encompasses both the will and the choice views, for we can think of those theories as specifying under which conditions (to protect a liberty or an interest) a state or community should invest a person with an 'entitlement.' Thus, a right is an entitlement to a certain freedom within a suitably specified scope of actions, or alternatively to a certain benefit (for which the right-holder should be the intended beneficiary).

The characterization of rights that we offer here does not take a stance between these views. It suffices for our argument to agree on a general characterization of the nature of rights as protecting the person's capacity for autonomous choice, which can be interpreted either within the choice conception or as a general interest. Such interest does not consist in a specific functional resource, but in the authoritative control over one's conduct. We do not argue further for this view but shall assume it as a starting point to conceptualize about rights and explore its implications.

With this clarification in mind, we can now proceed. In its most general understanding, a right is an entitlement a person has in virtue of a legal, moral, or membership[51] status she enjoys to free conduct within the scope defined by its content, under the guarantee that nobody can lawfully interfere with its exercise thereof.[52] In other words, a right protects the capacity of a person for autonomous choices.

---

[51] That is, as a citizen, a human being, as a member of a group, etc....

[52] A similar formulation we propose in Santoro and Kumar 2017 (unpublished manuscript). There we argue that 'right is an entitlement a person has to free conduct within the scope of action defined by the content of the right in question, under the guarantee that nobody can lawfully interfere with its exercise.'

Certain features of this characterization require clarification. First, we refer to the *scope* of a right; second, we speak of the *capacity* for action. Third, we insist on the idea of *autonomous* choice, not merely of non-interference.

As for the first feature, we can imagine of the scope of rights as defined by the union of two sets: the opportunity set given to the person under the circumstances of choice, and the set of possible actions the person can undertake given the opportunity set. For the sake of simplicity, we can think of such a space as given by O_n opportunities, with $n > 2$, multiplied by two possible actions, *acceptance* or *rejection*, for each given opportunity.

Opportunities do not require further definition here, for they can be taken at their face-value, that is as chances or provisions that an agent can accept or reject. A job offer is an opportunity in this sense, as well as the opportunity to access a higher education curriculum. Opportunities are thus the object of a choice.

As for the second feature, we distinguish between a capacity for action from the action itself. The distinction should also be familiar, for it assumes that any intentional action is performed in virtue of those cognitive and rational capacities that make it possible to ascribe (and crucially for the agent to self-ascribe) an action as one she is the author of. Persons are responsible for their actions insofar as judgments of responsibility, praise, and blame are grounded in such ascription. Thus, rights in this sense do protect not only the conduct but also the pre-condition for its exercise.

As for the third feature, we refer to such a capacity as deployed in *autonomous* choices to stress the significance of secrecy on the formation of choice. As we argued in the previous section, secrecy hinders the information available in the circumstances of choice, either by framing the opportunity set or by subtracting information about the opportunity set altogether. Hindrances of this sort affect the capacity of choice formation because they induce agents to act in ways they might not have acted *had* they been aware of a change in the opportunity set available to them. Affecting people's choices in this manner does not interfere with the action itself, but with the independence of choice formation.[53] Our selective reading of the concept of autonomy does not engage with the perfectionist views on the matter (see Raz 1986), but we instead assume that a conception of autonomy as a capacity for choice formation does not depend on a moral conception of autonomy. It insists instead on two epistemic features that are necessary for autonomy: the independence of one's deliberation from manipulation by others, and the capacity to give rules to oneself.[54]

---

[53] Joel Feinberg distinguishes four conceptions of personal autonomy: the *capacity* to govern oneself; the *actual condition* of self-government (and its associated virtues); an *ideal of character* derived from that conception; the *sovereign authority* to govern oneself (for collective agents such as nation-states) (Feinberg 1986: 28). Our understanding of autonomy relies on the first two closely related conceptions: the capacity of self-government granted by the conferral of rights. Gerald Dworkin (1988) lists a set of satisfactory criteria for a theory of autonomy.

[54] The distinction between autonomy and liberty is recurrent in the debate on the nature of autonomy. Autonomy and liberty (or freedom for some) are not identical, for the latter is only a necessary condition for the former. Gerald Dworkin nicely states where the difference lies when he

We are now able to provide a first characterization of the conception of right we defend here:

(R): A right is an entitlement a person X possesses, in virtue of a status she enjoys, to the capacity of making autonomous choices within the scope of a given opportunity set.

The definition above is an approximation. It lacks critical defining features for a comprehensive conception of rights, including the specification of the duties correlative to the rights. It can nonetheless help us to clarify an important distinction between different forms of interference (or invasion) a right-holder can suffer. The distinction is between what we may call as *direct* and *indirect* interference.[55]

A *direct* form of interference occurs when the opportunity set available to an agent is invaded either by impeding the set of choices or by preventing her conduct. A direct violation of rights invades the scope of the opportunity set available to an agent by constraining the formation of the intention to act. Such constraints are not a product of the cognitive and epistemic limitations of an agent but rather an arbitrary interference through deception or manipulation. Deception and manipulation are, more exactly, a product of an informational asymmetry whereby agents are either misled into believing information contrary to the fact or denied access to important information that aids in forming their judgment. When such is the case, the agent acts on partial information that she believes be complete. Thus, what they consider to be an act of freedom has been rather compromised through an intentional act of manipulation or deception.

Contrary to a direct violation which constitutes an interference in action, *indirect* violation involves precluding the knowledge of the background circumstances governing the execution of an act. A paradigm feature of free action involves an awareness of the antecedent circumstances governing an act within a rational agent's epistemic and cognitive limits. It also includes the awareness of possible, if any, impediments that preclude the realization of the action. An indirect violation does not preclude the realization of the action but rather the awareness that one's action has not been interfered with. When this is the case, the agent is devoid of a crucial set of information that aids in the formation of an intention to act. For if the agent were aware of any possible interference, she might have chosen to act otherwise, not to act, challenge the interference, or be agnostic about it and carry on like before. In either case, ignorance of interference affects the agent's capacity to choose autonomously by altering the opportunity set available to the agent. A paradigmatic case of

---

writes that autonomy cannot be identical to liberty since, when we deceive a patient, we are interfering with her autonomy, but not with her liberty: 'Deception is not a way of restricting liberty. The person who, to use Locke's example, is put into a cell and convinced that all the doors are locked (when, in fact, one is left unlocked) is free to leave the cell. But because he cannot—given his information—avail himself of this opportunity, his ability to do what he wishes is limited. Self-determination can be limited in other ways than by interferences with liberty' (G. Dworkin 1988: 14). Our view of autonomy does not insist on the aspect of 'authenticity,' 'exemplary validity' (Ferrara 1998), or 'reflective self-endorsement' (Korsgaard 1996).

[55] A similar distinction between direct and indirect violation we discuss in Santoro and Kumar 2017 (unpublished manuscript).

indirect interference is the secret acts of surveillance and wiretapping that invade the privacy of individuals. Surveillance and wiretapping do not involve direct interference with the conduct but rather with the belief that one's conduct is private. Had the agent been aware of such interference, she might have formed her intentions differently taking the impediments into account. Moreover, indirect interference impedes the assessment of the circumstances governing the formation of intention and thus the agent's choice whether the current action is in her best interest.

It is in this sense that real-world circumstances of secret operations by the executive impede the assessment of risks involved in forming a choice. While making the policy public will defeat its original purpose, its implications for individual rights are serious, since the secretive nature of the operations does not give a warrant to the citizens as to whether the policy is being run on reasonable grounds, or if it is justifiable. As we said above, surveillance and data mining also have important distributive consequences, when security policies mark out specific groups and communities as their targets. The surveillance of mosques in the USA is a case in point: members of a particular religious community were marked out as a potential source of the threat.[56] Singling out specific groups or communities for surveillance violates the distributive equality of the burdens and shared character of security. It cannot be the goal of a democratic public policy to single out specific groups and communities based on their ethnic, religious, or racial belonging. Secrecy, by violating this public purpose, obfuscates the distributive dimension of security since the community does not have the warrant of an equal enjoyment of their liberty (see Waldron 2006).

The second case of rights violation without the power of appeal is that of the 'no-fly lists' prepared by many Western governments, most notably the USA, of potential suspects. Sometimes, though, things do not go as they should. John Graham, an ex-member of the state department on security, was put on a no-fly list of the US Transportation Security Administration (TSA) (Graham 2005). Due process was denied to him, and no reasons were assigned for the limitation of his freedom of movement. The curious thing about the no-fly list is that once put on the list—he claimed—you remain on it, even when proven as not a threat to security. Such a listing not only curtailed Graham's liberty to move but also his livelihood, which was primarily linked to travel. 'No-fly' lists are one of the basic limitations of the modern freedom of movement; even more when such a limitation is not known to the citizens until and unless they want to fly. Secrecy denies the epistemic warrants that comes with the limitations of rights, and the possibility to contest those limitations, if and when they exist.

The third case of rights violation is when a secret policy affects the health of citizens. One of the essential features of secrecy is that it impacts individuals in endless ways. Secrecy can render life decisions uncertain and future projects at the mercy of unknown risks. Cases abound here. From the year 1952 to 1989, a secret nuclear power plant in the Rocky Mountains was producing over 70,000 plutonium triggers.

---

[56] A lawsuit filed by the American Civil Liberties Union and the Council of American-Islamic Relations alleges that the FBI was monitoring and using surveillance mechanisms against several mosques in south California. See Sacribey (2011).

The plant was maintained under the direction of the Atomic energy commission (later the Department of Energy) by Dow Chemicals till 1975 and Rockwell International till 1989. The facility severely impacted the environment and the health of the citizens exposed to the threats of radiation. These factors were hidden from the residents. Even the workers working in those factories were not aware of the nature of the risks they were indulging in. Secrecy around the plant prevented the assessment of risks involved in choosing whether to stay put or leave the region.

All these cases support the claim that secrecy impedes the enjoyment of rights in endless ways by denying the information one should ideally have in the assessment of risks involved in undertaking an action. It affects the individual's capacity to make informed choices by introducing an element of uncertainty with regard to the consequences of their action. The consequences can turn out to be so unpredictable that they cannot be evaluated based on the information any rational agent possesses. When such an assessment is denied, rights are violated because the denial precludes the possibility to know the conditions under which individuals can exercise their rights. Secrecy, thus, threatens a fundamental component of rights: its epistemic entitlement. Epistemic entitlement is the feature of rights that guarantees the most extensive amount of information necessary for a person to exercise one's autonomous choice (see Santoro and Kumar unpublished manuscript). In other words, it is the epistemic precondition for the enjoyment of rights because possessing a right entitles its holder to the fullest extent of available knowledge of the circumstances that may impede the enjoyment of a right. (ibid.).

Framing rights as an epistemic entitlement unveils a conflict with the prerogatives of governmental secrecy. It can be argued that such a view is too demanding and does not accommodate for genuine reasons of security. When such is the case, the epistemic entitlement requirement needs to be relaxed for those considerations where information needs to be secreted to prevent significant security breaches. In the absence of such accommodation not only the epistemic entitlement becomes too demanding to be realized in a real-world scenario, but full compliance may pose a threat to some basic civil liberties it seeks to protect in the first place. For instance, full compliance would demand complete information *a priori* of all those programs that can interfere with civil liberties either directly or indirectly. This would include full publicity of surveillance and data mining programs that seek to gather valuable information and often prevent security threats.

The epistemic entitlement allows for exceptions in cases of partial compliance. In conditions of partial compliance however, having a right entails a weaker condition, that the holder is still entitled to know under which conditions her exercise has been limited or suspended. This knowledge requirement in conditions of partial compliance is what we call the *right of assessment* (ibid.). The epistemic entitlement *entails* the right of assessment because it is a consequence of being entitled to the fullest extent of the available information about the circumstances of choice of a right, that one is also entitled to know when those circumstances change under non-ideal conditions (ibid.) A right of assessment is thus a second-order right that imposes a duty of justification on all those who seek to limit first order rights, because absent proper justification any interference is illegitimate.[57]

A right of assessment entails also that when secrecy practices outgrow their use, citizens or those affected by those practices are owed a proper justification as to why such restrictions were required in the first instance. Therefore, under the right of assessment, those affected by no-fly lists, and the residents of Rocky Mountains power plant are owed a ex-post justification. Under such a reading, the executive too is duty bound to justify secrecy practices that interfere with the rights of citizens. More in general, surveillance and data mining practices need to be adequately justified to the citizens and the judiciary for their scope, and proper warrants should be in place to ensure that they do not outrun their original purpose.

The right of assessment, by ensuring due ex-post justification of limitations of rights, determines the proper scope of secrecy in non-ideal circumstances. This ensures not only justice to those whose rights have been limited but also the accountability of democratic systems. But it might be argued that the very nature of secrecy conflicts with the normative requirements of both the epistemic entitlement and of the right of assessment. This is indeed true because it is in the very nature of unrestrained forms of secrecy to empower the secret keeper to determine its proper breadth and scope. When the concealment lies in the hands of the powerful, as often is in the case of the executive power, governments design ways to use it as they see fit and create safeguards against disclosure of their abuse of power. Secrecy, thus, opens up a possibility of unmitigated action often running against its intended publicly avowed and accepted purpose. When this happens, constitutional controls are undermined and rights threatened. In such circumstances, individuals are left not only uncertain regarding their legal standing vis-á-vis their enjoyment of rights but also the self-correcting nature of democracy, guaranteed by constitutional controls over abuses of power, is undermined.

4.8 Concluding Remarks

In this chapter we argued that the current conception of security derives from a metaphor of balance that does not do justice to civil liberties. Not only does the balance model allow for unrestrained practices of secrecy but it also allows for undermining of rights without any correlative justification why such limitation was warranted due to reasons of security. As we showed, the balance model is based on considerations of efficiency and lacks any principled justification. This we demonstrated through a historical reading of the relation between liberty and security. We argued that there are important reasons why democracies favor secrecy. But unrestrained secrecy opens up a paradox for democracy and tends to resist any form of control. We also showed that secrecy impacts the epistemic entitlement inherent in

---

[57] The right of assessment can be accommodated within the framework of constitutional rights. We show this in Santoro and Kumar (unpublished manuscript).

rights and opens up a space for abuse of power. Secrecy empowers those who have access to classified information by opening up a sphere of action unbeknown to others and official positions used to serve particularistic ends that deviate from the requirements of public office. In conclusion, unrestrained secrecy is the veil that protects corrupt acts and aids in deviating from publicly affirmed goals often leaving those affected by its operations with no awareness of limitation of their rights and with no possibility of redress.

The epistemic framework of rights that we presented here highlights the threat that secrecy poses to the realization of actions and choices protected under a right. We argued that secrecy not only interferes with an action but denies the possibility of assessment of the conditions of intentional and autonomous choice. The epistemic entitlement in ideal conditions, and the correlative right of assessment in non-ideal conditions, act as necessary constraints against arbitrary interference by determining the proper scope and purpose of secrecy. But such view is dependent on the realizability of the justification that is owed to right holders when their rights are limited. We argued that the very nature of secrecy empowers those who threaten rights in the first place thus increasing the possibility that the duty of justification will only seldom be realized. The duty of justification is owed from the very sources that threatens rights; when correlative controls are absent or do not work, it is not far-fetched to adopt a pessimistic view that they will never be realized. This indeed is a sorry state of affairs for any democracy premised on constitutional protection of rights.

In the absence of democratic controls over unrestrained secrecy, it is often the dissenting action of insiders, having privileged access to information, that ensures a degree of accountability. This is the act of whistleblowing that often reveals systemic acts of corruption and threat to rights that go unchecked through established democratic procedures. But do absent or missing democratic procedures of accountability justify acts of whistleblowing? This is an issue that we discuss in next chapter.

References

Ackerman, Bruce. 2004. The emergency constitution. *Yale Law Journal* 113: 1029–1091.
Ackerman, Spencer. 2014. US cited controversial law in decision to kill American citizen by drone. *The Guardian.* 23 June. https://www.theguardian.com/world/2014/jun/23/us-justification-drone-killing-american-citizen-awlaki. Accessed 8 Feb 2018.
Anderson, Elizabeth. 2006. The epistemology of democracy. *Episteme: A Journal of Social Epistemology* 3 (1–2): 8–22.
Arendt, Hannah. 1972. *Crises of the Republic: Lying in Politics, Civil Disobedience, on Violence, Thoughts on Politics and Revolution.* New York: Harcourt, Brace & Co.
Bentham, Jeremy. 1838. Principles of the civil code. In *The Works of Jeremy Bentham.* Part II, ed. John Bowring. Edinburgh: William Tait. https://books.google.fr/books?id=LU5ZAAAA cAAJ&printsec=frontcover&source=gbs_ge_summary_r&cad=0#v=onepage&q&f=false. Accessed 8 Feb 2018.

Berman, Emily. 2009. *Executive Privilege: A Legislative Remedy*. New York University School of Law, Brennan Center for Justice. http://ssrn.com/abstract=2112138. Accessed 8 Feb 2018.

Black, Edwin. 2012. *IBM and the Holocaust: The Strategic Alliance Between Nazi Germany and America's Most Powerful Corporation*. New York: Random House Inc.

Bobbio, Norberto. 1987. *The Future of Democracy. A Defense of the Rules of the Game*, ed. Richard Bellamy (trans: Roger Griffin). London: Polity Press.

Bok, Sissela. 1983. *Secrets: On the ethics of concealment and revelation*. New York: Vintage Books.

Brennan, William J. 1988. The quest to develop a jurisprudence of civil liberties in times of security crises. In *Israel Yearbook on Human Rights*, vol. 18, 11–22. Dordrecht: Martinus Nijhoff Publishers.

Breslow, Jason M. 2016. Colin Powell: U.N. Speech 'Was a Great Intelligence Failure'. *Frontline*. 17 May 2016. http://www.pbs.org/wgbh/frontline/article/colin-powell-u-n-speech-was-a-great-intelligence-failure/. Accessed 1 Mar 2017.

Calhoun, L. 2015. *We Kill Because We Can: From Soldiering to Assassination in the Drone Age*. London: Zed Books.

Chambers, Simone. 2004. Behind closed doors: Publicity, secrecy, and the quality of deliberation. *Journal of Political Philosophy* 12 (4): 389–410.

Chinen, Mark. 2009. Secrecy and democratic decisions. *Qunnipiac Law Review* 27 (1): 1–55.

Cohen, Joshua. 1986. An epistemic conception of democracy. *Ethics* 97 (1): 26–38.

Cole, David. 2003. Their liberties, our security democracy and double standards. *International Journal of Legal Information* 31: 290–311.

Dryzek, John S. 2000. *Deliberative Democracy and Beyond*. Oxford: Oxford University Press.

Dworkin, Gerald. 1988. *The Theory and Practice of Autonomy*. Cambridge: Cambridge University Press.

Dworkin, Ronald. 2002. The threat to patriotism. *New York Review of Books* 493: 44–49. http://www.nybooks.com/articles/archives/2002/feb/28/the-threat-to-patriotism/?pagination=false. Accessed 23 July 2013.

Ellsberg, Daniel. 2002. *Secrets: A Memoir of Vietnam and the Pentagon Papers*. New York: Viking.

Elster, Jon. 1995. Strategic uses of argument. In *Barriers to Conflict Resolution*, ed. K. Arrow. New York: Norton.

Estlund, David M. 2009. *Democratic Authority: A Philosophical Framework*. Princeton: Princeton University Press.

Feinberg, Joel. 1986. *The Moral Limits of the Criminal Law Volume 3: Harm to Self*. Oxford: Oxford University Press.

Fenster, Mark. 2005. The opacity of transparency. *Iowa Law Review* 91: 885–949.

Ferrara, Alessandro. 1998. *Reflective Authenticity*. London/New York: Routledge.

Fisher, Louis. 2007. The state secrets privilege: Relying on Reynolds. *Political Science Quarterly* 122 (3): 385–408.

Fuchs, Meredith. 2006. Judging secrets: The role courts should play in preventing unnecessary secrecy. *Administrative Law Review* 58 (1): 130–176.

German, Mike, and Jay Stanley. 2011. *Drastic Measures Required: Congress Needs to Overhaul US Secrecy Laws and Increase Oversight of the Secret Security Establishment*. https://www.aclu.org/files/assets/secrecyreport_20110727.pdf. Accessed 15 July 2017.

Gettier, Edmund L. 1963. Is justified true belief knowledge? *Analysis* 23 (6): 121–123.

Graham, John. 2005. Who is watching the watch list? *Alternate*. 6 July. http://www.alternet.org/story/23362/who%27s_watching_the_watch_list. Accessed 18 Feb 2018.

Greenwald, Glenn. 2017. Obama killed a 16-year-old American in Yemen. Trump just killed his 8-year-old sister. *The Intercept*. 30 January. https://theintercept.com/2017/01/30/obama-killed-a-16-year-old-american-in-yemen-trump-just-killed-his-8-year-old-sister/. Accessed 8 Feb 2018.

Gutmann, Amy, and Dennis Thompson. 1996. *Democracy and Disagreement*. Cambridge, MA: The Belknap Press of Harvard University Press.

Herring, George C., ed. 1993. *The Pentagon Papers*. Abridged edition. New York: McGraw-Hill.
Hobbes, Thomas. 1996. *Leviathan*. (1651). ed. Richard Tuck. New York: Cambridge University Press.
Horton, John. 2010. *Political Obligation*. London: Palgrave Macmillan.
Jones, Peter. 1994. *Rights*. London: Palgrave Macmillan.
Julius, A.J. 2003. Basic structure and the value of equality. *Philosophy & Public Affairs* 31 (4): 321–355.
Korsgaard, Christine M. 1996. *The Sources of Normativity*. New York: Cambridge University Press.
Kramer, Matthew H., N.E. Simmonds, and H. Steiner. 1998. *A Debate Over Rights*. Oxford: Oxford University Press.
Lazar, Nomi C. 2009. *States of Emergency in Liberal Democracies*. New York: Cambridge University Press.
Locke, John. 1980. In *Second Treatise of Government*. (1689). ed. C.B. Macpherson. Indianapolis/ Cambridge: Hackett Publishing Co.
Mill, John S. 1863. *On Liberty*. (1859). 2nd ed. Ticknor and Fields.
———. 1879. *Utilitarianism*. (1861). 7th ed. London: Longmans Green and Co.
Moore, Adam. 2011. Privacy, security, and government surveillance: The new accountability land-scape. *Public Affairs Quarterly* 25 (2): 141–156.
Moynihan, Daniel P. 1998. *Secrecy: The American Experience*. New Haven: Yale University Press.
Neocleous, Mark. 2002. Privacy, secrecy, idiocy. *Social Research: An International Quarterly* 69 (1): 85–110.
———. 2008. *Critique of Security*. Montreal: McGill-Queen's University Press.
Norton-Taylor, Richard. 2013. MI6 and CIA were told before invasion that Iraq had no active WMD. *The Guardian*. 18 May. https://www.theguardian.com/world/2013/mar/18/panorama-iraq-fresh-wmd-claims. Accessed 8 Feb 2018.
Parry, Robert, and Peter Kornbluh. 1988. Iran-Contra's untold story. *Foreign Policy* 72: 3–30.
Pogge, Thomas W.M. 2008a. *World Poverty and Human Rights*. London: Polity Press.
———. 2008b. Making war on terrorists—Reflections on harming the innocent. *Journal of Political Philosophy* 16 (1): 1–25.
Posner, Richard. 2006. *Not a Suicide Pact: The Constitution in a Time of National Emergency*. Oxford: Oxford University Press.
Posner, Eric A., and Adrian Vermeule. 2007. *Terror in the Balance: Security, Liberty and the Courts*. Oxford: Oxford University Press.
———. 2011. *The Executive Unbound: After the Madisonian Republic*. Oxford: Oxford University Press.
Pozen, David. 2010. Deep secrecy. *Stanford Law Review* 62 (2): 257–340.
Priest, Dana, and William M. Arkin. 2016. A hidden world, growing beyond control. Top Secret America. A Washington Post Investigation. *Washington Post*. http://projects.washingtonpost.com/top-secret-america/articles/a-hidden-world-growing-beyond-control/. Accessed 1 Mar 2017.
Rawls, John. 1999. *A Theory of Justice*, revised edition. Cambridge, MA: The Belknap Press of Harvard University Press.
Raz, Joseph. 1986. *The Morality of Freedom*. Oxford: Clarendon Press.
Rozell, Mark J. 2002. *Executive Privilege: Presidential Power, Secrecy, and Accountability*. Lawrence: University Press of Kansas.
Sacirbey, Omar. 2011. Muslims and ACLU sue FBI over mosque surveillance. Religion News Service. *The Huffington Post*. 25 May. http://www.huffingtonpost.com/2011/02/23/muslims-and-aclu-sue-fbi-_n_827339.html. Accessed 7 June 2013.
Sagar, Rahul. 2007. On combating the abuse of state secrecy. *The Journal of Political Philosophy* 15 (4): 404–427.
———. 2009. Who holds the balance? A missing detail in the debate over balancing security and liberty. *Polity* 41 (2): 166–188.

Santoro, Daniele, and Manohar Kumar. 2017. *Liberty, secrecy, and the right of assessment.* Unpublished manuscript. Available with the authors.

Savage, C., Eric Schmitt, and Mark Mazzetti. 2016. Obama expands war with Al Qaeda to include Shabab in Somalia. *The New York Times.* 27 November. https://www.nytimes.com/2016/11/27/us/politics/obama-expands-war-with-al-qaeda-to-include-shabab-in-somalia.html?_r=0. Accessed 8 Feb 2018.

Shenon, Philip, and Stephen Engelberg. 1987. Eight important days in november: Unraveling the Iran-Contra affair. *The New York Times.* 4 July. http://www.nytimes.com/1987/07/05/world/eight-important-days-in-november-unraveling-the-iran-contra-affair.html?pagewanted=all. Accessed 8 Feb 2018.

Simmel, Georg. 1906. The sociology of secrecy and of secret societies. *The American Journal of Sociology* 11 (4): 441–498.

Solove, Daniel J. 2008. Data mining and the security-liberty debate. *University of Chicago Law Review* 75: 343–362.

Steiner, Hillel. 1994. *An Essay on Rights.* Oxford/Cambridge, MA: Blackwell.

Stiglitz, Joseph. 1999. *On Liberty, the Right to Know, and Public Discourse: The Role of Transparency in Public Life.* Oxford Amnesty Lecture. January 27, 1999. http://citeseerx.ist.psu.edu/viewdoc/download?doi=10.1.1.594.93&rep=rep1&type=pdf. Accessed 23 Feb 2018.

Sunstein, Cass. 1986. Government control of information. Symposium: New perspectives in the law of defamation. *California Law Review* 74 (3): 889–921.

———. 2002. *Conformity and Dissent.* University of Chicago Law & Economics, Olin Working Paper No. 164; and University of Chicago, Public law research paper No. 34. Available at SSRN: http://ssrn.com/abstract=341880 or https://doi.org/10.2139/ssrn.341880. Accessed 20 July 2012.

The European Convention on Human Rights. 1950. Council of Europe. Rome.

Thompson, Dennis. 1999. Democratic secrecy. *Political Science Quarterly* 114 (2): 181–193.

Van Buren, Peter. 2012. Obama's unprecedented war on whistleblowers. From Manning to Kiriakou. *Salon.* February 9.

Vermeule, Adrian. 2014. Security and liberty: Critiques of the tradeoff thesis. In *The Long Decade: How 9/11 Changed the Law,* ed. David Jenkins, Amanda Jacobsen, and Anders Heriksen, 31–44. Oxford/New York: Oxford University Press.

Waldron, Jeremy. 2003. Security and liberty: The image of balance. *The Journal of Political Philosophy* 11(2): 191–210, now included in Waldron, Jeremy. 2012. *Torture, Terror, and Trade-Offs: Philosophy for the White House,* 20–47. Oxford/New York: Oxford University Press.

———. 2006. Safety and security. *Nebraska Law Review* 85: 454–507.

Weber, Max. 1978. *Economy and Society: An Outline of Interpretative Sociology.* Vol. 1. Berkeley: University of California Press.

Wenar, Leif. 2011. Rights. In *The Stanford Encyclopedia of Philosophy,* ed. Edward N. Zalta. http://plato.stanford.edu/archives/fall2011/entries/rights/. Accessed 18 Feb 2018.

Williams, Bernard. 1996. Truth, politics and self-deception. *Social Research: An International Quarterly* 63 (4): 603–617.

Zedner, Lucia. 2005. Securing liberty in the face of terror: Reflections from criminal justice. *Journal of Law and Society* 32 (4): 507–533.

———. 2007. Seeking security by eroding rights. The side-stepping of due process. In *Security and Human Rights,* ed. Benjamin J. Goold and Laura Lazarus, 257–276. Oxford/Portland: Hart Publishing.

———. 2009. *Security.* London/New York: Routledge.

Chapter 5
A Justification of Political Whistleblowing

Abstract In this chapter we provide a justification of political whistleblowing and articulate some criteria for the permissibility of disclosures. In the first part we discuss the main criticisms against political whistleblowing. In particular, we address the objections from the breach of obligation and trust, lack of patriotism, harm to national security, vigilantism, lack of accountability, and imperfect information. In the second part we define the epistemic circumstances of disclosure, and we specify three conditions for the permissibility of political whistleblowing: the communicative constraints, intent, and public interest.

Keywords Political whistleblowing · Justification · Public interest · Communicative conditions · Permissibility

5.1 The Case for Political Whistleblowing

We so far discussed the literature concerning forms of civic whistleblowing, cases of disclosures that do not commit to a breach of the law. As we said at the end of Chap. 3, governments do recognize acts of civic whistleblowing and provide some channels of disclosure especially when the information concerns gross mismanagement of funds, abuse of authority, or hazard to public safety or health. Complications arise when the breach of the law concerns the disclosure of information and material classified for reasons of national security. This is the case of *political* whistleblowing, an act of public disclosure of classified government information concerning violation of rights or illegitimate governmental secrecy.

Unauthorized disclosures not only have the potential of making public information to the enemies of the state, but they may also render many policies ineffective. It is the troubling aspect of national security and the concerns for public safety that has polarized the debates on political whistleblowing.

At the same time, such disclosures come at a heavy cost for the whistleblowers. It is not uncommon for political whistleblowers to face charges of treason, breach of trust, or disloyalty towards one's country, and unprecedented retaliation in recent

© Springer International Publishing AG, part of Springer Nature 2018   123
D. Santoro, M. Kumar, *Speaking Truth to Power – A Theory of Whistleblowing*,
Philosophy and Politics - Critical Explorations 6,
https://doi.org/10.1007/978-3-319-90723-9_5

times (Rottman 2014). While some political commentators have defended the action of political whistleblowers as genuine acts of dissent or disobedience (Lewis 2013) others have called it an isolated act of betrayal (Brooks 2013). Some have also termed these actions as espionage (Epstein 2014, 2017). For instance, the Federal Court of the Eastern District of Virginia charged Edward Snowden with 'theft of government property', 'unauthorized communication of national defense information' and 'willful communication of classified communications intelligence information to an unauthorized person' (these last two charges were brought under the 1917 Espionage Act). Despite the public importance of the information disclosed, the breach of national security remains a serious harm. Escaping in these cases is one option, but it is often subject to asylum granted by a foreign country, and insecurity all the way along. The sense of betrayal can make loyal government employees who blow the whistle miserable. As much as their feelings can be eased by support campaigns (but not every whistleblower is a Snowden), they are generally alone when they face prosecution, charges of treason, and years of prison.

Most national legislations passed to protect whistleblowers, do not protect political whistleblowers, especially when they are part of the intelligence services community. The US Whistleblowers Protection Act of 1989 and the Whistleblowers Protection Enhancement Act of 2012 exclude the intelligence services from the scope of their authority. This is also the case of many European Legislations on whistleblower protections that end up treating any form of security disclosures as illegitimate. Political whistleblowing raises suspicion on the motives behind the disclosures and—as we discussed in Chap. 2—invites comparisons with spies and enemies.

For the sake of simplicity, we can group the arguments against the permissibility of political whistleblowing under the following headings: (i) it is a breach of an obligation; (ii) it is a breach of trust; (iii) it is unpatriotic; (iv) it harms national security; (v) it is a form of vigilantism; (vi) it fails to show public accountability; (vii) there are good epistemic arguments against non-disclosure. In the following we discuss and reply to each of these criticisms. The purpose of this discussion is to obtain a more defined profile of political whistleblowing before we move, in the second part, to provide the conditions for the permissibility of disclosures.

5.1.1   Breach of an Obligation

Political whistleblowing is a breach of the moral and professional obligation to maintain confidentiality. The premise of this criticism is that the agent who enters the rank of a secret agency, does so by promising to honor the obligation of her office. It is this promise the agent has freely made that imposes on her the obligation of confidentiality. When the agent decides to blow the whistle on information or material she has gained access to in virtue of her office, she violates her promissory obligation. Moreover, whistleblowing disclosures undermine the constitutional mandate of government agencies handling classified information. Disclosures of such information represent a disobedience against the democratic procedures that enact laws to that count. For instance, Rahul Sagar has argued that unauthorized disclosures disobey 'not only their supervisors, but also the public, whose representatives have enacted laws and regulations relating to the handling of classified information' (2013b, para 4).

In response to these criticisms, the first thing we should notice is that the violation of a promissory obligation is justified when the disclosure concerns government abuses of power. This is, for instance, the case of confidentiality clauses that undermine the public interest. Second, confidentiality is valuable only insofar as it does not deviate from its constitutional purpose. The Snowden affair is a case in point. Although his disclosures represent a *prima facie* moral wrong due to breach of an organization's confidentiality, many have justified his actions by referring to a more basic right to know. For instance, Seumas Miller has argued that the US public 'had a right to know what its intelligence agency was doing in this area, given that it was engaged in widespread infringements of the privacy rights of US citizenry.' (2017b: 486) Snowden was morally justified in disclosing NSA's program, even though the scale and the manner of disclosures 'was unnecessary in terms of what the public had the right to know, and harmful to US security interests' (ibid.: 492). While Miller's latter claim regarding the harm to security interests is debatable, the larger claim still stands: in a clash between duties of confidentiality and upholding citizen's right to know, the latter trumps when the disclosed information is in the public interest.

Second, since confidentiality is an obligation made in conditions that prevent the employee from foreseeing some of the most morally controversial circumstances she will be exposed to in course of duty, it is open to debate how fair it is to demand full compliance. Daniel Ellsberg puts this point nicely:

> a promise to keep secrets is a special kind of promise. If what you are about to learn—on condition you keep it secret—is presumptively knowledge you do not already have, you are making a commitment whose exact content and bearing you do not know. It's like agreeing to do something without knowing at all in advance what you may be asked to do. You can't foresee confidently how it might relate to other obligations you might have—to warn others or keep them informed—or to your own various interests. In that light, a promise to keep a secret might seem intrinsically less binding than a promise made with full foresight of its implications (2010: 776–777).

Ellsberg rightly points out that compliance in matters of secrecy is rather contingent upon the circumstances that force individuals to make a moral choice. Given that a prospective employee is at an epistemic disadvantage in assessing the proper terms of engagement that a contract entails, demanding full compliance with laws would amount to complicit silence when those orders command operations that are morally or even legally questionable. It is the conflict between the duty of allegiance and the distress from complicity that imposes an unfair burden on employees.

Yet, some might argue that it is not up to the employee who is subject to a legal obligation to decide when the law harms the public interest. A general criticism in this direction comes from Joseph Raz, who has defended the view that the duty to obey the law is an exclusionary reason (Raz 1990: 35–84). His argument, in brief, is this: being subject to an obligation gives the person a first-order reason to act according to the obligation. An exclusionary reason is a second-order reason to refrain from acting for any other reason conflicting with that obligation. Second-order reasons *insulate* an obligation 'from the general competition of reasons'(Green 2012). In the case under examination, no balance of reasons should be allowed in matters of secrecy, since the obligation derives from secrecy norms, which give both a first-order reason not to disclose, and a second-order reason to exclude other reasons in favor of disclosing, among which are the reasons of public interest. Raz calls these kinds of norms 'mandatory' (1990: 49–84). Kimberley Brownlee and Candice Delmas have both argued against the Razian argument. Delmas argues that these conflicts open to debate, following on this point Brownlee who argues that there is a conceptual and evaluative gap between codified and rigid laws and non-codifiable moral responsibilities.[1] We agree that the exclusionary reason argument as it is generally understood does not apply to the breach of promissory obligations of secrecy, but for different reasons that can be reconciled with the Razian point of view. First, Raz's argument seems to apply to ordinary cases of commands, but hardly to exceptional circumstances where the authority of a commander may order a person to commit an atrocity.[2] Exclusionary reasons have a prevailing force when the authority from which it is derived is generally accepted as legitimate. In cases of a major harm to a vast collective of people, we should not presume public officials defer their judgment. Doing so would imply that public officials should not reason at all: they should be just executioners of commands. This seems an implausible reductio of the Razian argument.

The second Razian argument is that the scope of the exclusionary reasons depend on the scope of the authority from which they derive (1990: 46–47). The obligation the public official has to fulfill a certain order *qua* order will presumably depend on a higher-rank official commanding him certain operations. It might be the case that a certain operation is ordered from the top of the chain, in which case the official may give the order extreme importance; but in other circumstances the order can be less authoritative. Treating all commands as providing the same exclusionary reasons to obey them seems again implausible, even more because we must assume that the ultimate authority in a constitutional democracy is the constitution itself. It is implausible to assume that an obligation is mandatory when its fulfillment implies a violation of constitutional rights. This leads us to the point about the public interest. We saw in chap. 3 that the core aspect of public interest consists in a set of all-purposive rights. Since the interpretation that we have given of these rights is the constitutional model of representative democracy, we argued that whistleblowing disclosures are justified only when they safeguard the public interest in this constitutional sense. Hence, our answer to the question whether whistleblowers are always unjustified should be reframed, within the Razian context, as a question about the justification of those very obligations the whistleblower has broken. Sometimes it is the obligation itself that does not provide good reasons for obeying it; in other cases

---

[1] See Delmas (2015: 86), who also refers to Brownlee (2012: 86–87) on the 'gap thesis'.
[2] See the discussion of the Jeremy's case for a hint on this point (Raz 1990: 38).

it is the authority that commands it that is unauthoritative. At any rate however, what confers authority to any law is its constitution. Whistleblowers who break the law and their obligations may still act under the authority of the constitution.

5.1.2   Breach of Trust

Political disclosures are also wrong in another way. They undermine the institutional purposes of the secret services by breaching their trust in confidentiality. Confidentiality is a 'constitutive institutional good' that enables these organizations to achieve their purposes (Miller 2017a: 218). Complex organizations like a secret service, 'cannot achieve its aims in the absence of loyalty and faithfulness on the part of its members' (Sagar 2013a: 110). According to this view, whistleblowing is ethically wrong because it compromises a collective enterprise that the whistleblower has freely submitted to, and whose success is based on a strict compliance by its members.[3]

In response to this criticism, we agree that, *in general,* failing to keep confidentiality is a failure of the contributory role the individual has to uphold the enterprise. But is this the case also for those collective enterprises where abuses or wrongdoings are committed? In such cases the individual does not benefit akin to a free rider who enjoys the benefit without contributing their fair share to the collective enterprise. The whistleblower does not accrue any personal benefit by withdrawing their contribution, rather they risk retaliation, personally and professionally. Loyalty and fair contribution to a collective enterprise are contingent upon the enterprise not demanding acts that entails a wrongdoing.

5.1.3   It is Unpatriotic

Perhaps the most common argument against political whistleblowing is that it is unpatriotic, or worse, an act of treason.[4] The former accusation was famously manifested in President Obama's news conference at the White House on August 9, 2013.[5] In response to a question he suggested that he does not consider Edward Snowden to be a patriot. Snowden, for him, not only discounted due procedures for disclosures and hampered national security by exposing intelligence gathering techniques, but also side-stepped due process by escaping the law.

---

[3] See Sagar 2013b: 'The first thing to bear in mind is that employees such as Snowden volunteer to be entrusted with classified information. When they disclose secrets, they are violating the trust that they have asked to be placed in themselves'.

[4] Epstein (2014, 2017) calls Snowden's disclosure a foreign espionage operation.

[5] See transcript of President Obama's August 9, 2013 news conference at the White House available on *The Washington Post.*

In circumstances of governmental secrecy, the charge of espionage and treason acts as a form of deterrence against future disclosure. It is also internalized by most members of the intelligence community. Daniel Ellsberg writes:

> The mystique of secrecy in the universe of national security, even beyond the formal appa-
> ratus of classification and clearances, is a compelling deterrent to whistleblowing and thus
> to effective resistance to gravely wrongful or dangerous policies. In this realm, telling
> secrets appears unpatriotic, even traitorous. That reflects the general presumption—even
> though it is generally false—that the secrecy is aimed not at domestic, bureaucratic, or
> political rivals or the American public but at foreign, powerful enemies, and that breaching
> it exposes the country, its people, and its troops to danger (2010:773).

A failure to keep a secret is almost tantamount to giving it away to the enemy, thus inviting the accusation of spying and treason. We already clarified in Chap. 2 the distinction between whistleblowing and espionage. Whistleblowing mostly involves public disclosure contrary to spying that requires instead stealth and non-disclosure of identity. Spying involves infiltration of an agency with the defined purpose to steal information for purposes that run counter to the agency one has infiltrated in. Whistleblowing does not require infiltration. A whistleblower does not intend to join an organization with the purpose of disclosing information but it is a conscientious action of disclosing a wrongdoing that she becomes aware of while partaking her duties. Contrary to whistleblowing, espionage is not in the public interest of domestic constituencies.

The charge of treason though is a serious one. It involves a betrayal of the country one owes allegiance to. One can still betray a country without being a spy. Public disclosures can aid the enemy by exposing the secrets of the government. Disclosures also expose fissures in the security apparatus of the government machinery. In these circumstances, disclosures are considered a sign of betrayal. The logic goes that disagreements over the scope of secrecy should be resolved internally through established procedures. The whistleblower is someone who, rather than appealing to those procedures, chooses to expose their weaknesses, and thus weakens state security.

The charge of treason can be a rhetorical device too. Accusing someone of treason or betrayal, when everyone else observes the rules of the game, is to shift the burden of explanation on the accused. It is not uncommon to hear the use of 'traitors' in everyday parlance to describe dissidents. As a rhetorical device it serves to shift attention from the content of the disclosure to the dubious moral character of the actor.

What about the betrayal of the country? The notion of patriotism that equates whistleblowing with disloyalty conflates patriotism with following the dictates of the government of the day (see Delmas 2015).[6] One can be a patriot yet without that implying being a blind executioner of the dictates of the government.

---

[6] See Nathanson (1993) for an account of patriotism that can be consistent with Snowden.

5.1.4   Harm to National Security

Whereas the patriotism argument insists on the moral character of whistleblowers, its political correlative among political thinkers in the realist tradition is that whistleblowing harms national security. Disclosure of national security information, when unedited, can often threaten life of soldiers and informers who often work covertly for national security. In addition, such disclosures put at risk national security by divulging strategic information. This goes against the genuine requirements of secrecy that allows governments and the executive to ward of potential dangers from outsiders. This was one of the arguments that followed post the NSA disclosures by Edward Snowden. The former director of US National Intelligence James Clapper declared that Snowden's leaks represented the 'most damaging theft of intelligence information in our history', adding that 'terrorists and other adversaries of this country are going to school on U.S. intelligence sources, methods and tradecraft, and the insights that they are gaining are making our job much, much harder'.[7]

Rahul Sagar argues that disclosures can undermine security and 'reveal sources and methods used to obtain secret intelligence', hampering the ability 'to collect intelligence in the future' and fostering cooperation with other countries on ventures that although are 'morally troubling or politically embarrassing....are nevertheless vital for national security' (2013a:108).[8] Moreover, public disclosures thwart the possibility of national security agencies to recruit informers who would be reluctant to come forward in absence of proper procedural safeguards to their identity.

However, national security depends on the interests it is meant to serve. Even though there is a presumption towards confidentiality of national security information, that presumption only holds when the information being gathered is not against either what has been constitutionally mandated or the public interest of the constituent group of a polity. In absence of correlative controls, it is difficult to ascertain that the cloak of secrecy is not being used to protect malicious acts of corruption and injustice. For, even though secrecy enables effectiveness in dealing with security threats, it also enables the opposite: the utilization of public offices for causes that fall outside the constitutional mandate. When public offices are usurped to forward personal ends, or ends deleterious to constitutional essentials, and in the process they subvert democratic controls, the justification of confidentiality is rather weak. Any disclosure under such circumstances that highlights the wrongdoing is then permitted.

Even though the dangers of malicious leaks are real disclosures often end up upholding the public interest. Even more so is the case when disclosures reveal

---

[7] As cited in Dilanian (2014).

[8] Sagar concedes that not all unauthorized disclosures are unjustified. If a disclosure reveals a wrongdoing or an abuse of public authority, then it is justified. The justification of disclosures should be public, employ the least drastic measure to disclose, be backed by clear and convincing evidence, and should not pose a disproportionate threat to public safety. See (2013a: ch. 5).

information of wrongdoing that are of embarrassment to the government, and thus require more, not less transparency. As a matter of fact, no empirical evidence has ever pointed that disclosures of government wrongdoing, from Ellsberg to Snowden, have ever compromised national security as government officials have claimed.

5.1.5   Vigilantism

Candice Delmas presents (but does not subscribe) an intriguing argument for the wrongfulness of political whistleblowing. She argues that an unauthorized disclosure 'amounts to an impermissible form of vigilantism that undermines the rule of law' (2015:92). Following Youngjae Lee (2012), who defines Foreign Relations Vigilantism as a breach 'of the moral duty to respect the allocation of state power', Delmas argues that 'the prosecution of government whistleblowers as traitors and spies seems to suggest that they might be engaged in exactly the kind of transgression of the boundaries of state power that Lee describes' (ibid: 93).[9] She finds that this view of vigilantism is not helpful to capture the features of whistleblowing.[10] Political whistleblowing is rather another form of vigilantism i.e. political vigilantism. For her 'vigilantism at the heart of whistleblowing consists in *transgression of the boundaries around state secrets, for the purpose of challenging the allocation or use of power*' (ibid: 94, emphasis in the original). 'Political vigilantes' for Delmas, 'aim to expose to the public, and thus question the legitimacy of, the boundaries around state secrets that they cross' (ibid.).

Is whistleblowing a form of political vigilantism? We do not think so. Although whistleblowing shares with vigilantism[11] some features, it is not an instance of it. We agree that whistleblowers challenge the proper scope of secrecy and use of power. But they do not, as she claims, challenge the allocation of power. They rather challenge the abuse of power in a particular instance. They do not disagree with secrecy per se but its particular realization in a given context that shields wrongdoers. It is rather their deep commitment to democratic authority, the judgement of the people, and the procedures of democratic self-correction, which motivate

---

[9] Notice that Lee's point is not to define vigilantism, but identify the wrong-making features of espionage. Similarly, Delmas' attempt is not to work out a characterization of vigilantism but to provide 'a persuasive rationale' for the wrongfulness of governmental whistleblowing (2015: 94). The fact of political vigilantism and the disrespect for state power do not imply that political whistleblowing is always unjustified (ibid.).

[10] She also refers here to the Dumsday's normal version of vigilantism (2009).

[11] Les Johnston argues that vigilantism shows the following features: it involves planning and premeditation by those engaging in it; its participants are private citizens whose engagement is voluntary; it is a form of autonomous citizenship and, as such, constitutes a social movement; it uses or threatens the use of force; it arises when an established order is under threat from the transgression, the potential transgression, or the imputed transgression of institutionalized norms; it aims to control crime or other social infractions by offering assurances (or 'guarantees') of security both to participants and to others (1996:220).

their appeal to those very same procedures to correct gross wrongdoings. This is unlike the case of the vigilante, who consider themselves to be the source of authority and thus do not trust the allocation of power. Moreover, a vigilante action can be deeply undemocratic, aimed against targeting groups or constitutionally protected minorities.

The case of whistleblowing, as we said, is the opposite. It is not geared towards establishing a new order or protecting a threatened old order. Unlike vigilantism, it is not a product of a disbelief in democratic laws, but a radical manifestation of constitutional values when these are subverted by particularistic interests.

5.1.6   Accountability

In a series of works Rahul Sagar has questioned the accountability of anonymous whistleblowers and leakers towards democratic constituencies. The argument is that unauthorized disclosures neither have the consent of the public, nor those resorting to them have been chosen by the public or their elected representatives. In this regard, unauthorized disclosures constitute a form of usurpation, since they undermine 'the public authority that we have created through law and armed with expertise and information' (2013a: 113).

> [W]e establish procedures and authorities—such as elections and courts—in order to balance and arbitrate between conflicting interests. These authorities and procedures allow us to collectively determine what is in the public interest. Consequently, to permit these authorities and procedures to be undermined on the basis of private judgments about what constitutes the public interest plainly seems a recipe for disorder (ibid.: 114)

Moreover, unauthorized disclosures are a product of private judgements that are unavailable for public scrutiny, and thus it is difficult to hold those disclosing accountable for rash and malicious disclosures (ibid.: 114–115).

We agree with Sagar that the allocation of political authority is violated in the process of unauthorized disclosures, but it is also a fact that it is only through such a violation that disclosures can be realized. Sagar seems to believe that such violations do not respect the democratic allocation of power, but the fact that power is democratically allocated does not imply a duty of full compliance when those institutions overstep their constitutional limits, and do not conform to the very reasons for which they were created. It is in this precise sense that unauthorized disclosures should be read as an act of dissent. Such disclosures negotiate the scope and extent of political authority and in doing so test its legitimacy.

5.1.7   Imperfect Information

Finally, an important argument against unauthorized disclosures concerns the informational aspect of disclosures. Rahul Sagar argues that, for a disclosure to be justified, the whistleblower needs to be aware of the context surrounding a decision to classify a particular information. He argues that:

> since adventurous exercises of executive power usually take place in the midst of complicated and fast-moving events, an official cannot rely on a rigid definition of what constitutes wrongdoing. In determining whether a prima facie violation of the law constitutes a genuine abuse of authority, she will need to take account of the broader context within which the violation has occurred (2013a: 129).

A potential whistleblower, especially someone in a subordinate role, is not always in the position to ascertain the circumstances, constraints, and reasons behind a certain activity they perceive to be wrong. Decisions are often a product of and necessitated by the circumstances they respond to. Absent contextual information provides a weaker ground for disclosure. Rather than being muted by the lack of information, a subordinate should rather approach superior officials to gather evidence (ibid.: 130).

The argument from imperfect information is compelling. We agree with Sagar that prospective whistleblowers should have some initial evidence of a wrongdoing, be truthful in making their claims, and demonstrate adequate care in gathering additional evidence to back their disclosures. But it is equally true that they might fail in obtaining adequate knowledge of the context in which of the suspicious activies, especially when they are of a subordinate rank. Approaching superiors is an option, but petitioning a superior for information is fraught with personal risks and rarely effective to the process of exposing the wrongdoing itself.

We rather believe that disclosures addressing a wrongdoing that undermines the public interest is prima facie justified when reasonable care has been taken to gather sufficient evidence and avoid exposing innocent individuals to risks. In the following section we discuss in detail which conditions satisfy a full justification of political whistleblowing.

5.2   When Is Whistleblowing Justified?

Criticisms of political whistleblowing leaves us with scattered positions. First, scholars often disagree, if not talk past each other, on the constitutive elements of its permissibility and justification.

To recapitulate the discussion so far, those working within the field of business ethics elaborate criteria for corporate whistleblowing that insist on principles of loyalty and responsibility towards the firm, conceding at times that loyalty cannot be absolute when firms operate in violation of the law. Civic disclosures in such cases are justifiable only *pro tanto*, when overriding duties of statutory law requires whistleblowers to betray the firm. However, considerations of loyalty and trust should never be set aside, and insofar as whistleblowing disclosures can reinforce the mutual trust between the corporation and its stakeholders, they are more or less welcomed.

Scholars interested instead in government whistleblowing, insist on the duty of confidentiality as the yardstick against which to determine whether the disclosures are permitted. Here too loyalty plays a role, but in the sense of the political allegiance citizens (should) have towards democratic institutions on whose legitimacy the authority of the law fundamentally rests. Political acts of whistleblowing might be *excused*, as last resort measures, when any other channels of internal disclosures are fended off, or inexistent. A full justification cannot be obtained, since the duty of allegiance and confidentiality clauses can be hardly met. In any case, disclosures should not conflict with overriding interests of national security, even when emergency threats require procedures that may affect the privacy of citizens.

Notwithstanding the rich debate we have tried to account for, it is our conviction that some crucial points go missing. There are three crucial elements of whistleblowing, in our opinion. First is the idea that acts of whistleblowing are communicative acts directed at the public or audience. Such acts can be successful, but can also fail. A would-be whistleblower who doesn't properly evaluate the circumstances of her disclosure, may fail despite her best intentions.

Second, the debate is remarkably silent about the nature of the good faith requirement that a justification would require. We have seen that some scholars and legislators are skeptic about the very idea of a good faith requirement, for a variety of reasons. Morality may require an evaluation of the intent as a condition for the permissibility of act. However, intentions, desires, motivations more often can only contribute to explain the aims of the action, but they are not an appropriate ground for praise or blame of the action, which often depend on the reasons the agent has to act the way she does. What is good faith then? A form of intent in the sense of a predictive intention, or should it be rather assessed in terms of reasons?

The third point concerns the public interest argument. In our opinion, failing to see that acts of whistleblowing are communicative acts directed to a public audience is partly the cause why the current debate has paid so little attention to the public justification of whistleblowing in terms of public interest. Yet, as we argued in Chap. 3, public interest is the standard of assessment for the justification of civic whistleblowing, and—as we argue here– plays an important contributory role in defining the public relevance of politically motivated disclosures. Even more, it offers an argument in favor of whistleblowing as a form of civil dissent (see Chap. 6).

In what follows we propose some necessary and sufficient conditions for permissible acts of *political* whistleblowing. In Kumar and Santoro (2017) we have provided a blueprint of these conditions. Here we analyze them in detail, especially in the light of the public interest requirement, and show that they are sufficiently general to include both civic and politically motivated whistleblowing. Not all cases of leaking count as cases of whistleblowing. Leaking a secret information may in fact serve several purposes, some of which are morally impermissible. Thus, under which conditions an act of whistleblowing is morally permissible?

5.2.1   The Informational Circumstances of Whistleblowing Disclosures

Whistleblowing disclosures arise in conditions of informational asymmetry. Informational asymmetry can result from different circumstances: because those having informational privileges (call it X) deliberately hide the information from another subject or group (call it Y); or because X gets access to a source which Y does not have. It can also arise when Y is unaware of the very existence of the information and does not have the resources to access it. We have reviewed some of these cases with respect to secrecy in Chap. 4. Here we are concerned with the informational circumstances that lead to justifiable disclosures. Not all cases of information asymmetry justify disclosures. For instance, an employee who has information regarding her own health condition does not usually have any obligation to disclose it to her employer. Such knowledge confers the employee an informational advantage over the employer, especially when her health conditions could lead to losing the job. The mere fact that X possesses an information that Y does not possess constitutes only a generic case of informational asymmetry and is not a wrong *per se*.

An individual or institution can also claim property rights over information they possess, and in virtue of this claim justify informational asymmetry. Patents, client portfolios, and assets are often cases of a company's privileged information. States can also claim property rights over sensitive documents or information they possess. The location of nuclear power plants and the movement of troops along the border are examples of legitimate secrecy that constitutes information asymmetry. Information of this sort is usually protected under secrecy laws that are constitutionally mandated.

The informational circumstances of whistleblowing are instead cases of *unjustified* asymmetry. Unjustified asymmetries is part of everyday life: for instance when the car dealer sells a lemon to the unaware client; or, much worse, when a person who suffers from a sexually transmitted disease has unprotected sex with a partner without informing the partner. Other cases are less straightforward as, for instance, in the requirement to disclose health data to procure services from institutions like hospitals and insurance companies. The request of a hospital in having updated information on the health conditions of a blood donor is justified in the name of the general interest of not harming the blood recipients. However, a medical insurance company requesting information on pre-existing conditions will illegitimately refuse assistance if based on that information, although it might legitimately request disclosures in assessing the premium.[12]

These examples tell us that asymmetry is unjustified in two cases: when Y has a legitimate interest in obtaining the information that is *intentionally* denied by X; or

---

[12] A different scenario is one in which the withdrawal of information is not due to intentional denial, but to mere failure to request it. Citizens might fail to obtain social services because they simply do not solicit them for lack of adequate information. In such a case, if the provider has sufficiently publicized the service, it can be hardly held responsible for the failure to deliver the service.

when X has an illegitimate interest in hiding access of the information to Y, and no further reasons justify a restriction to access the information. We can thus say that:

> Within the epistemic circumstance defined by two subjects X and Y, such that X possesses an information i that Y does not possess, X's informational advantage over Y is unjustifiable *if and only if:* (i) X intentionally withholds i from Y; (ii) Y has a legitimate interest to access i, or (iii) X has an illegitimate interest in hiding i, and (iv) no other reasons justifies the restriction to access i. (5.1)

Consider now the case of whistleblowers. The opportunity for legitimate disclosures arises within the epistemic circumstance where all these conditions are met, and the whistleblower reasonably believes that they obtain. More precisely:

> Within the epistemic circumstance defined by three subjects X, Y, Z such that the informational asymmetry of X over Y is unjustified, and Z has access to i, a disclosure by Z is justified *if and only if* Z has a justifiable belief that the asymmetry is unjustified. (5.2).

Only within the context of informational asymmetry described by (5.2), claims of justification can be vindicated. Call it the context of *justifiability* for whistleblowing disclosures.[13]

The context of justifiability presents features that deserve some attention. First, we should stipulate at the outset that when the information is not withheld intentionally, disclosures may render the information public without any further need to provide justification for an act that is already permissible (other things staying equal).

The second feature is the idea of an interest. When we say that a third-party (Y in our formula) has a legitimate interest to access information we do not imply that the interest should necessarily be claimed by the party. Sometimes parties may not be aware of an interest they may have. Consider an example similar to the case discussed in Chap. 4 of a community living in a neighborhood whose water is being polluted unbeknown to them.[14] Their failure to advance a request of disclosure on the level of pollution and the liability involved does not debunk the interest in question.

Now consider the case of illegitimate interests. We may ask: does the fact that X has an illegitimate interest in hiding information imply that Y has a legitimate interest to acquire that information? The answer is yes. The reason is that these are

---

[13] It can be argued that disclosures are justified when the institution has lost claim over the information. This can happen in several cases: in cases of corruption described in Chap. 3, when the abuse harms the public interest; in the abuse of the secrecy privileges; or when the classifying privileges have expired, or public regulations have changed, but it is in the interest of the organization to avoid this information to become of public domain. Strictly speaking we cannot say a disclosure of this information is a case of whistleblowing, since there is no wrongdoing implied in these circumstances.

[14] The example recalls the real story of the late 1980s case of Hinkley, California, a small town in the Mojave Desert whose inhabitants had been suffering from several forms of cancer due to the high-level of hexavalent chromium (10 times the maximum allowed) in the groundwaters used by the community. After a lengthy legal battle, the State gas provider PG&E was found guilty of polluting the waters due to leaks from a nearby compressor station. The story hit world attention thanks to the movie *Erin Brockovich*, starring Julia Roberts, which tells the story of the woman who discovered and pursued the case.

competing interests in conditions of relative scarcity of resources such that any increment in the satisfaction of the interests of one side correspond to a decrement of satisfaction on the other. We already discussed this point in Chap. 3. We argued that the public interest of a polity is affected by influential social groups who feed their own special interests by plundering the common pool or resources. The public interest, we said, is an adversarial notion that stands opposite to those special interests. The context of justifiability models this situation by considering both kinds of interests as alternative ways to identify an unjustified asymmetry. The 'or' in the formula should be read inclusively: whistleblowers can make a legitimate public disclosure when they have a justifiable belief that the public interest is harmed in either one of these two forms (i.e. *either* to redress or prevent a harm to legitimate interests, *or* to report or contrast the protection of illegitimate interests), if not both.

The third condition of justifiable belief also requires some consideration. A whistleblower may hold information that is later revealed to be false, although she sincerely believes it is not. She may even have gathered accurate information that yet turns out to be fake. But within the limited circumstances of her disclosures, she can only take some precautions before going public. Such is the possibility of checking the facts, or outsourcing the check to platforms or media that can do the research properly. At times whistleblowers just disclose rough evidence of the wrongdoing, documents whose authenticity—once released—can be later confirmed, or verified in the public eye. For instance, in the Snowden case, the NSA did not deny the authenticity of the documents, but denied the right to their public access. In the Watergate case instead, the 'deep throat' source asked the press (notably Woodward and Bernstein of the Washington Post) to run an extensive fact-checking before going public, while the White House had denied any allegation. Most importantly however, it is not up to the whistleblower alone to verify the truthfulness in the information she discloses. Other institutions, including the press, and the public opinion, play a subsidiary role when checking the facts is not feasible without going public first. Instead, the whistleblower should *not* release information that she knows to be false. This knowledge requirement is weaker than a full justification of evidence, and yet sets a minimal but important threshold for permissible disclosures which is meant to avoid manipulation effects and deception. This is how the requirement of justifiable belief should be interpreted above.

The epistemic circumstances of disclosures determine the context of justifiability, but are not sufficient alone to justify the act of whistleblowing itself. In addition to the epistemic circumstances, we need to formulate the conditions for the permissibility of whistleblowing.

The argument comes in three steps. First, we identify what we call the communicative constraints on the act, which fit the 'justifiable belief' requirement for disclosure. Second, we discuss the aspect of intent, which insists on the normative reasons for justification; third we provide an account of public interest along the lines of the argument defended in Chap. 4.

Our claim is that an act of whistleblowing disclosure is *permissible* if and only if:

(i)   it fulfils specific communicative constraints on the disclosure;
(ii)   the disclosure is made with the right kind of intent;
(iii)   the disclosure addresses wrongdoings relevant to the public interest; (5.3)

5.2.2   *Communicative Constraints*

The starting point is that whistleblowing is essentially a communicative act. As such, for an act of leaking to count as whistleblowing, the act must satisfy some communicative constraints.

(i)   The act should be informative as far as possible for a targeted audience;
(ii)   The act does not convey information known to be false;
(iii)   The act does not convey information for which adequate evidence is lacking;
(iv)   The act is performed with the intention to convey information that cannot be obtained by other means than by performing the act of whistleblowing;
(v)   The information ought to be relevant to the targeted audience, that is the revealed information contributes to their legitimate interests. The audience may consist the general public opinion, the citizenry, or a specific group thereof. (5.4)

A brief explanation is in order. Taken together, the conditions (i) and (ii) concern the felicity conditions of the illocutionary act of disclosure. By this we mean they are constraints modelled after the speech act theory (see Grice 1989). In particular, they express the requirement of informativeness and truthfulness. For Grice the maxims were meant to provide a guidance in the hearer-speaker situation. Similarly, here the constraints also have a linguistic significance. This insight owes also to Habermas' (1984) analysis of the validity claims for successful speech acts (truth, sincerity, and rightness). Such claims are 'equivalent to the assertion that the conditions for the validity of an utterance are fulfilled' (ibid.: 38). For Habermas the validity claims are requirements of the rational discourse in a speaker-oriented situation. Likewise, in the context of disclosures, informativeness and truthfulness apply to the situation of the speaker-discloser as normative constraints on the permissibility of the communicative act.

Another important function of the validity conditions is to avoid cases of manipulation and deception. Deception (see Chap. 4) may happen when partial disclosures are made with the intention of leading the public to draw conclusions that would not stand had full disclosure been made. When the public is led to believe conclusions contrary to the facts, ill-intentioned disclosures have usually perlocutory effects of manipulation, for they lead people to act in ways they would not have acted in presence of full information.

Condition (iii) is a constraint on available evidence. As we said, whistleblowers are not always able to provide evidence confirming the truthfulness of their disclosure, unless documents themselves are official and count as evidence without further checking. Other times, facts of wrongdoing can only be reported orally. In this case, it is important that leaks are susceptible to confirmation by fact-checking. The press can play an important role in this regard, filtering news to the public that can be backed up by evidence. This is after all what important news outlet like *The*

New York Times, The Guardian, The Washington Post, and *The Intercept* more recently, have done in the last decade. More controversial is the role of leaking platforms like Wikileaks, which releases, unfiltered, any material they deem worth publishing.

Condition (iv) is more controversial, for it can be interpreted in three different ways. One way to read it is by saying that whistleblowing disclosures would be permissible only when nobody else within the organization in possession of the same information is willing to make the disclosure. But this reading is exposed to several problems, one of which is the unwelcome situation in which the whistleblower would be responsible for blowing the whistle as a consequence of an omission by the others. The second interpretation is that the whistleblower is the only one who possess an information worth disclosing. Should she be then obliged to disclose? The answer is unclear. For one thing, it is very unlikely that only one person knows that something is wrong in an organization. But even if that was the case, we should consider that employees who find themselves in this predicament also have countervailing reasons not to disclose, among which is the fear of retaliation. We should rather say that when employees are in such predicament, they should not be judged blameworthy at face value. We will come back to this dispute in the last part of the section. The final interpretation of this clause is that the whistleblower would have a legitimate reason to disclose when every other channel has been attempted, or no channels are available. This is the most reasonable interpretation of the clause, for it justifies the permissibility as an act of last resort after due effort has been made to follow internal procedures.

The last of the conditions listed above (v) requires the information to be of relevance to a specific audience. We include it here because it links the communicative constraints to the content of the disclosure. This condition says that leaks should have a communicative purpose; othersive they would be just a message in a bottle floating in the ocean of information, and fail their aim of addressing specific interests of public concern. Let's move now to the intent and public interest requirements.

5.2.3   Intent

As many have argued, the good faith requirement in whistleblowing disclosure is hard to identify, even more when the intent is interpreted as a psychological motive. Moreover, the determination of the intent may be legally irrelevant vis-à-vis the political or legal value of the potential wrong being revealed. There is, however, a reason for insisting on the intent requirement. Acts of whistleblowing are often on the edge of the law, and they call into question a moral and not only a strict legal or political dimension.

A theory of whistleblowing should be able to outline which considerations should be relevant in the deliberative circumstances of the potential whistleblower. Whistleblowers are often stuck in a dilemma between disclosure and the breach of oath, which may involve sentiments of guilt and treason, and may have long-term consequences for their life. The 'situational' aspect of this problem should not be overlooked as a resolute choice will depend, in these circumstances, upon the intention the person forms given the limited time and pressure. On a different note, we should also consider the role of blameworthy intents, especially when revenge and resentment trigger the disclosures. When a disclosure is made to harm a specific person, regardless of the legitimate interests the disclosure may unveil, it is legitimate to wonder whether the act is justified. In order to assess whether a disclosure is made with a justifiable intent, we can formulate a tentative test. Call it the harm test:

> The harm test: a disclosure is *prima facie* justified when the agent foresees that the probability of harm she may suffer from disclosing the information is higher than the probability she assigns to any personal benefit she may enjoy.[15] (5.5)

The idea of the test is that in order to assess whether the whistleblower's intent is licit, we should look at the risk of harmful consequences (as specified above) the whistleblower expects from making the disclosure. If this chance is higher than the chance of the advantages she may obtain, the risk she takes should be taken as a proxy for the right kind of intent. But why so? The reason is that when the whistleblower makes the disclosure, on the balance of reasons, she acts against her best interests given the higher risk of harm she is willing to take. Notice that the test does not exclude that a personal interest may also be among the reasons for disclosure. It only excludes that preponderant blameworthy motives may justify the disclosure.

The test bears some resemblance to the principle of double effect.[16] According to this principle, an act is permitted when the aim of the action is good (or at least indifferent), the good effect, not the evil effect, is intended; the good effect is not produced by means of the bad effect; and finally, the good effect must be sufficiently desirable to compensate for permitting the evil effect.[17] The fourth condition does establish a proportionality between good and bad effects, thus 'determining if the extent of the harm is adequately offset by the magnitude of the proposed benefit' (McIntyre 2014: §1). Our insight is that an examination of the whistleblower's intent should be subject to the same evaluation. However, we do not require the further condition that the evil effect should not be intended, neither that the realization of the good effect should depend on the realization of the bad effect. These constraints may apply in case of killing for self-defense, but they seem too strict in cases of public interest disclosures in which motives of revenge may also be present.

Thomas Scanlon (2008) is skeptic about the nature of the intent considered in this doctrine. He writes:

---

[15] The harm test is not a version the Harm Principle provided by John Stuart Mill in *On Liberty* (Mill 2003). See also Kumar and Santoro (2017: 675–676) for a discussion of the test.

[16] Thomas Aquinas is credited for the earliest formulation of the doctrine in his *Summa Theologica* (Part II.II, Question 64, Art.7). See Aquinas (1988).

[17] The conditions are a reformulation of Mangan (1949: 4), as cited in McIntyre (2014: §1).

> An agent's aim in acting, her plan in acting, her beliefs about the likely effects of her action, and her evaluation of various features of her situation […] are, taken together, an important part of our basis for predicting the effects that her action will have. They are not, however, a complete basis for predicting those effects. An agent's understanding of her situation is often incomplete or mistaken, and the effects of a planned action may be quite different from what the agent expected. (2008: 12)
>
> […]
>
> [The agent's] intention is relevant ... only because it tells us something about those effects. This is what I will call the *predictive* significance of intent (2008: 13, emphasis in the original).

Therefore it is one thing to intend in a predictive sense, another is to deliberate upon reasons that a normal agent should be able to consider:

> The question of permissibility is a question that can be asked by a deliberating agent, and one that a normal agent can be expected to be able to answer. The answer to this question is not just a matter of what is in fact the case (whether anyone could know it or not). But at the same time, permissibility is not merely a matter of what a particular agent believes the facts to be. It depends also on what it is reasonable for the agent to believe in the situation, what it is reasonable for the agent to do to check those beliefs, and whether the agent has done those things (ibid.: 51–52).

Thus, while the predictive intent takes into account the aim of the person before acting, (ibid.: 13), also—and more crucially for Scanlon—the critical standpoint of what is reasonable to do, which reasons the agent *should* come up with, is relevant to the question of the moral permissibility. It may seem though then that the harm test fails to account for the right kinds of reasons an agent should have about the action. These reasons, not the immediate motives of the action, are relevant.

Scanlon's critique of the doctrine of double effect captures an important distinction between the intent and the reasons for action that impinge on the question of permissibility. A similar distinction can be drawn in the legal doctrine of the intent assessment, especially within the framework of court trials. What really matters in determining whether a person is guilty, or innocent of a crime, is not the mental states of the agent in the moment she was acting. The practice of taking and attributing responsibility presupposes, for a competent agent facing a trial, a more robust capacity of being responsive to the request of explanation and justification for her act.[18]

We agree on this point. Within the scope of our discussion, the permissibility of the disclosure cannot be assessed by the aims of the actions alone, perhaps in connection with their expected consequences. There are reasons that confer meaning to the action itself that the agent should consider, and such a duty of reasonableness ought to count in the justification of disclosures. Our view on the public interest captures this insight. However, such critical standpoint cannot at the same time be the exclusive ground for permissibility (Scanlon is indeed not clear on whether it

---

[18] The capacity of being responsive to reasons is for instance implicit in our mastery of counterfactual judgments, when we are able to discern between ways agents have acted, and how they should have acted (this of course holds also in the case of normative self-appraisals of one's own action). This view is defended in Santoro (2013).

should be so or not). As we have highlighted above, what makes a disclosure permissible is also the fact that the disclosure realizes its public aim, and thus for a whistleblower what counts as a reason for action is the likelihood of reaching a certain audience, whether the larger public or a particular group. The communicative constraints cannot be disregarded.

We shall ask at this point: is the harm test alone sufficient to justify an act of whistleblowing? Some difficulties arise here, when considering the communicative constraints. Here we consider two main scenarios.

The first is when the disclosure satisfies the harm test, but not the constraints: the exposure to risk by the whistleblower is sufficiently high to prove that the intent is not malicious, and yet she acts within unfavorable circumstances where the likelihood of reaching her targeted audience is small or absent. This is for instance the case of disclosures in weak institutional contexts where corrupt practices are the norm. In such contexts, the internal channels of disclosures are usually absent or ineffective, the judiciary is compromised, and the media, for lack of concern, weak influence, or bent to special interests, are not prone to assist the whistleblower. If—despite the odds—the whistleblower decides to expose herself, her act would be noble, but she would fail to act successfully. Is this a case of permissible disclosure? In one sense yes, for it is a supererogatory act and thus also permissible. Moreover, the whistleblower may decide to make the disclosure to colleagues or to the public immediately available to her, acting out of what we may call testimonial justice, in the hope that she will be heard at one point. But in another sense it is not a politically significant act, for she would not only fail to act prudentially, but her action would turn out against her and even compromise her position, more so if the value of the information she might want to disclose is higher. Here the harm test clashes with the communicative constraints, and a solution to this predicament doesn't seem to be easy to provide.

The second scenario is the one in which the whistleblower may act for personal interests alone (which would not pass the test) and yet her disclosure is properly addressed. This is the case, for instance, of a revenge a whistleblower takes on a boss who she knows has committed a crime. If the personal circumstances had been different, perhaps the whistleblower would not have reported him but given their personal conflict, she resolves to act. Anonymous disclosures, tit-for-tat agreement with the authorities in exchange for preferential treatment in court are often cited as cases of this sort of dubious good faith. Even more, it might be objected that when effective protection is ensured, whistleblowers' risk of exposure is limited, incentivizing thus instrumental disclosure which can yet bring beneficial effects. The reward system adopted in some jurisdictions seems to work exactly on this form of incentive. Here the harm test seems to be redundant to assess the permissibility of disclosure. It should not be forgotten though that purely instrumental disclosures may also have perverse effects on the very public the disclosure is meant to reach. For the incentives to disclosures may also enhance an atmosphere of mutual suspicion among colleagues. More importantly, the lack of sincerity in the disclosure does not contribute to a public evaluation of the wrongdoings, but rather to ignite polarized reactions among the public where populist attitudes are widespread. Disclosures of this sort are often not made in the public interest.

It seems, in conclusion, that the harm test provides a minimal threshold for the deliberative conditions of disclosure. It does not provide a justification per se to the permissibility of the act, although it has a heuristic function, especially in the legal assessment of disclosures that usually follows successful disclosures.

We come now to the third condition of permissibility, the public interest. We have defended in Chap. 3 a characterization of the public interest as a 'presumptive interest for all-purposive rights.' We will not resume here the earlier discussion, but only recall the idea and generalize it to fit the conditions of permissibility for any form of whistleblowing, civic and political.

5.2.4   Disclosures in the Public Interest

Our conclusion in Chap. 3 was that a policy is in the public interest when there is a presumption that: (i) it may affect the rights and duties of the members of a polity that supervise the distribution of social benefits; or (ii) there is a private interest that may harm the rights and duties of those members. In either case, public interest concerns assume that (iii) there is an institutional authority accountable for addressing wrongdoings that arise due to the pursuit of illegitimate interests. We specified that 'presumptive' interest refers to an information that everybody being part of that public may have an interest to be informed about as it may concern them, and that such presumption holds only insofar as the public validates it once it is made available. We provided an account of the core content of a public interest justification, claiming that it consists in the set of rights that are all-purposive for the attainment of social benefits. That is, the public interest does not primarily consist in a specific list of benefits, primary goods or resources, but in the rights (and relative schemes of distribution) that supervise the arrangement of those benefits. According to this view, the public interest includes a set of fundamental rights which enable the enjoyment of more substantive rights and particular social benefits.

Following such characterization, we argued that an act of whistleblowing of civic kind is justified *inter alia* if the disclosure is made in the presumptive interest of a polity or social group with regard to instances of wrongdoing that affect the enjoyment of rights (including the case when these effects are unbeknown to the members of the polity), and when the disclosure reveals the failure of procedures that are meant to provide measures of accountability.

In Chap. 3 we limited this argument to the case of civic whistleblowing. The *inter alia* qualification expressed the idea that other conditions may apply, and thus the public interest condition is not sufficient for a full justification of disclosures.

The purpose of this section is to generalize the argument presented above. We do this in two steps. First, we discuss how the public interest condition fits with the communicative and intent conditions. Second, we argue that within this framework, we can also justify the permissibility of disclosures of a political kind.

To recall from the earlier discussion, the communicative constraints on whistle-blowing require the disclosure be informative, truthful, fact-based, necessary to address the wrongdoing, and directed towards an audience. In addition, the information is to be relevant to the legitimate interests of the public. These conditions define what we may call genuine public interest disclosures.

First, a genuine public interest disclosure is addressed towards an audience that may include the general public or a group thereof. When it concerns the public, the disclosure is referred to non-assignable individuals (see *infra,* Chap. 3 for a discussion of non-assignability). Second, a genuine public interest disclosure is informative of a crime or wrongdoing that harms the public (or group). Given the secretive nature of corrupt practices, the informative value of disclosure is generally high. As for the third condition, a genuine public interest disclosure is usually documented and makes evidence available for investigation.

Fourth, a genuine disclosure usually follows internal channels of report, especially to the public administration equipped for this purpose. When there are no such channels, civic whistleblowers often resort to the press as a consequence of a lack of alternatives.

Last, a genuine public interest disclosure is relevant to the legitimate interests of the public, for it addresses crimes that are of immediate or long-term harm to the collectivity. Harm to the public does not only consist in the very perpetration of a crime of corruption, but also in the rights affected by those crimes. The common opinion may sometimes be scandalized by the news of embezzlment, fraud, misappropriation by politicians but tends to overlook this deeper aspect of rights violation, as there is no immediate or short-term effect of private appropriation of public money over public services. Corruption though also harms citizens' full enjoyment of social services that may be cut due to lack of financial resources; even more directly the right to employment, health, social security, personal safety. Examples abound here, too. A general fact though seems confirmed: in countries with high perception index of corruption, social services tend to have lower standards.

Let's consider now the condition of the intent. We said in the previous section that the evaluation of the intent comprises two aspects: a deliberative aspect, and the aspect of assessment. The deliberative aspect is that of the concrete circumstances in which the whistleblower has to decide whether to make a disclosure. A genuine public interest disclosure provides aims and reasons for the right kind of intent. It provides the right kind of intent under the harm test for obvious reasons. When the aim of disclosure in the predictive sense is to address the public about information concerning legitimate interests of the polity, the test is passed. Likewise, in the case of assessment, what Scanlon takes as the locus of the question about permissibility, the public interest identifies an objective reason for disclosure that every moral person would reasonably endorse. More precisely, we may say that, within Scanlon's contractualist view of reasons—the morality of whistleblowing consists in the hypothetical endorsement of the reasons every member of the public would reasonably accept as a reason for the disclosure.

We have shown so far that public interest disclosures of a civic kind fit the requirement of communication and intent for the permissibility of whistleblowing. We now want to show that this tripartite argument also holds for disclosures of a political kind.

The most important distinction between whistleblowing of political and civic kinds is that only the former requires a breach of a statutory law. Political whistleblowers betray their duty of confidentiality, especially when they require non-disclosure of classified material. The value of their disclosure is even higher when, in virtue of their secrecy privileges, they dispose of information that only a handful of people can legally access.

Of course their betrayal comes at a high cost. While civic whistleblowers are commended, at least in public, for their sense of civility, political whistleblowers are often accused of treason, espionage, threat to national security, and often charged under theft of government material or national security laws. We have discussed these features at length in this chapter and in Chap. 2, so we will not add more here. The question we should ask now is whether the breach of confidentiality affects the conditions of permissibility of the act.

It is important here to underline that 'permissibility' in the sense being employed in this discussion refers to the moral conditions of the disclosures, not to its legal counterpart. But, in our opinion, the morality of disclosures has an obvious political import, for the whistleblower who, in full consciousness, decides to breach the laws of a country to which she has pledged allegiance, also performs a political act of criticism and dissent.

We shall assume here that the communicative and intent conditions are met for the same reasons provided above. The case of a breach of the duty of secrecy meets the same conditions of permissibility for civic disclosures. As for the intent, it suffices to notice that the breach increases enormously the risk for the whistleblower of a long-term punishment, thus passing the threshold set by the harm test.

The crucial question is rather whether the breach of duty can be still said to be in the public interest. Considered as a question about the legitimacy of democratic authority, the answer will depend on which conception of political obligation one is willing to endorse. Voluntarist conceptions of political obligation claim that the bonds of political allegiance in democratic societies are justified by the consent given to democratic institutions who act on behalf of citizens they represent. A different version of the same paradigm insists on the hypothetical nature of such consent, rather than the historical roots of polities. Justifications of political obligations are also given in terms of a duty of 'fair-play' and of a natural duty to uphold just institutions.[19]

The ideal view of political obligation is unsatisfying for different reasons. In a nutshell, these views remove the problem rather than addressing it. Political disclosures made in violation of the law highlight conflicts between different allegiances in historically rooted constitutional democracies. Despite the common

---

[19] See Horton (1992: 27–41; 70–108) for a concise reconstruction of the debate on political obligation.

framework of the constitution, real-world democracies are characterized by powerful adversarial interests and conflicts of obligation. Whistleblowers are often in this
predicament, owing fidelity towards the law against their best moral and political
convictions. These are conflicts that do not emerge within conceptions that assume
public institutions to be generally just. It is thus within the framework of competing
claims that whistleblowers may take recourse to public interest arguments in justifying their breach of the law. Our conviction is that the question, whether public interest disclosures may justify such breach, is an open one that cannot be resolved
within the confines and terms of ideal theory. Public interest disclosures have—as
we argued here—a presumptive value for the public and as such should be made
available to a democratic polity.

Perhaps, the main argument against the permissibility of political disclosure is
that by making the disclosure, the whistleblower harms the public interest. Thus she
cannot seek excuse or justification under this heading. In Chap. 4 we have discussed
a realist version of this argument. Championed by Richard Posner, Eric Posner and
Adrian Vermeule, and partly Rahul Sagar (along with several legal and political
experts), the argument simply says that national security is an overriding interest of
the public. Insofar as secrecy ensures the security of the country, without subtracting too much liberty, secrecy measures are justified. A consequence of the argument
is that whistleblowers who disclose classified information are outlaws.

We have argued that this argument, a consequence of the balance model, does not
account for unrestrained secrecy, whose impact on fundamental constitutional rights
is much wider than what realists assume. In Chap. 4 we have provided an argument
to this effect. We said that secrecy affects the epistemic entitlement of citizens to
know under which circumstances their rights are limited or interfered by secrecy
practices. We have shown that while the epistemic entitlement holds in ideal context, it does not account for the practice of legitimate secrecy under the non-ideal
circumstances of constitutional democracies. However, the epistemic entitlement
justifies what we called a right of assessment of the circumstances in which rights
have been limited or violated. Such a right holds ex-post and in due time. Some
limitations on the time of disclosures are justified by the need of large scale investi-
gations in cases of emergencies countries may face in the events of terrorist attacks.
Some other limitations instead are illicit, when such practices widen their scope
over time and space, and the judiciary branch defers to the government in deciding
who to spy on and what to classify. We argued that a right of assessment holds in
these circumstances, granting citizens the power to appeal against the government,
to file court petitions, and also publicly express their opposition when the government refuses to disclose the requested information in due time. When, despite
the constitutional guarantees, such procedures of assessment of the terms governing
the state limitation of fundamental rights are not granted, rights can be violated
outright, limited, or suspended without proper justification. It is then in the public
interest of the citizens, who enjoy those rights, to be informed of the nature and
extent of these violations, limitations, and suspensions.

If –as we believe– this argument holds, then political disclosures are justified in
virtue of a specific right to information, the right of assessment, citizens have

regarding the legal standing of their rights. A political disclosure is therefore in the public interest of citizens when it exposes (i) the violation or limitation of fundamental rights of citizens unbeknown to them; and (ii) the absence of mechanisms of assessment of the reasons for the limitation of those rights.

It follows that public interest disclosures are justified by their appeal to the constitutional protection of fundamental rights in those circumstances where practices of secrecy exceed proper constitutional checks.

The idea that constitutional rights are in the public interest of a polity generalizes the proposal we have defended in Chap. 3. We can then say that public interest consists of the core set of rights that supervise the equal recognition of liberties and the fair distribution of social benefits. More precisely, we can define the core set of rights that constitute the public interest as those constitutional rights which enable the enjoyment of more substantive rights and particular social benefits. Political and civil rights, and the socio-economic rights to education, employment, health-care etc. are rights that figure in this set. In the third chapter, we provided a definition of a policy in the public interest (see 3.7). We can reformulate it as follows:

> For any policy or action x: x is in the public interest when:
>
> (i)   there is a presumption x may affect the members of a polity (...); *or*
> (ii) x may affect the constitutional rights of the members of a polity that supervise the equal recognition of liberties and the fair distribution of social benefits; *or*
> (iii) a private interest y opposed to x may harm the constitutional rights of those members.
> (iv) There is an institutional authority accountable for addressing wrongdoings due to the pursuit of illegitimate interests. (5.6)

As we said in Chap. 3, these are sufficient conditions for a policy to be 'in the public interest'. Once we generalize the idea of public interest as a *constitutional* public interest, political disclosures made in its name are up for conditions of permissibility. We can then say:

> Political whistleblowing is in the public interest when it satisfies at least one of the following conditions:
>
> (a) it discloses information of presumptive interest for a polity or a group thereof;
> (b) it discloses the violation of a constitutional right perpetrated against and unbeknown to some members of that polity;
> (c) it discloses a private interest that potentially or actually harms a constitutional right;
> (d) it exposes deficits of procedures within those institutions that are accountable for addressing wrongdoings incurred by the pursuit of illegitimate interests. (5.7)

Three main consequences follow from the conditions of permissibility for political disclosures. The first is that the requirement that whistleblowing must be directed to enhance public interest is crucial to dismantle the objection that acts of whistleblowing are just acts of espionage, for espionage is performed with the knowing intention that the act can potentially harm the public interest. We have already discussed above why political whistleblowing is not a case of espionage, thus we will not pursue this argument further here.

The second is the more controversial argument that we have already discussed with regard to the communicative constraints: an act of whistleblowing is not only permissible, but morally *demanded* when nobody else other than the potential whistleblower possess the information of a public interest. This condition is meant to express the idea that cases of whistleblowing that seem to be morally required are exactly those when no other means are available to address public interest issues. As Sissela Bok wrote: 'Certain outrages are so blatant, and certain dangers so great, that all who are in a position to warn of them have a *prima facie* obligation to do so' (1983: 219). We must be careful however with demanding too much. We already criticized in Chap. 2 those views of whistleblowing whose justification rests on civic duty and the avoidance of complicity. The common problem of these views is that they impose over-demanding burdens for agents who operate in non-ideal conditions where there is no guarantee of due and fair process, and even anonymity in the long term. Our impression is that asking whether whistleblowing is a duty without considering those limitations is an exercise of armchair philosophy that we should avoid to the extent we can.

Third, nothing that we have argued for here excludes that anonymous disclosures may also be permissible in the name of public interest. We believe that when protective mechanisms are absent, expecting whistleblowers to disclose information while facing personal and professional risks, puts an unfair burden on individuals who seek to uphold the public interest and ensure accountability of democratic institutions. We will not discuss these points further here.

5.3 Concluding Remarks

In this chapter we argued that political whistleblowing is justified when it satisfies normative conditions of communication, intent, and public interest. We spelt out these three conditions in detail and generalized the argument on the public interest presented in Chap. 4. In doing so we also rebutted the existent criticism against unauthorized disclosures and whistleblowing. We also insisted on the role of public interest against many of these critiques.

The view that emerges is that whistleblowing should be an act of last resort, which is required when mechanisms of assessment and accountability are absent, and grants redress when fundamental constitutional rights are violated, limited, or suspended. This is typically the case when unrestrained secrecy halts those mechanisms. Since political whistleblowing requires a breach of the law, its justification has to fulfill high bars. Whistleblowing is not inherent to the democratic process of self-regulation, amendment, and reciprocal check, but it is a necessary correction when this process fails. In these circumstances, the appeal to the public interest of common constitutional rights justifies—so we argued—the breach of confidentiality provisos.

From this angle, whistleblowing is a form of dissent, but of a democratic kind. It is a subversion of the normal democratic process in the name of the constituting values of a democracy. In the next chapter we will argue in favor of this view, offering some arguments to the effect that political whistleblowing is compatible with a certain form of civil dissent.

References

Aquinas, Thomas. 1988. Of Killing (Summa Theologica II-II, Q. 64, art. 7). In *On Law, Morality, and Politics*, ed. William P. Baumgarth and Richard J. Regan, 226–227. Indianapolis/ Cambridge: Hackett Publishing Co.

Brooks, David. 2013. The Solitary Leaker. *The New York Times*, June 11. http://www.nytimes.com/2013/06/11/opinion/brooks-the-solitary-leaker.html. Accessed 8 Feb 2018.

Brownlee, Kimberley. 2012. *Conscience and Conviction: The Case for Civil Disobedience.* Oxford: Oxford University Press.

Bok, Sissela. 1983. *Secrets: On the ethics of concealment and revelation.* New York: Vintage Books.

Delmas, Candice. 2015. The ethics of government whistleblowing. *Social Theory and Practice* 41 (1): 77–105.

Dilanian, Ken. 2014. Report puts Snowden-like leaks as the no. 2 threat to U.S. security. *Los Angeles Times*. 29 January. http://articles.latimes.com/2014/jan/29/world/la-fg-worldwide-threats-20140130. Accessed 1 Feb 2018.

Dumsday, Travis. 2009. On cheering Charles Bronson: The ethics of vigilantism. *The Southern Journal of Philosophy* 47 (1): 49–67.

Ellsberg, Daniel. 2010. Secrecy and national security whistleblowing. *Social Research* 77 (3): 773–804.

Epstein, J. Edward. 2014. Was Snowden's heist a foreign espionage operation? *The Wall Street Journal.* May 9. https://www.wsj.com/articles/edward-jay-epstein-was-snowdens-heist-a-foreign-espionage-operation-1399674409. Accessed 8 Feb 2018.

———. 2017. *How America Lost Its Secrets: Edward Snowden, the Man and the Theft.* New York: Alfred A. Knopf.

Green, Leslie. 2012. Legal obligation and authority. *The Stanford Encyclopedia of Philosophy*, ed. Zalta (ed.), https://plato.stanford.edu/archives/win2012/entries/legal-obligation/. Accessed 20 Feb 2018.

Grice, Paul. 1989. Logic and Conversation (1975). In *Studies in the Way of Words*, 22–40. Cambridge, MA: Harvard University Press.

Habermas, Jürgen. 1984. *The Theory of Communicative Action Vol. 1. Reason and the Rationalization of Society.* Cambridge: Polity Press.

Horton, John. 1992. *Political Obligation.* London: Macmillan.

Johnston, Les. 1996. What is vigilantism? *The British Journal of Criminology* 36 (2): 220–236.

Kumar, Manohar, and Daniele Santoro. 2017. A justification of whistleblowing. *Philosophy & Social Criticism* 43 (7): 669–684.

Lee, Youngjae. 2012. Punishing disloyalty? Treason, espionage, and the transgression of political boundaries. *Law and Philosophy* 31 (3): 299–342.

Lewis, Paul. 2013. Veteran civil rights leader: Snowden acted in tradition of civil disobedience. *The Guardian.* 7 August. https://www.theguardian.com/world/2013/aug/07/john-lewis-civil-rights-edward-snowden. Accessed 8 Feb 2018.

Mangan, Joseph. 1949. An historical analysis of the principle of double effect. *Theological Studies* 10: 41–61.

McIntyre, Alison. 2014. Doctrine of double effect. In *The Stanford Encyclopedia of Philosophy*, ed. Edward N. Zalta. https://plato.stanford.edu/archives/win2014/entries/double-effect/. Accessed 15 Mar 2017.

Mill, John S. 2003. *On Liberty* (1859). ed. David Bromwich and George Kateb. New Haven/ London: Yale University Press.

Miller, Seumas. 2017a. *Institutional Corruption: A Study in Applied Philosophy.* Cambridge: Cambridge University Press.

———. 2017b. The ethics of whistleblowing, leaking and disclosure. In *The Palgrave Handbook of Security, Risk and Intelligence*, ed. Robert Dover, Huw Dylan, and Michael Goodman, 497–494. London: Palgrave Macmillan.

Nathanson, Stephen. 1993. *Patriotism, Morality, and Peace*. Maryland: Rowman & Littlefield.

Raz, Joseph. 1990. *Practical Reason and Norms (1975)*. Oxford: Oxford University Press.

Rottman, Gabe. 2014. On leak prosecutions, Obama takes it to 11. (Or should I say 526?). *ACLU blog*, 14 October. https://www.aclu.org/blog/leak-prosecutions-obama-takes-it-11-or-should-we-say-526?redirect=blog/free-speech/leak-prosecutions-obama-takes-it-11-or-should-we-say-526. Accessed 8 Feb 2018.

Sagar, Rahul. 2013a. *Secrets and Leaks: The Dilemma of State Secrecy*. Princeton: Princeton University Press.

———. 2013b. Who decides what's secret: Obama or Snowden? *CNN*. 14 June. http://edition.cnn.com/2013/06/14/opinion/sagarsnowden-secrets/. Accessed 8 Feb 2018.

Santoro, Daniele. 2013. Legal responsibility. A pragmatic perspective. In *Pragmatism, Law, and Language*, ed. Graham Hubbs and Douglas Lind, 98–114. London/New York: Routledge.

Scanlon, M. Thomas. 2008. *Moral Dimensions. Permissibility, Meaning, Blame*. Cambridge, MA: Belknap Press of Harvard University Press.

Transcript of President Obama's August 9, 2013 news conference at the White House. *The Washington Post*. 9 August. https://www.washingtonpost.com/politics/transcript-president-obamas-august-9-2013-news-conference-at-the-whitehouse/2013/08/09/5a6c21e8-011c-11e3-9a3e-916de805f65d_print.html?Post%20generic=%3Ftid%3Dsm_twitter_washingtonpost. Accessed on 8 Feb 2018.

Chapter 6
Charting Dissent: Whistleblowing, Civil Disobedience, and Conscientious Objection

Abstract How should one qualify political whistleblowing within a democratic system, governed by the rule of law? Whistleblowing is often considered a form of principled, sometimes even democratic dissent. In this last chapter, we discuss what kind of dissent whistleblowing is. We discuss various forms of dissent and argue that whistleblowing is neither a case of conscientious objection nor a case of civil disobedience. However—we conclude—it is a distinctive form of civil dissent against the threat of unruled government secrecy.

Keywords Political whistleblowing · Civil disobedience · Civil dissent · Conscientious objection · Dissent

6.1 Is Whistleblowing a Form of Dissent, After All?

In the previous chapter we argued why political whistleblowing—acts of disclosure of government classified information—is a justified form of dissent against state secrecy. However, we left aside the issue of whether whistleblowing is a form of civil disobedience under special circumstances, or rather an act of conscientious objection. This chapter explores some similarities with these forms of principled dissent and highlights its distinctive nature.

From a general point of view, dissent is an act of resistance or disagreement against the state by a political agent who has a reasonable belief that: a given law or policy differs from its stated purpose; a policy or a law is morally wrong (or wrongfully applied in a given context); or is contrary to what their conscience dictates. In some cases dissent is also manifested against the authority of a legal regime, and not just against a single law or executive order. Acts of dissent motivated by one or more of these convictions may take different forms: revolutionary, political protests, militant action, petitioning, infractions of the law, evasion of duty, acts of conscientious objection, or civil disobedience. Some of these forms also involve the exercise of free speech by dissenting voices.

Whistleblowing is clearly not a revolutionary act since its aim is not to subvert the authority in power.[1] Successful whistleblowing requires the infringement of a legal duty of secrecy exclusively when this act is necessary to disclose information of public interest. It is equally clear that whistleblowing is not a form of petition. Petitions to concerned authorities might precede an act of whistleblowing, and demand the disclosure of classified information (for instance, by request through the Freedom of Information Act), but they are not a public disclosure.

Whistleblowing is also not merely an infraction of law or evasion of duty. In a very narrow sense it involves both: a law is intentionally broken and the duty of confidentiality is violated. But it is not a significant case of evasion, which merely requires the failure to fulfill a role obligation. The intention in evasion is to covertly refrain from a duty one is otherwise legally obliged to perform. Evasion does not fulfill the felicity conditions for a successful act of whistleblowing (what we called the communicative constraints) since it does not require evidence or fact-checking; it is not communicative in character, and it is not necessarily done keeping in mind the interest of others, although it might be guided by moral convictions. Moreover, evasion does not comply with the disclosure requirement of whistleblowing because it is covert in character. Although whistleblowing can be done covertly, the disclosure itself is not. Likewise for the intent, the act of evasion is meant to be secret, while whistleblowing obviously has the opposite aim. Besides, evasion is not necessarily in the public interest. Any fulfillment of public interest is merely incidental to the primary purpose of the act, which is rather guided by personal motives.

Rawls identifies another form of evasion in what he calls conscientious evasion (1999: 324), which arises when an agent evades a duty because it does not agree with their own firmly held moral beliefs and conscience. The example Rawls gives is a covert infraction of fugitive slave law (ibid.). The kind of evasion we refer to here is different from Rawls'. First, a whistleblower may act covertly for pragmatic reasons, but only insofar as the covert action is needed to protect their identity or source until the disclosure is made public. Second, conscientious evasion is an omission of the duty to report information (e.g., the identity of a fugitive) to the authorities, while whistleblowing is an act of reporting wrongdoing against the duty not to do so. Both conscientious evasion and whistleblowing disobey an authority but in different manners.

A different way of conceptualizing whistleblowing is to conceive of it as a form of free speech. Employees who speak against corporate practices that are detrimental to workers' rights and dignity, or who reveal corruption in their workplace, are often seen as exercising their right to free speech, despite their duty of confidentiality. The argument has some plausibility, especially when whistleblowers stand up and speak out against the background of a silent majority.

This view bears directly on the justification of whistleblowing that we presented in Chaps. 4 and 5. According to this argument, free speech is a fundamental right,

---

[1] Joseph Raz defines revolutionary disobedience as 'a politically motivated breach of law designed to change or to contribute directly to a change of government or of the constitutional arrangements (the system of government)' (1979: 263).

which deserves strong protection.[2] Because whistleblowing is a form of free speech, the protection of free speech entails the protection of whistleblowing. Although whistleblowing is a form of free speech, it is difficult to see how whistleblowers could enjoy a *right* to free speech. One consideration is that the right to free speech is a universal human right, while a supposed right to whistleblowing would belong to employees or government representatives, in virtue of their role within an organization. Therefore, even if there is a right to whistleblowing, it would not have the same strength of the human right to free speech. Another consideration is that employees who blow the whistle inevitably break the institutional obligations they have themselves freely accepted. Part of these obligations includes waiving the right to divulge confidential information. Therefore, they do not have a prima facie right to speak freely on sensitive matters.[3]

Of course, free speech has several restrictions, most notably those arising from hateful, discriminatory, offensive and racially biased abuses of free speech; defamation laws also limit free speech. However, such restrictions are side constraints on the action set by the moral inviolability and the equal right to free speech of others.[4] Free speech is always permitted *unless* it violates the side constraints that limit its expression. The logic of its justification is reversed in the case of whistleblowing: whistleblowing is never permitted unless it meets certain conditions that justify the disclosure. Whistleblowing is a form of *fearless* speech, but not of free speech.

A related aspect that distinguishes these two forms is the justification underlying their protection: the right to free speech is independent of the content of the speeches. It is a right that cannot be alienated even when it is limited under the law.[5]

On the contrary, whistleblowing depends on the content of its disclosure, and on the context in which the whistleblowers operate, such as the public they disclose to. Therefore, it is prima facie prohibited, unless there is a further compelling reason,

---

[2] Strong protection means that free speech overrides other considerations of societal benefits that may result from limiting such right.

[3] Of course, employees may also decide to speak as citizens on matters they become aware of as employees. However, this argument seems to conflate different statuses of the person, as a citizen and as an employee. A whistleblower enjoys the right to free speech, but as an employee that right does not excuse, nor justify the violation of her contractual obligations. If there is a right to whistleblowing, it should apply to the person disclosing information qua member of the organization, not as a citizen. Another case is when the whistleblower is not a member of the organization and discloses information she has come to know indirectly from a primary source within the organization. These are the so-called third-party whistleblowers, who reveal classified material but are not part of the organization who claims ownership of the material. Third-party disclosures might be justified by free speech or freedom of the press; they may also be justified by a more general right to know, as in the case of Wikileaks when it publishes material obtained from its sources. But from the fact that the third-party exercises the right to free speech, it does not follow that there is a right to whistleblowing. It only follows that there is a valid legal justification for protecting the whistleblowing source and not revealing its identity.

[4] For a conception of side constraints, see Nozick (1974: 31–35).

[5] In this sense, free speech is a more fundamental right than personal liberty: personal liberty can be alienated by incarceration, whereas a person sued for defamation does not lose her right to speak freely.

given the content and context of the disclosure, that makes it permissible. No such justification is required for the exercise of free speech.

There is a related point that is worth discussion here. In Chaps. 4 and 5 we defended a justification for whistleblowing set in terms of public interest. Now, it is often maintained that free speech is in the public interest. Free speech is often justified as a public interest by drawing on the overall benefits accrued in society by protecting speech even when in some cases such freedom results in harm (in which case, the side constraints apply). We may then wonder whether the same consequentialist justification applies for whistleblowing. For instance, we may say that raising public awareness on important matters overrides any potential negative consequence. This is obvious in the case of corruption, where there is no countervailing reason not to expose corporate crimes, but also in the more delicate case of government secrecy, where such damage is more immediate and concrete. However, there is a difference between saying that a practice, in general, is *in* the public interest, and saying that one acts to reveal information *of* public interest. Whistleblowers do not make disclosures because they want to contribute to the practice of disclosing, but because they judge the disclosure to be of public interest. These two ways of justifying the public interest are mutually independent, but only the latter provides a cogent argument for the protection of whistleblowing.

We must now address whether (political) whistleblowing is either a form of conscientious objection or civil disobedience. There is already an ongoing debate on these topics, especially after Snowden's NSA disclosures.[6] We will start with the case of conscientious objection.

6.2   Conscientious Objection

Conscientious objection as a term gained currency in the 1890s and during the first World War to define pacifist resistance to military conscription (Brownlee 2012b: 9). Conscientious objection is a form of resistance against laws, directives, or injunctions that put unfair burdens on the conviction or deeply held beliefs of an individual (ibid.: 10). A doctor refusing to perform an abortion, a pacifist refusing to serve in the military, researchers refusing to perform experiments on animals, and even the refusal by civil administrators to marry same-sex couples are all examples

---

[6] In the aftermath of the revelation, many have in fact accused Snowden of treason (see Keck 2013). Former director of the NSA Michael Hayden even called Snowden 'a traitor' (see Foley 2013). Some have claimed he had committed espionage (see Epstein 2014), while the CIA asserted that his leaks helped the ISIS Paris terrorists in avoiding detection (See Austin 2015; Simcox 2015). Some authors, especially in academia, have defended these acts as cases of conscience (see Berkowitz 2014), and conscientious objection (see 'Edward Snowden: More Conscientious Objector than common thief', *The Guardian* June 10 2013; see also Friedersdorf 2014; Bromwich 2014), or civil disobedience (Brownlee 2016; see also Scheuerman 2014a, b, 2016; Celikates 2016).

of conscientious objection. Conscience is essentially related to the moral identity and autonomy of a person: it reflects not only who the person is but how they choose to represent themselves to the others. In other words, a conscientious action is a reflection of the practical identity of a person and of her sense of moral integrity. This is particularly true in the case of medical objection (see Childress 1979; Wicclair 2000). According to this view, integrity can only be maintained by staying faithful to commitments one deeply identifies with, or what persons 'consider their life is fundamentally about' (Cox et al. 2013; Giubilini 2016). An appeal to the conscience is thus meant to preserve a person's identity, which certain demands by the state or society can jeopardize (Childress 1979: 327). Integrity has a general scope: preserving one's identity is a practical conflict between self-regarding and other-regarding duties. The significance of conscience thus extends to all sorts of role obligations (Greenwalt 2010a), and the extent to which a person is willing to face hardship to stay truthful to themselves depends on the many contexts in which professional obligations conflict with the duty of confidentiality.[7]

Phrased this way, the concept of conscientious objection seems to share two conditions of legitimacy with whistleblowing: the idea that, in the conflict between what a person's conscience dictates and her role obligations, her moral integrity, and thus making the public aware of an evil, has to prevail.[8]

Not everybody agrees though. Rawls argues that conscientious refusal is not a public act since it does not address the sense of justice of the majority. He defines conscientious refusal as a 'noncompliance with a more or less direct legal injunction or administrative order. It is refusal since an order is addressed to us and, given the nature of the situation, whether we accede to it is known to the authorities' (1999: 323). But manifesting one's refusal to the authority is not necessarily based on political principles, and would rather be founded on 'religious other principles at variance with the constitutional order' (ibid.: 325).

Hugo Bedau proposes a different argument to support the same claim: the main purpose for conscientious objection is 'not public education but private exemption, not political change but (to put it bluntly) personal hand-washing.' A conscientious objector violates the law 'primarily in order to avoid conduct condemned by personal conscience even though required by public law.' Any regard of committing exemplary action for others or 'forcing them to re-evaluate their support for the law is a secondary consideration' (2002: 7).

Protection for conscientious objection is also defended on the grounds of respect for diversity (Cohen 1968), pluralism and autonomy (Raz 1979), and freedom of conscience (Martinez-Torrón 2015). However, while considerations of diversity, pluralism, autonomy, and freedom of conscience may justify conscientious objection in a pluralistic society, they are hardly sufficient to justify whistleblowing on

---

[7] The same view sometimes appeals to moral perfectionism, when conscientious objection is a way for a person to identify with who she really is, with one's own character (Blustein 1993: 294).

[8] See George Brenkert (2010). Whistleblowing disclosures demonstrate the commitment to one's own values and principles. Blowing the whistle is dictated by the ideal and the kind of person the whistleblowers choose to be. For a more detailed discussion of this point, see Chap. 2.

moral grounds.[9] These accounts do not have a direct bearing on the justification of whistleblowing because while conscientious refusal is a necessary means for whistleblowing, it is by no means its goal, which rather consists in exposing wrongs, crimes, and raising public awareness. A state that protects whistleblowing on these grounds would, by the same token, preemptively justify any breach of the duty of confidentiality on those moral grounds alone, and recognize whistleblowing as a right per se. We are skeptical about the idea that whistleblowers should have a right to blow the whistle but diversity, autonomy, and non-interference are values that a democratic society should promote. Insofar as whistleblowers uphold them through conscientious action, conscientious objection and whistleblowing may be both regarded as forms of dissent that contribute to democracy.

Another feature of conscientious objection is that is only incidentally illegal (Brownlee 2012a, b: 12).[10] It may involve a refusal that would be liable to punishment, penalty or removal from office, as for soldiers who refuse to combat in war, citizens who refuse to pay taxes, or public officials who refuse to marry same-sex couples. More often, democracies recognize the right to conscientious objection in so far as it does not conflict with the enjoyment of equal rights by others, and at least in two cases, military service and the medical profession, the law protects the objectors and grants them exemptions.[11] This is clearly not the case of whistleblowing. Political whistleblowing necessarily—not incidentally—involves a breach of the

---

[9] To elaborate: respect for diversity demands the state protect conscientious acts that have great consequences for its citizens, if such protection does not impose great costs on the state. Such protection honors variety in the community in manner, moral conviction, and style of life that 'not only adds richness and interest to the life of the whole but may prove essential to the long life of the community' (Cohen 1968: 270). An autonomy based view demands protection of those actions that reflect 'essential personal goals' and are crucial to the sense of identity and self-respect of citizens whereby they are not forced to be 'false to their moral convictions'(Raz 1979: 280–281). A freedom of conscience view, on the other hand, demands the state to avoid interference in action or thought that arise out of deeply held convictions. For instance, Martinez Torrón argues that such freedom consists not only 'in the individual's right to choose the moral principles that guide his life; it also entails the right to maintain behavior in conformity with the binding rules stemming from those moral choices—both in ordinary and in extraordinary circumstances' (2015: 191). Freedom of conscience has yet another important epistemic function: policies and laws may be based on erroneous or false presumptions or might be simply wrong (see Mill 2003, chapter 2). When conscientious objection is defended as witnessing the wrongness of a policy, its democratic function bears a stronger resemblance to our account of whistleblowing.

[10] Doctors refusing to perform abortion or euthanasia on religious grounds, or soldiers refusing conscription based on their religious convictions are examples of conscientious objection. The right to refuse service is often allowed by the law when exemptions are a relatively costless measure that does not entail a substantive threat to the policy itself since there is a general expectation of sufficient compliance by other members of the community. For a discussion of conscientious objection in health care see Wicclair (2008, 2011), Savulescu (2006), Greenwalt (2006), R. F. Card (2007, 2011, 2014), Meyers and Woods (2007).

[11] See Raz (1979). Brownlee (2012a) argues that civil disobedience has a better claim to rights-based protection than personal disobedience (conscientious objection) due to its non-evasive, constrained, and communicative properties. For more see Chaps. 4 and 5.

law. No exemption under a higher order statute, nor other constitutional protection is extended to whistleblowers of this sort.

Martinez-Torrón has argued that the freedom of conscience protected under the principle of conscientious objection is itself in the public interest:

> Citizens' freedom to live according to their conscience is not merely an individual or private interest. From the state's perspective, being freedom of conscience a fundamental right, its protection is a public interest—*and indeed a public interest of the highest rank*. This applies to all cases of conscientious objection, independently from their bigger or lesser social significance (2015: 199, emphasis in the original).

The argument deserves attention as it closely recalls the justification of whistle-blowing that we presented in Chaps. 4 and 5. Conscientious objection is in the public interest even when it does not have a major social significance *because* it is an instance of a fundamental right in the public interest, which deserves protection independently of the social significance of conscientious objection.[12]

However, the similarity does not survive scrutiny. Torrón's argument is based on the premise that fundamental rights are in the public interest. Then, since conscientious objection is an expression of freedom of conscience, which is a fundamental right in the public interest, conscientious objection is also in the public interest.

The argument from public interest shares the same premise but assigns to whistleblowing a different status with regard to the value of fundamental rights. Whistleblowing can contribute to the protection of fundamental rights, but it is not a right per se. When disclosures reveal infringements of fundamental rights, then whistleblowing is in the public interest and thus deserves protection in virtue of the right that it protects. However, its justification depends on the content and the context of its disclosure, not the conscience of the whistleblower. Conscientious objection can be in the public interest, but only because it upholds and protects fundamental rights.

There is also another difference in the appeal to the public interest by conscientious objectors and by whistleblowers. *Pace* Torrón, upholding the public interest is merely incidental and not the primary goal of the conscientious act. As we said, conscientious objection can be invoked by the objector for reasons of public interest. Take the example of a soldier who refuses to participate in a war they view as unjust, or unconstitutional. However, conscientious objection may also conflict with the public interest: when a massive appeal to conscientious objection undermines the enjoyment of another right in the public interest, i.e., doctors refusing to perform

---

[12] Joseph Raz argues that 'laws protecting public interest have traditionally been the main focus of attention of those who claim a right to conscientious objection' (1979: 286). This is because laws protecting public interest have similar characteristics to those laws that provide for common goods (ibid.). He further argues that: 'laws protecting the public interest normally allow for certain flexibility because of the insignificance of each individual's contribution. Consider taxation, anti-pollution laws, etc. Most of the time exempting a single individual from the duty will make little or no discernible difference to the protected good. This is generally the case in all public interest laws concerned with the provision of common goods, whose availability to an individual does not depend on his personal contribution and where the value of individual contributions to the generally available benefits is small.' (ibid: 285–6)

abortions. Italy has seen a rising number of doctors refusing to perform abortions in the last decade, sometimes creating extremely painful situations.[13] In 2017, a woman in Northern Italy seeking an abortion was refused by 23 hospitals.[14] While conscientious objection can be in the public interest, its goal is not to promote the public interest: conscientious objection is often self-regarding and only contingently in the public interest, while public interest is necessarily other-regarding. Whistleblowing is one such case. The self-regarding attitude of conscientious objectors also has a further consequence: conscientious objection is not meant to change the law or the practice that it seeks to oppose (Brownlee 2012a, b: 12). Conscientious objectors merely seek non-interference of the law, and any public communication of the reasons for refusal is merely incidental (2012b: 12).[15] Communication is incidental to conscientious objectors because their goal is not to convince a broader audience to repeal laws or seek remedies to injustices (ibid.). Admittedly, it is possible to find professional objectors such as doctors and nurses among anti-abortion advocates, but if they do act in public support of such campaigns, these persons act as citizens, not as medical professionals.

Sometimes scrutiny is deemed necessary to assess requests of conscientious refusal. Giving some evidence, or at least a reasonable account that a person is truthful may be invoked for granting exemption.[16] However, even if such a standard of assessment were in place, it would be merely testimonial. Claims based on faith, conviction, and belief are so intimate to one's conscience that they can only be taken at face value. The case of whistleblowing is different altogether. As discussed in Chap. 5, the communicative success of disclosure depends on the public assessment of the truthfulness of the claims supported by evidence.

Another difference between political whistleblowing and conscientious objection concerns its mode of action. When the objector refuses to perform a specific role, they communicate it directly to an intended receiver, usually a member of the organization who occupies a higher office. As a communicative act, it is a claim on others, in most cases the state officials. The claim is thus made in the form of an

---

[13] The strategic use of conscientious objection is a matter of extended debate in Italy. See Torrisi (2017) and Sala (2017) for recent assessments. See Chavkin et al. (2017) for a comparative analysis of the laws on medical conscientious objection.

[14] The story dates back to April 2017. For details, see Bêche-Capelli (2017).

[15] Henry David Thoreau is an exception to this claim; he refused to pay taxes because the state imposing taxation promoted slavery, and he therefore thought that the tax was illegitimate. He thus refused to let his own income be used to advance what he considered to be unjust. See Thoreau (2002). See also Bedau (1970), Lyons (1998), Herr (1974) for a different interpretation of Thoreau's stance.

[16] For a detailed investigation of the problems related to the right to conscientious objections, see Raz (1979: 286–89). See also Greenwalt (2010b). Greenwalt (2010a) claims that evidence regarding the sincerity of beliefs is very hard to gather. It is easier in cases where the individual has already suffered losses but to test whether a claim is sincere would be difficult to assess by others (906). Reflecting on conscientious objection in healthcare, R.F. Card argues that conscientious objection can only be honored if the agent is also able to demonstrate to others (not necessarily convince) the reasonableness of her views (2014: 321–322; see also 2007, 2011)

objection not open to negotiation. We may say that, in these cases, conscientious objection is a direct act of refusal presented to an interlocutor.

On the contrary, whistleblowing is a communicative act that does not necessarily demand the presence of the intended audience. The presence or absence of an audience is merely contingent upon and depends on the mode chosen by the whistleblower. Whistleblowing is direct when the whistleblowers present themselves for public scrutiny and explain the reasons for the disclosure, for instance in front of a hearing committee. It is indirect when the information is disclosed anonymously. What counts in cases of disclosures is the content of the information, not the agent. In conclusion, whereas conscientious objection and whistleblowing share some incidental similarities, they are in many other ways distinct, if not incompatible forms of dissent. We move now to civil disobedience.

6.3   Civil Disobedience

There is a general tendency in the current debate to conceive of whistleblowing as a form of civil disobedience. There are several competing accounts of civil disobedience, some of which incorporate a defense of the right to disobedience, in one form or another. For instance, neo-republicans argue that disobedience is justified when laws or policies steer away from the sovereign will of the people and are rather designed to cater to individual or particular wills. When certain partisan interests seek to divert or manipulate democracy to their own design, disobedience is not only legitimate but a duty of the citizen (see Markovits 2005).[17] Civil disobedience can also arise when policies or laws are insufficiently deliberative. A deliberative account of civil disobedience seeks to justify civil disobedience in virtue of the role it plays in the public sphere of a democratic society (Smith 2011: 146).[18]

---

[17] Markovits calls it democratic disobedience. Unlike the liberal view, whose primary concern is to oppose unjust laws or policies, democratic disobedience seeks to counter 'democratic deficits' in both laws and policies that threaten every democracy. Deviation from collective wills or manipulation causes deficits in the democratic process, and sometimes cannot be filled through institutional processes since these are inadequate and petitioning is frustrating at best (ibid.: 1934–35). When political institutions are caught in the inertia and thus inimical to change, citizens have no alternative other than to disobey them; such disobedience not only removes inertia but also, when applied properly, can enhance democracy (ibid.: 1928). By limiting people's awareness of the intentions and actions of the government, secrecy generates a democratic deficit by compromising democratic checks and balances. An act of whistleblowing that uncovers illegitimate acts would thus constitute a form of civil disobedience under a Republican conception. For a deliberative account of civil disobedience see Habermas (1985) and Smith (2004, 2011, 2013), for a communicative account see Brownlee (2012a). For other general liberal accounts of civil disobedience see Cohen (1969), Bedau (1961), Raz (1979).

[18] In Smith's account, civil disobedience upholds the norms of deliberative democracy and thus is a way of publicizing issues that receive scant attention due to the 'stifling effects of prevailing orthodoxies' (ibid.). Civil disobedience is thus justified as an act of protest against the failure to respect principles of deliberative democracy in three cases: when deliberation is insufficiently

However, since the liberal conception of civil disobedience is the point of reference in this debate, we will focus exclusively on this conception in what follows. John Rawls made an essential contribution by establishing what is considered the standard account of civil disobedience in contemporary liberal political philosophy. For Rawls, civil disobedience is a 'public, nonviolent, and conscientious act contrary to law usually done with the intent to bring about a change in the policies or laws of the government' (Rawls 1999: 181). It is a political conception because it is 'an act justified by moral principles which define a conception of civil society and the public good' (ibid.). It is also essentially public and communicative because its goal is to address 'the sense of justice of the majority in order to urge reconsideration of the measures protested and to warn that, in the sincere opinion of the dissenters, the conditions of social cooperation are not being honored' (ibid.). For Rawls, the circumstances for civil disobedience emerge from a 'persistent and deliberate violation' of basic liberties over an extended period which 'cuts the ties of community and invites either submission or forceful resistance'(ibid.: 182). Moreover, civil disobedience in itself 'manifests a respect for legal procedures' and 'expresses disobedience to law within the limits of fidelity to law' (ibid.). Fidelity to law establishes the sincerity and the conscientious aspect of the act. Finally, civil disobedience is an act of last resort, only to be carried out when normal political appeals to the majority have been rejected, and 'standard means of redress have been tried' (ibid.: 183).

When phrased this way, civil disobedience shares some basic features of whistleblowing.[19] For instance, William Scheuerman has equated whistleblowers like

---

inclusive; when it is manipulated by powerful participants; and when it is insufficiently informed (Smith 2004: 363–64). Civil disobedience is also a way to counter the inertia that arises when a 'law and policy is determined by discursive frameworks that are less adept at identifying and resolving vital policy issues than marginalized alternatives' (Smith 2011: 154). Such inertia inhibits the 'cognitive function of the public sphere' by limiting the likelihood of alternative perspectives to have a say in the deliberative process, and by excluding important discourses from participating in the policy-making process (ibid). A deliberative act of civil disobedience is carried out 'not with the aim of self-promotion, but with the intention to publicize discourses that identify and address problems of demonstrable and urgent import to the democratic community' (ibid: 156). It is an act of 'will formation' geared towards enlisting the support of citizens to force the government to take note of issues of urgent import (ibid: 158).

[19] Sissela Bok (1983) had indeed already touched upon this issue, arguing that whistleblowing and civil disobedience are two distinct forms of dissent.While they resemble each other in their openness and intent to act in the public interest, whistleblowing does not often constitute a breach of law and is protected by the right to free speech. Whistleblowing is a violation of loyalty and an accusation against specific officials. Neither of these features is a case of civil disobedience. However, the two can be combined in the case of 'former CIA agents [who] publish books to alert the public about what they regard as unlawful and dangerous practices, and in doing so openly violate, and thereby test, the oath of secrecy they have sworn' (Bok 1983: 214ft). Interestingly, for Bok, whistleblowing is a case of civil disobedience when the disclosure of information is an open violation of the oath of secrecy to reveal information that the whistleblower feels is unlawful and dangerous. Frederick Elliston makes a similar comparison between civil disobedience and whistleblowing, by using civil disobedience to shine a light on whistleblowing. For more see Elliston (1982).

Snowden with historical figures like Gandhi, Thoreau, and Martin Luther King. Except for the requirement of the fidelity to the law, Snowden fulfills in fact the Rawlsian requirements of justified civil disobedience under the rule of law. Snowden's public disclosures are civil, conscientious, and are enacted as a measure of last resort. Moreover, the failure to comply with fidelity to the law does not make the action any less justifiable since the Espionage Act under which Snowden has been indicted is not consonant itself with the ideal of a rule of law. Instead, Snowden's actions are 'potentially supportive...not destructive of the rule of law', and of its virtues of publicity and openness, especially when criminal proceedings 'rest on vague and poorly defined legal norms, suffer from excessive politicization so as to impair the possibility of a fair trial, and regularly mete out draconian sentences.'[20] (2014a: 619) These same virtues, rather underdeveloped in the present constitutional context, make the situation of whistleblowers very precarious (ibid.: 620). Given that the law is uncertain, and plausible grounds of argument exist on both sides, citizens using their judgment on complex constitutional matters ought to be encouraged (when it can be done with less damage to other policies), and tolerated in the name of conscience (ibid.: 621).

Not everybody agrees with the claim that whistleblowing is civil disobedience in the Rawlsian sense.[21] Kimberley Brownlee (2016) argues that, under Rawls' narrow conception of civil disobedience, Snowden's actions do not qualify as disobedience in a civil sense since they do not meet the condition of fidelity and Snowden did not give prior notice to authorities. The failure to qualify as such, however, does not make his actions any less civil under a broader reading of civil disobedience. Giving warning in advance of a disclosure is a feature of civil disobedience that is contingent upon an assessment of the context of the disclosure. In conditions where prior publicity would inhibit the very possibility of a dissenting action, it is prudent for the dissenter to remain silent.[22] The publicity of motives and reasons for the disclosure should rather follow—not anticipate—the disclosures (Brownlee 2016: 966). The fact that an articulate argument by Snowden followed the PRISM

---

[20] In another paper, Scheuerman elucidates this argument further by arguing that '[w]hen criminal proceedings potentially violate basic legal virtues (generality, clarity, and publicity), or where the independence of courts is badly compromised, sound reasons can be adduced for avoiding criminal punishment. A dissenter who accepts the legitimacy of criminal proceedings which are secret, irregular, or arbitrary does not, in fact, necessarily help to uphold law's highest aspirations. On the contrary, by participating in them, they inadvertently risk becoming complicit in the regime's assault on the rule of law' (2015: 446).

[21] Evgeny Morozov argues that DDOS attacks cannot be construed as an act of civil disobedience because they do not fulfill the fidelity to law criteria laid down by Rawls. See Morozov (2010)

[22] The literature on publicity is quite contested. While on one hand Carl Cohen (1966) and Marshall Cohen (1969); Gewirth (1970); Habermas (1985); Bedau (1961; 1970); Singer (1973); Smith (2013); Childress (1985) argue for advanced warning as a commitment to sincerity and seriousness, Raz (1979), Smart (2002), Simmons (2010), Brownlee (2004) disagree. They argue that sometimes advance warning can inhibit the act of disobedience, thus in such circumstances, the requirement of publicity should be relaxed. The dissenter should instead be required to explicate their motives ex-post.

revelations is thus sufficient to justify it as civil disobedience in this broader non-Rawlsian sense.

Brownlee also disagrees with the idea that whistleblowing demonstrates fidelity to the law by upholding the rule of law. The fidelity to the law under Rawls' narrow view applies only to a nearly just society, and thus fails to consider real-world circumstances (ibid.: 967).[23] However, under non ideal circumstances 'the legality of law does not depend on the morality of law' and 'the rule of such law need not... [to] protect against substantive injustices, such as those to be visited upon whistleblowers who are charged and convicted under the US Espionage Act 1917' (ibid.: 968). Therefore, the unwillingness to accept punishment under the valid law does not show a lack of fidelity 'because the punishment for an offense may be the very thing that the disobedient opposes and which she seeks to highlight by breaching the law in question' (ibid.). Snowden's disclosure of information represents an act of civil disobedience because it 'satisfies a more modest and more plausible condition for civil disobedience, which is non-evasiveness broadly construed.'[24] The exposure of his identity after the disclosure suggested 'that he was willing to bear the risk of being punished as well as to endure the substantial losses of his citizenship rights and residence rights in the USA' (ibid). So his actions constitute civil disobedience in a broader sense as 'a constrained, conscientious and communicative breach of law that demonstrates one's opposition to a law or policy and one's desire for lasting change' (ibid.: 968).

Candice Delmas (2016) argues that the government whistleblowing exemplified by Snowden is neither civil disobedience in the narrow (Ralwsian) sense nor in the broader non-ideal sense. Civil disobedience requires the cooperation of other individuals and cannot be carried out alone, whereas whistleblowing can. Moreover, civil disobedience is carried out over a stretch of time while whistleblowing is a more circumscribed event. Most importantly, though at times civil disobedience hurts the interests of other individuals, it does not undermine national security, and consists of minor infractions of the law, while some of the infractions caused by Snowden invite penalties under US law for crimes jeopardizing national security.

Elsewhere, she argues that Snowden's conduct can be justified on the basis of the public interest, namely the information revealed to the public. So, although

---

[23] Like most features of Rawlsian civil disobedience, fidelity to the law has also sparked major debates. Fidelity to the law is supposed to demonstrate the sincerity of conviction, concern for other law-abiding citizens, and public mindedness (Rawls 1999). Andrew Sabl defends fidelity on the basis of the benefits for future cooperation that it entails (2001: 317). Robin Celikates argues instead that fidelity to law is inimical to political and social changes that are transformative in character. Fidelity shows bias towards constitutional and legal systems that are badly in need of an overhaul (Celikates 2014: 216). On the other hand, David Lefkowitz (2007) argues that while the protester need only submit to the law for strategic reasons, the state should have the liberty to penalize, but should refrain from punishing dissenters. See also Brownlee (2008) for a critique of Lefkowitz suggesting that accepting a moral right to public disobedience also includes claims against penalization by the state. On the same debate, see also Brownlee (2007), Zinn (1968).

[24] See also Brownlee (2012a) on the communicative aspect of civil disobedience.

whistleblowing is not civil (in the manner civility is defined in the literature[25]), whistleblowing shares 'with civil disobedience its "defensive" and "proactive" functions, working both as a "stabilizing device" and as an "agent for change and innovation"' (Delmas 2017: 210). This type of whistleblowing provides a means for overcoming 'deliberative ignorance' and cognitive deficits that emerge due to the secrecy of information, which halts deliberation on important policy matters. Whistleblowing is an important device in the vicinity of civil disobedience and brings about the same benefits: respect towards fellow citizens, and a concern for the integrity of democratic procedures that they manifest in the risk undertaken for the act (ibid.). Thus, even though 'illegal, conscientious and political acts' (she has obviously in mind government whistleblowing of classified information) 'are incompatible with the standards of civility, yet appear justified on the same general grounds that justify civil disobedience.' (ibid.: 211)

6.4 Whistleblowing as Civil Dissent

We have said that whistleblowing does not fit within the classic liberal understanding of civil disobedience, although there is some agreement that, under more relaxed non-ideal circumstances, blowing the whistle is an act of civility in disobeying the law. Whether or not whistleblowing is a form of civil disobedience in the liberal sense depends then on the extent to which we are ready to relax the circumstances of ideal theory. Perhaps this is just a forced theorization of whistleblowing, as Delmas suggests, and thus not an interesting issue per se, but the alternative does not seem any better. We are referring to the idea that civil disobedience should be rather understood as rooted in group activism. This view however neglects the fact that civil disobedience often arises out of individual conscientious actions whereby an appeal is made to a majority. If whistleblowing is part of the reputable legacy of civil resistance, we must not forget that it is in virtue of the fact that conscientious individuals may also act outside, even against, group activism.

   Yet, it is true that the recent debate on whistleblowing as a form of dissent has a narrow scope. The attempt so far has been to examine whether individual instances of whistleblowing do constitute acts of civil disobedience. Unsurprisingly, Edward Snowden's situation is often cited because of how well his situation embodies the features of conscientious actions that fit within a relaxed Rawlsian account. Even the media's coverage of Snowden tends to cast him as a civil disobedient. However, Snowden is not the only, and hopefully not the last whistleblower to disclose secrets in a world of growing government surveillance. Other forms of disclosures are emerging, especially on digital platforms, both in public and in an anonymous form. More needs to be said to give a thorough account of what democratic benefits practices of whistleblowing can offer. As creative forms of democratic engagement

---

[25] She primarily deals with the conception of civility proposed by Smith (2013).

appear in the face of new threats to civil liberties and democratic accountability, theories of civil disobedience need to be more alert and open to such changes.

We believe that whistleblowing is a form of civil dissent, distinctive in its aim and character. It shares features of civil disobedience but stands alone as a theoretical category. In Chap. 5 we set out conditions for the justification of whistleblowing. The rest of this chapter will attempt to contrast its constitutive features with some aspects of civil disobedience.

The intended aim of whistleblowing disclosures is less disruptive of everyday activities than other forms of civil disobedience such as organized protest movements, which seek to garner attention through grassroots activities and use the public medium to advance a partisan agenda.[26] Whistleblowing is non-partisan in this sense. It merely seeks to communicate rather than to advance a political agenda. It injects vital informational resources hitherto missing in public space. Since whistleblowers do not advance an agenda, their scope is limited to enhancing public awareness over matters of public interest. By doing so, the impact of whistleblowing can be even more disruptive of normal state affairs by disclosing information that a state wants to keep secret. The impact of disclosures made by Wikileaks regarding the Arab Spring is a sample of the influence disclosures can have in revolutionary contexts.

Whistleblowing is also distinct in its character. By character we refer to a non-exhaustive yet comprehensive set of descriptive features and justificatory conditions that are associated with whistleblowing as a political act. Although civic whistleblowing shares some of these features, we only address here the political variety of whistleblowing. Whistleblowing only arises within the informational circumstances in which disclosures are made. As we said earlier in this chapter, its justification rests both on its content and the context of engagement. It is content-dependent because its justification depends on the public value of the information the whistleblower decides to reveal (for instance the information refers to crimes against other countries' governments and citizens, or to the violation of fundamental rights that are in the public interest of a constitutional democracy). It is contextual because the public value of those revelations is sensitive to the time and situation of disclosure. Revealing surveillance techniques used by secret agencies to trace terrorists may be less appropriate, and more damaging in fact, than when the same information is disclosed in less critical moments. Moreover, the attempt of disclosures can be more or less successful depending on the professional and political context in which the whistleblowers operate. As we argued in Chap. 5, when the likelihood that blowing

---

[26] Piero Moraro (2014) argues that sometimes road-blocks or forcing people to take notice of a protest by inconveniencing them does not undermine their autonomy because the mode of protest is aimed at seeking attention, and thus enhances dialogue with others who in ordinary circumstances would not take note. The process of dialogue can be a way for the protesters to help others to identify with their desires and choices which would not have been possible if not for the forced dialogue. The use of force, in this case, allows others to access a wide variety of choices which would not have been available to them due to lack of information or other factors which they would not consider in making a choice. Moraro cites the blockade of Stansted Airport in 2008 by protestors to draw attention to the dangers to the ecosystem within it. See Moraro (2014).

the whistle will be successful is low, the would-be whistleblowers should be prudent about the time of disclosure. If whistleblowers deem that the public opinion would not be ready to appreciate the value of the information, or remain insensitive to what they have to reveal, or even if they predict that the media will not help their cause, they should reconsider disclosing the information. The quantity and quality of information should also be factors in determining whether to go public. It is unlikely that a small amount of poor information will have an impact on an audience. Both Daniel Ellsberg and Edward Snowden spent months storing material (Ellsberg's photocopying the Pentagon papers was notoriously painstakingly lengthy) before coming out in public.

The privileged access that whistleblowers have to information is another circumstance of disclosures. The injustices whistleblowers disclose are generally secret, either because the content is difficult to retrieve and the public is unaware of how to get information that in theory is of public access, or else because the content threatens the power at many levels with evidence supporting public claims of state accountability.

Privileged information contrasts with civil disobedience. The circumstances that give rise to civil disobedience are often known publicly and open to public scrutiny. There is thus a shared epistemic basis, at least in principle, that can be easily accessed when matters are disputed. Disobedience arising out of ecological concerns, racial segregation, social or policy exclusions are generally visible in the public domain.[27] In a Rawlsian framework, this shared epistemic basis is instrumental for the dissenter to be able to appeal to the sense of justice of the majority.

Another distinction worth noting is that the aims of disclosure in whistleblowing are not motivated by interests that directly affect the whistleblower. Political protests, boycotts, marches, public unrest, and even violence,[28] are all cases of civil

---

[27] Secrecy disclosures can also be instrumental to civil disobedients as in the case mentioned above of the Arab Spring. Disobedience can also arguably be a product of policies that deprive citizens of assessment of certain secret actions of the government. In this case, disobedience may take the form of a demand for general transparency.

[28] The recourse to violence is debated in the literature on civil disobedience. For Rawls (1999) a justified act of civil disobedience should be non-violent since as a mode of address 'civil' disobedients cannot resort to threatening the rights of others. Andrew Sabl adds that resorting to violence is also not pragmatic since it can invite retaliation from the majority and preclude any form of just cooperation in the future (2001: 314–15). However, rational persuasion can often fail when the majority is unwilling to address the concerns of the disobedient groups. Protesters can use violence as a mechanism to draw attention to issues they feel are important, where either the majority or those in power would not take note if not for the inconvenience caused due to the violent action. Thus certain forms of disobedience such as sit-ins, mass tax-refusals, and public disruption would constitute a legitimate form of action if they helped in furthering the cause, initiating a hitherto non-existent dialogue, or when violence may help to stop the oppression of innocent persons (Morreall 1976). Recourse to violence sometimes does not undermine demands of equal opportunity or deny the legitimacy of the state machinery (Smart 2002: 205–6). Rather, at times, recourse to non-violent lawful action can have even more harmful consequences, such as in the case of strikes by ambulance workers (Raz 1979: 267). Violence, if used discriminately, with prudence, and with great reluctance, can communicate the dissenter's frustration and the importance of the issues being addressed, and to that extent, it is non-coercive given the enormity of the issue at hand

disobedience that often involve actors who are directly affected by a policy. For instance, the American Civil Rights movement was primarily, but not exclusively, sustained by African-Americans who were subjected to racial segregation in the Southern states. Whistleblowing is not self-regarding in this sense, but it can be other-regarding in a way in which civil disobedience sometimes is, but not necessarily so. Indeed, Thoreau's refusal to pay taxes to a state that upheld slavery, political protest in Europe and public outcry expressed by college students and other non-affected parties in America against the Vietnam war, are examples of people who acted in the interest of others. However, the party affected by an unjust law may or may not be the civil disobedient themselves. The other-regarding nature of whistle-blowing also does not necessarily share the character of public advocacy inherent in civil disobedience. The success of whistleblowing lies in its ability to reach a wide audience, and in gaining the support of media houses, journalists, and advocacy groups. Whistleblowing is thus informative in that it offers information relevant for deliberation on important public policy matters. Whistleblowing disclosures can be followed by a public advocacy for garnering support against the wrongful policy, but as far as whistleblowing is concerned, this is not required for the act to be successful.

Another important distinction lies in the standing of the whistleblower with respect to the law. Civil disobedience is a reaction to the injustice of the law. Thus, disobeying is itself a moral act of testifying against that injustice. In a slightly different way, we may say that the act of disobeying is also exemplary of the resistance against injustice. The case of whistleblowing is different, for disclosing classified information is not a moral act of testifying against injustice per se. It does have a moral worth which lies in the aim of the act, but not in the act as such. There is nothing moral in disclosing secret information unless independent reasons are provided for why that information pertains to morality or justice. Unlawful disclosures are moral exactly when they reveal information about the wrong the whistleblower seeks to address. It is the wrongness disclosed that makes the disclosure moral. Whistleblowing is then an *indirect* manifestation of a wrong or injustice. Often, the law the whistleblowers disobey and the secrecy privilege they are bound to as public officials (or contractors), are not per se unjustified, and they do not necessarily have to oppose the right to secrecy privilege. However, whistleblowers do express dissent against a particular application of secrecy, namely when it is used to cover crimes, wrongdoings, and violations of rights that affect unaware citizens.[29]

Another feature distinguishing feature of whistleblowing is the publicity condition. Advance warning to public officials can not precede whistleblowing. The

---

(Brownlee 2004: 349–50). A.J. Simmons considers violence to be an appropriate political act when it is 'carefully presented to the public as protest, if it is isolated (an unusual act in an otherwise non-violent life), if it has been preceded by passive political efforts, and if it is followed by non-evasion and acceptance of punishment'(Simmons 2010: 1808).

[29] Whistleblowing can also represent a *direct* manifestation of a wrong or injustice when it signals the wrong conducted by colleagues or members of an institution. In this case, the violation is directly related to the law one is bound to comply with. This is chiefly the case of civic whistleblowing.

success of the act is dependent upon maintaining secrecy until the information is communicated. Thus, whistleblowing can only operate under a restricted condition of ex-post publicity regarding the reasons for disclosure. One needs to relax the Rawlsian account of civil disobedience to meet whistleblowing at the other end. Brownlee (2016) advocates precisely this point in defending Snowden's action. However, it does not seem that the revised account admits anonymous unauthorized disclosures. Under the revised account, a failure to explicate reasons and motivations for disclosures would not only cast doubts on the sincerity of motivations and conscientiousness of the actor but on the civility of the act itself.

In Chap. 2 we defined publicity as an attribute of the act of disclosure, not of the agent. The act must be public in the sense of being directed at an audience, as well as its justification must satisfy the public interest. However, the anonymity of the agent does not make an act less conscientious and uncivil. Demands of identity disclosure constrain the feasibility of an action when the contextual institutional, societal, and legal circumstances limit the alternatives open to a potential whistleblower. If the only option available for a whistleblower is whether or not to disclose, then it will be preferable not to disclose. This is especially true when institutional, societal, and legal circumstances impose unfair burdens on the whistleblower by exacting personal and professional costs. The absence of constitutional safeguards or retaliatory attitudes often makes disclosures costly for whistleblowers. Individual biographies suggest that they do put themselves at risk of consequences (no matter what protections they may enjoy) for career opportunities, financial stability, psychological, emotional balance, and even freedom. Full blown crusades against political whistleblowing by the administration are bound to waver the conscience of well-meaning agents as well (see Greenberg 2014; Ackerman and Pilkington 2015). When the risk of blowing the whistle is high, prudence might advise against undertaking any such course of action. Blowing the whistle when social and constitutional support are absent (or tenuous) constitutes an act of courage, and the failure of public disclosure is less a shortcoming by an agent of disclosure; it is more often a symptom of a structural failure to provide due guarantees for conscientious acts by the legal system and the society at large.

Moreover, when the disclosed information is in the public interest, the anonymity of disclosure is justified by the appeal to public interest, thus demanding due consideration and scrutiny. If the disclosures qualify as a genuine subject of democratic debate, then revealing one's identity is not essential in justifying the disclosure. The identity of the person disclosing is more critical when revelations are dubious, but genuine acts of whistleblowing made in the public interest do not fall into that category. Whistleblowing can thus be considered an act of civility in conditions of anonymity, yet not of civil disobedience.

Anonymity also explains why fidelity to the law is less important for whistleblowers. When they are not guaranteed due process, and constitutional protection is missing, whistleblowers are justified in not submitting to the law. Demanding submission to the law, and acceptance of punishment in such circumstances puts an unfair burdens on whistleblowers and discourages future disclosures. Indeed, we may say that whistleblowers express a higher form of fidelity to the democratic values of the law. What law, after all, is the whistleblower bound to? The constitution, or instead the secrecy laws that they have duty to obey in virtue of their role? It seems that the idea of constitutional fidelity leaves too much space for arbitrary interpretation. We are not saying that whistleblowers cannot intend to act in the name of constitutional values, but we do believe that it is not their prerogative to decide whether their disclosures have constitutional value. Once whistleblowers have made a disclosure, they lay the task of interpreting the constitutionality of the information on the public and the relevant authorities. Stretching the notion of fidelity to law also include the disobedience of the law, or more precisely the evasion from the consequences of disobedience, seems to be incompatible with the understanding of civil disobedience defended by Rawls.

One aspect of the Rawlsian view that whistleblowing shares with civil disobedience is that both are acts of last resort. Whistleblowing is often resorted to when internal procedures for disclosures and system of redress have been exhausted, or preclude the possibility of seeking redress. This can happen, as we said in Chap. 2, when disclosures concern higher officials, who may have a conflict of interest, or are in the position to thwart the very possibility of disclosure. Thus, when the likelihood of a possible censure is high, sidestepping from established procedures is justified on the grounds of justice and public interest. Similarly, civil disobedients act upon considerations of what the last course of action could be, once more lawful means are ruled out for manifest inefficacy. How can their claim be heard, if no representative authority is willing to listen? How can a larger inattentive public be woken to what they have to say if not by striking initiatives that would call for attention? Civil disobedients often choose to break the law as part of a larger strategy of civil action when other means fail. Sometimes, in circumstances where there is an extensive violation of rights, direct action is the only and last resort for them, and as such is justified even for Rawls. We may also add that: exposing oneself to lawful action precludes the very possibility of seeking redress and compromises the cause—but alerting officials of the petitioner's intentions whose interest is in sabotaging a campaign—direct action can be more effective than mere peaceful protest. Admittedly, whistleblowers often act alone or without the support of a group in making resolutions of last resort. However, both whistleblowers and civil disobedients appear to share the idea that breaking the law should not be taken lightly and should only be sought when all other options have been fully explored.

Is whistleblowing then just another form of civil disobedience, spurred on by the greater access to information that digital communication offers? We argued that it is not. Practices of civil disobedience share features that define acts of whistleblowing as well, but they are conceptually independent notions. Contingent similarities come along with obvious differences. Differences depend on the contextual circumstances (essentially the information conditions for disclosure) the whistleblower is exposed to, which narrows the scope and modes of action. The reality of informational asymmetry between the whistleblower and the public, the informational privilege that it entails, and the dangers that it involves, impose communicative and prudential constraints that distinguish whistleblowing from other kinds of civil action.

6.5 Concluding Remarks

In this chapter we placed political whistleblowing within the general category of dissent. We argued that whistleblowing is a distinctive form of civil dissent. It is not conscientious objection, for concerns of public interest that are essential to justify whistleblowing are only incidental to conscientious objection. We concluded that conscientious objection is done with the purpose of maintaining personal integrity in one's own deeply held beliefs and convictions. We then investigated whether the best way to characterize political whistleblowing is a form of civil disobedience. We concluded that whistleblowing does not fit within commonly accepted conceptions of civil disobedience, but that it does share the same civil nature of a democratic act of dissent.

Whistleblowing shares with civil disobedience its 'civil' aspect, that is the thought that disobeying the law is justifiable only in the name of fundamental rights and of the democratic values of openness, accountability, and equal consideration of interests. It is civil because it is an act of citizenship, an expression of disobedience that refuses to submit to laws that protect wrongdoing and abuse of power. It is also civil because it is a communicative form that addresses the public in a non-coercive, and non-violent manner, and seeks to elicit a public debate upon the content of the disclosures.

In conclusion, what ultimately distinguishes political whistleblowing from other forms of dissent is its civil opposition against government secrecy. Unlike other practices of civil disobedience, whistleblowers face conditions of secrecy, and their civil commitment is measured by their willingness to stand up against the threatening power of government interests.

References

Ackerman, Spencer, and Ed. Pilkington. 2015. Obama's war on whistleblowers leaves administration insiders unscathed. *The Guardian*. March 16. https://www.theguardian.com/us-news/2015/mar/16/whistleblowers-double-standard-obama-david-petraeus-chelsea-manning. Accessed 31 Oct 2016.

Austin, Jon. 2015. Traitor Edward Snowden 'taught ISIS Paris terrorists to avoid detection'. *Express*. November 18. http://www.express.co.uk/news/world/620270/Traitor-Edward-Snowden-taught-ISIS-Paris-terrorists-avoid-detection-NSA-CIA-John-Brennan. Accessed 28 June 2016.

Bêche-Capelli, Malika. 2017. Although legal, Abortion Remains a Major Challenge for Women in Italy. *The Civil Liberties Union for Europe*. April 18. https://www.liberties.eu/en/news/abortion-in-italy-is-still-a-challenge/11685. Accessed 10 Feb 2018.

Bedau, Hugo Adam. 1961. On civil disobedience. *The Journal of Philosophy* 58 (21): 653–665.

———. 1970. Civil disobedience and personal responsibility for injustice. *The Monist* 54 (4): 517–535.

———. 2002. Introduction. In *Civil Disobedience in Focus*, ed. Hugo Adam Bedau, 1–12. London/New York: Routledge.

Berkowitz, Roger. 2014. The conscience of Edward Snowden. *Hannah Arendt Center Blog*. http://www.hannaharendtcenter.org/the-conscienceof-edward-snowden/. Accessed 28 June 2016.

Blustein, Jeffrey. 1993. Doing what the patient orders: Maintaining integrity in the doctor-patient relationship. *Bioethics* 7 (4): 289–314.

Bok, Sissela. 1983. *Secrets: On the Ethics of Concealment and Revelation*. New York: Pantheon.

Brenkert, G. George. 2010. Whistle-blowing, moral integrity, and organizational ethics. In *The Oxford Handbook of Business Ethics*, ed. George G. Brenkert and Tom L. Beauchamp, 563–601. Oxford: Oxford University Press.

Bromwich, David. 2014. The question of Edward Snowden. *The New York Review of Books*. http://www.nybooks.com/articles/2014/12/04/question-edward-snowden/. Accessed 28 June 2016.

Brownlee, Kimberley. 2004. Features of a paradigm case of civil disobedience. *Res Publica* 10 (4): 337–351.

———. 2007. The communicative aspects of civil disobedience and lawful punishment. *Criminal Law and Philosophy* 1 (2): 179–192.

———. 2008. Penalizing public disobedience. *Ethics* 118 (4): 711–716.

———. 2012a. *Conscience and Conviction: The Case for Civil Disobedience*. Oxford: Oxford University Press.

———. 2012b. *Conscientious Objection and Civil Disobedience*. Warwick School of Law Research Paper no. 2012/15. https://ssrn.com/abstract=2091045. Accessed 28 June 2016.

———. 2016. The civil disobedience of Edward Snowden: A reply to William Scheuerman. *Philosophy & Social Criticism* 42 (10): 965–970.

Card, Robert F. 2007. Conscientious objection and emergency contraception. *The American Journal of Bioethics* 7 (6): 8–14.

———. 2011. Conscientious objection, emergency contraception, and public policy. *Journal of Medicine and Philosophy* 36 (1): 53–68.

———. 2014. Reasonability and conscientious objection in medicine: A reply to Marsh and an elaboration of the reason-giving requirement. *Bioethics* 28 (6): 320–326.

Celikates, Robin. 2014. Civil disobedience as a practice of civic freedom. In *On Global Citizenship. James Tully in Dialogue*, ed. David Owen, 207–228. London: Bloomsbury.

———. 2016. Civil disobedience. *The International Encyclopedia of Political Communication*. https://doi.org/10.1002/9781118541555.wbiepc092. Accessed 28 June 2016.

Chavkin, Wendy, Laurel Swerdlow, and Jocelyn Fifield. 2017. Regulation of conscientious objection to abortion. An international comparative multiple-case study. *Health Human Rights* 19 (1): 55–68.

Childress, James F. 1979. Appeals to conscience. *Ethics* 89 (4): 315–355.

———. 1985. Civil disobedience, conscientious objection, and evasive noncompliance: A framework for the analysis and assessment of illegal actions in health care. *Journal of Medicine and Philosophy* 10 (1): 63–84.

Cohen, Carl. 1966. Civil disobedience and the law. *Rutgers Law Review* 21 (1): 1–17.

———. 1968. Conscientious objection. *Ethics* 78 (4): 269–279.

Cohen, Marshall. 1969. Civil disobedience in a constitutional democracy. *The Massachusetts Review* 10 (2): 211–226.

Cox, Damian, Marguerite La Caze, and Michael Levine. 2013. Integrity. In *The Stanford Encyclopedia of Philosophy* (Spring 2017 edition), ed. Edward N. Zalta. http://plato.stanford.edu/archives/fall2013/entries/integrity/. Accessed 1 Mar 2018.

Delmas, Candice. 2016. That lonesome whistle. *Boston Review*, 14 June. http://bostonreview.net/world-us/candice-delmas-lonesome-whistle. Accessed 1 Mar 2018.

———. 2017. Disobedience, civil and otherwise. *Criminal Law and Philosophy* 11 (1): 195–211.

Editorial. 2013. Edward Snowden: More conscientious objector than common thief. *The Guardian*. June 10. http://www.theguardian.com/commentisfree/2013/jun/10/edward-snowden-conscientious-objector. Accessed 28 June 2016.

Elliston, Frederick A. 1982. Civil disobedience and whistleblowing: A comparative appraisal of two forms of dissent. *Journal of Business Ethics* 1 (1): 23–28.

Epstein, Edward J. 2014. Was Snowden's heist a foreign espionage operation? *The Wall Street Journal*. 9 May. https://www.wsj.com/articles/edward-jay-epstein-was-snowdens-heist-a-foreign-espionage-operation-1399674409. Accessed 28 June 2016.

Foley, Elise. 2013. Michael Hayden 'Drifting' toward calling Edward Snowden a 'Traitor'. *The Huffington Post*. December 30. http://www.huffingtonpost.com/entry/michael-hayden-edward-snowden_n_4515705.html?section=india. Accessed 28 June 2016.

Friedersdorf, Conor. 2014. The national- security state persecutes conscientious objectors. *The Atlantic*. July 8. http://www.theatlantic.com/politics/archive/2014/07/the-pattern-of-persecuting-dissenters-in-the-national-security-state/374051/. Accessed 28 June 2016.

Gewirth, Alan. 1970. Civil disobedience, law, and morality: An examination of justice Fortas' doctrine. *The Monist* 54 (4): 536–555.

Giubilini, Alberto. 2016. Conscience. In *The Stanford Encyclopedia of Philosophy*, ed. Edward N. Zalta. http://plato.stanford.edu/archives/spr2016/entries/conscience/. Accessed 1 Mar 2018.

Greenberg, Jon. 2014. CNN's Tapper: Obama has used Espionage Act more than all previous administrations. *Pundit Fact*. January 10. http://www.politifact.com/punditfact/statements/2014/jan/10/jake-tapper/cnns-tapper-obama-has-used-espionage-act-more-all-/. Accessed 20 Oct 2016.

Greenwalt, Kent. 2006. Objections in conscience to medical procedures: Does religion make a difference. *University of Illinois Law Review* 4: 799–825.

———. 2010a. The significance of conscience. *San Diego Law Review* 47: 901–918.

———. 2010b. Refusals of conscience: What are they and when should they be accommodated. *Ave Maria Law Review* 9 (1): 47.

Habermas, Jürgen. 1985. Civil disobedience: Litmus test for the democratic constitutional state. *Berkeley Journal of Sociology* 30: 95–116.

Herr, William A. 1974. Thoreau: A civil disobedient? *Ethics* 85 (1): 87–91.

Keck, Zachary. 2013. Yes, Edward Snowden is a traitor. *The Diplomat*. 21 December. http://thediplomat.com/2013/12/yes-edward-snowden-is-atraitor/. Accessed 28 June 2016.

Lefkowitz, David. 2007. On a moral right to civil disobedience. *Ethics* 117 (2): 202–233.

Lyons, David. 1998. Moral judgment, historical reality, and civil disobedience. *Philosophy & Public Affairs* 27 (1): 31–49.

Markovits, Daniel. 2005. Democratic disobedience. *Yale Law Journal* 114 (8): 1897–1952.

Martínez-Torrón, Javier. 2015. Conscientious objections: Protecting freedom of conscience beyond prejudice. In *Routledge Handbook of Law and Religion*, ed. Silvio Ferrari, 191–207. Abingdon/New York: Routledge.

Meyers, Christopher, and Robert D. Woods. 2007. Conscientious objection? Yes, but make sure it is genuine. *The American Journal of Bioethics* 7 (6): 19–20.

Mill, John S. 2003. *On liberty* (1859), ed. David Bromwich and George Kateb. New Haven/London: Yale University Press.

Moraro, Piero. 2014. Respecting autonomy through the use of force: The case of civil disobedience. *Journal of Applied Philosophy* 31 (1): 63–76.

Morozov, Evgeny. 2010. *In defense of DDoS*. Slate, December 13. http://www.slate.com/articles/technology/technology/2010/12/in_defense_of_ddos.single.html. Accessed 29 Sept 2016.

Morreall, John. 1976. The justifiability of violent civil disobedience. *Canadian Journal of Philosophy* 6 (1): 35–47.

Nozick, Robert. 1974. *Anarchy, State, Utopia*. New York: Basic Books.

Rawls, John. 1999. *A Theory of Justice*. Revised edition. Cambridge, MA: Harvard University Press.

Raz, Joseph. 1979. *The Authority of Law: Essays on Law and Morality*. Oxford: Clarendon Press

Sabl, Andrew. 2001. Looking forward to justice: Rawlsian civil disobedience and its non-Rawlsian lessons. *Journal of Political Philosophy* 9 (3): 307–330.

Sala, Ilaria M. 2017. Abortion in Italy, a right wronged. *The New York Times*. 13 November. https://www.nytimes.come/2017/11/13/opinion/abortion-italy-conscientious-objectors.html. Accessed 10 Feb 2018.

Savulescu, Julian. 2006. Conscientious objection in medicine. *BMJ* 332: 294–297.

Scheuerman, William E. 2014a. Whistleblowing as civil disobedience The case of Edward Snowden. *Philosophy & Social Criticism* 40 (7): 609–628.

———. 2014b. Snowden and the ethics of whistleblowing. *Boston Review*. May 21. http://bostonreview.net/books-ideas/scheuerman-snowdengreenwald-harding-sagar. Accessed 28 May 2016.

———. 2015. Recent theories of civil disobedience: An anti-legal turn? *Journal of Political Philosophy* 23 (4): 427–449.

———. 2016. What Edward Snowden can teach theorists of conscientious law-breaking. *Philosophy & Social Criticism* 42: 958–964.

Simcox, Robin. 2015. Don't listen to Edward Snowden's supporters—His leaks have been a gift to terrorists. *Independent*. June 9. http://www.independent.co.uk/voices/comment/dont-listen-to-edward-snowdens-supporters-his-leaks-have-been-a-gift-to-terrorists-10307959.html. Accessed 28 June 2016.

Simmons, A. John. 2010. Disobedience and its objects. *Boston University Law Review* 90 (4): 1805–1831.

Singer, Peter. 1973. *Democracy and Disobedience*. Oxford: Clarendon Press.

Smart, Brian. 2002. Defining civil disobedience. In *Civil Disobedience in Focus*, ed. Hugo Adam Bedau, 189–211. London/New York: Routledge.

Smith, William. 2004. Democracy, deliberation and disobedience. *Res Publica* 10 (4): 353–377.

———. 2011. Civil disobedience and the public sphere. *Journal of Political Philosophy* 19 (2): 145–166.

———. 2013. *Civil Disobedience and Deliberative Democracy*. Abingdon: Routledge.

Thoreau, Henry David. 2002. Civil disobedience. In *Civil Disobedience in Focus*, ed. Hugo A. Bedau, 28–48. London/New York: Routledge.

Torrisi, Claudia. 2017. Abortion in Italy: How widespread 'conscientious objection' threatens women's health and rights. *Open Democracy*. June 15. https://www.opendemocracy.net/5050/claudia-torrisi/abortion-italy-conscientious-objection. Accessed 10 Feb 2018.

Wicclair, Mark R. 2000. Conscientious objection in medicine. *Bioethics* 14 (3): 205–227.

———. 2008. Is conscientious objection incompatible with a physician's professional obligations? *Theoretical Medicine and Bioethics* 29(3): 171–185.

———. 2011. *Conscientious Objection in Health Care: An Ethical Analysis*. Cambridge: Cambridge University Press.

Zinn, Howard. 1968. *Disobedience and Democracy: Nine Fallacies on Law and Order*. Vol. 4. Cambridge, MA: South End Press.

Chapter 7
Conclusion

Keywords State duty · Right to whistleblowing · Whistleblowing protection

In this book we have argued that whistleblowing is an act of civil dissent. By civil dissent, we mean that whistleblowing is part of a more general conception of the role dissent plays in democracy. Whereas most accounts of democratic theory in the liberal tradition have focused on the procedures of consent formation to justify democracy, we have insisted on the opposite view that the justification of democracy depends on its capacity to safeguard the expression of dissent. This was one important aim of this book. We wanted to stress the function of dissent in exposing the limitations of the democratic procedures that undermine equality and accountability. Forms of dissent that uphold the public interest are not only justified but also perform a civic role in democracy.

In our understanding, whistleblowing plays such a distinctive role. Whistleblowers are witness to the capacity of governmental and corporate institutions to evade structures of accountability and impose unfair burdens on people through covert acts of corruption and injustices. The fact that whistleblowers, more so in recent times, have been subjected to retaliation, stands testimony to the quality of contemporary democracies. Their lack of protection raises troubling questions on the commitment of contemporary democracies.

We all agree that ideally democracy is a system of government based on fair procedures that accommodate multiple voices and devise methods of redress in the face of conflicting claims. If such procedures were in place, no extra-legal methods of redress like whistleblowing would be legitimate. But real world democracies are far from ideal, and so are the procedures. In this book we have shown that one of the major limitations that democracies face is how they can justify legitimate claims of governmental secrecy. The need to accommodate governmental secrecy for concerns of security, confidentiality of trade practices, and considerations of independence in government deliberations, often lead to far reaching consequences beyond the control of the established procedures of self-correction. This is due to the very nature of secrecy that allows actions to grow unnoticed beyond their original intended purpose, and give rein to particularistic or unconstitutional interests in the comforting knowledge that they will never be noticed. No ideal theory can *ex-ante* accommodate the far reaching consequences of secrecy, except at its own peril. The answer to this predicament often lies in the conscientious acts of those who have privileged access to information and who, despite fear of reprisal, seek to disclose it to the public.

History abounds with examples of individuals who have sought to defy institutional procedures to stand for what they deemed to be the right. Whistleblowing as a concept emerged originally to accommodate conscientious acts of individuals within business settings who sought to signal acts of corruption, often after having attempted to draw attention within the organization they worked for. But the roots of whistleblowing lie much deeper than its etymology suggests. In Chap. 2 we offered a brief reconstruction of some famous historical cases, whose examples stand testimony to the whistleblowers' capacity to speak truth to power (often with a disregard for personal and professional retaliation). We argued that such capacity resembles the ancient Greek practice of parrhesia, the fearless act of speaking truth without resorting to rhetoric or manipulation, based on the speaker's belief that they stand for truth.

In contemporary representative democracies public and corporate institutions have become a *locus* of such fearless speech. Direct accountability in the *polis* has been replaced by accountability through procedures of transparency and publicity. It is in this context that whistleblowing plays the function of upholding the ideals of publicity and transparency. And it is the failure of institutions to conform to the norms of publicity that prompts the need for whistleblowing disclosures. Whistleblowing in this regard testifies to the often complicated relations between truth and politics. By ensuring publicity of wrongful government actions and policies, whistleblowing exposes the capacities of deception and manipulation that are products of secret policies, as Hannah Arendt had already pointed out over fifty years ago in her reflections on the Pentagon Papers.

We distinguished between two forms of whistleblowing: civic and political. They represent different aims of disclosure. Civic whistleblowing, we said, arises when an individual reveals cases of corruption within an institution, whether private or public. It is civic because it fulfills a civic function that promotes the public good, is a fulfillment of civic duty, and upholds the law of the land by denouncing its violation. Political whistleblowing, on the other hand, refers to the disclosure of classified information protected by the law. It is political because its purpose is to reveal the democratic deficits that arise from the arbitrary exercise of state power.

Civic and political whistleblowing carry intents and justifications that are sensitive to the context of disclosure. They share the *conduct* since both disclose information that is not supposed to be disclosed, to an audience or public which has a legitimate interest in the content of the disclosure. However, the *act* varies according to the specific intent, and so does the justification for the act, and of course the circumstances of disclosure.

The role that whistleblowers, both civic and political, play in a democracy can be properly understood within a conception of public interest. Civic whistleblowers uphold the public interest by exposing the wrongs of political corruption. The injustice of political corruption lies exactly in undermining the public interest by diverting public funds for personal advantages and dumping the costs of diversion on the polity at large. But what conception of public interest captures best the function of civic whistleblowing?

In Chap. 3 we argued that the aggregative model of non-competing interests faces severe constraints as it assumes that public interest is based on convergent preferences, and thus cannot account for the fact that public interest is often not in the interest of every member that constitutes a public. The common good conception of public interest instead faces distributive problems, as it can make the provision of public goods costly for certain social groups to the advantage of others. Finally, the deliberative and proceduralist accounts are limited because they offer an ideal conception of public interest based either on the rational constraints on deliberation, or on the shared framework of procedures that embed the ideal of equal respect. However—we argued—within the context of real-world democracies, such framework and constraints are only part of a normative ideal, unattainable in most if not all cases, and corrective measures must be deployed in order to guarantee that the common rules of discussion, and deliberation, as well as the outcomes of procedures, are not thwarted.

In contrast to these views, we argued that the public interest should be conceived as a presumptive interest. By this we mean that everybody being part of a public may have an interest to be informed of policies or actions that may affect them. Moreover, instances of public interest are often negatively identified by competing private interests that may harm the rights of those members. We defended this characterization by showing that it is based on a common core of equal rights, thus widening the scope of public interest beyond the actual or present interests of a polity at any point in time. Moreover, this view accounts for some important aspects of the proceduralist conception of justice.

Still in Chap. 3 we argued that a civic whistleblowing disclosure is justified if the information it conveys is of presumptive interest for a polity, that is when it reveals crimes affecting all-purposive rights, and when it exposes deficits of procedures that provide measures of accountability, sanction, and redress. Civic Whistleblowing contributes to the public interest when it unveils crimes and wrongdoings that cause an unfair allocation of the burdens of cooperation. By doing so, civic whistleblowers contribute to more accountable practices in both the corporate and the public sectors, and often pay a high price for their public service. New laws provide them with some protections nowadays, in part thanks to the growing support of civil society activism. However, civic whistleblowing is often less controversial than political whistleblowing. There is a large consensus that corporate loyalty is not unconditional. When corporate interests are detrimental to the interests of a society at large, and when the pursuit of corporate interests leads to crime and corruption of public officials, whistleblowers have a moral justification for breaking their duty of fidelity.

   The controversy arises when whistleblowers call into question the legitimacy of democratic states to classify information. Of course, democracies require protection of sensitive information, for public disclosures could otherwise endanger their stability, and sometimes even their existence. Democratic secrecy, as it is sometimes called, is necessary for the requirements of security and for conducting diplomatic negotiations that would be impossible in the face of full publicity. But many contemporary views of security are largely framed under a conception of trade-off between competing considerations of liberty and security. We argued that the trade-off model threatens the structure of rights: not only the balance view lacks a proper justification, but it also paves the way for unrestrained practices of secrecy. This is the problem of democratic secrecy. Democratic secrecy allows for wrongdoing and illicit conducts when specific clauses of a policy or government decisions are hidden from the control of designated oversight committees. The unregulated use of secrecy in real-world circumstances encourages individuals to use classified information they possess as they see fit. It enables—in other words—an abuse of office by public officials.
   Democratic secrecy gives rise to a dilemma: democracy requires transparency, but there is no protection and stability for democratic institutions without secrecy. Is this a genuine dilemma, and how can democratic theory resolve it? In Chap. 4 we laid the groundwork for a reconciliation of these opposites in terms of what we call an epistemic entitlement of rights. Our thought is that one cannot genuinely enjoy a right, such as free speech, without knowing the conditions under which the right can be hindered. Mass surveillance was our case in point: how reasonable is it to say that a person enjoys freedom of speech when they fear that someone is eavesdropping on them? And who decides when a person can be surveilled? We argued that by paying attention to what we called the epistemic entitlement of rights, secrecy precludes the very possibility of an assessment of the circumstances that may affect the enjoyment of those rights. We argued that once we recognize the plausibility of a right of assessment, citizens should be accorded the knowledge and public justification of the conditions that lead to a limitation or suspension of their rights. The right of assessment is a right in non-ideal circumstances, which—in our opinion—offers a shield against arbitrary interference by determining the proper scope and purpose of secrecy. When such conditions are not met, and the possibility of redress of wrongs is denied, acts of whistleblowing done in the public interest remain a last resort to ensure the accountability of democratic institutions. Our view is that the value of whistleblowers is to shine light on the political conflict between democratic authority and citizens' rights.
   These features show why political whistleblowing is in the public interest. According to the characterisation of public interest that we offered in Chap. 3, it is not only in the public interest to know when rights have been violated but it is also in the public interest to know when the arrangement that supervises the distribution of those rights has been compromised. Whistleblowing as a communicative act not only addresses issues of public interest by exposing potential harm to it, but also ensures forms of democratic accountability by exposing limitations of constitutional safeguards. This way, whistleblowing aims to fill a democratic void caused by

the lack or weakness of democratic system of checks and balance. By revealing the breadth and the scope of governmental secrecy, whistleblowing demonstrates not only the absence of restraints on illegitimate secret acts, but also exposes the fact that governmental policies are insufficiently deliberative. Whistleblowers inject the missing informational component that citizens require to judge the action of state institutions and of its political actors, deliberate on important public policy matters, and hold public officials accountable for their actions. The information whistleblowers divulge is also important to nudge institutions and citizens out of their passivity and challenge commonplace views that defy possibilities of change.

The informational asymmetry between the whistleblower and the people, the informational privilege that it entails, and the dangers that it involves, impose moral, communicative, and prudential constraints that distinguish justified whistleblowing from other kinds of disclosures. The communicative dimension of whistleblowing, we said in Chap. 4, demands it to be truthful, and backed by sufficient evidence. The fact that whistleblowing is a moral act of testimony, a form of witness to a wrongdoing, demands the disclosure be performed with good intentions and a truthful account of the facts, while in the process exercising caution to avoid harming others. Such care demands also that the whistleblower, when faced with doubt regarding the importance of information and its impact for the general public, should seek advice or elicit support from other sources in order to identify avoidable harms to innocent people. When an act of whistleblowing demonstrates such ethical care, communicative conditions, a permissible intent, and fulfills the public interest, we claim it is justified.

To assess the rightfulness of intent, we formulated what we called the 'harm test': a disclosure is *prima facie* justified, we said, when the agent foresees that the likelihood of harm they may suffer from disclosing the information is higher than the likelihood they assign to any personal benefit they may enjoy. However, the harm test alone does not justify the disclosure. The third criterion of permissibility we provide is exactly the public interest. We showed in Chap. 5 that the characterization of the public interest provided in Chap. 3 fits the communicative and intent conditions of permissibility.

The question of the permissibility of whistleblowing lead to the final question that we deal with in this book. In Chap. 6 we asked: How should one qualify an act of political whistleblowing within a democratic system governed by the rule of law? In other words, does whistleblowing qualify as a distinctive form of democratic dissent? Two forms of dissent (conscientious objection and civil disobedience) compete for consideration here. The existing literature has largely relied on these two forms to distinguish whistleblowing within the general category of dissent. The communicative features of whistleblowing, its conditions of justified intent, and its public interest nature stand in contrast to the private nature of most forms of conscientious objection. In addition, the legal character of conscientious rejection is starkly opposed to the illegal nature of political whistleblowing. It is thus clear that whistleblowing is not a legitimate case of conscientious objection as is sometimes popularly argued.

Whistleblowing also does not fit within the classical liberal understanding of civil disobedience. It is rather a form of dissent that is distinctive in its character and aim, less partisan and disruptive than other forms of dissent. Whistleblowing, unlike civil disobedience, represents an indirect manifestation of the injustice of the law in instances that are against the public interest. Moreover, unlike civil disobedience, whistleblowing operates under constrained publicity conditions and can be public, partially anonymous, or fully anonymous depending upon the assessment of the context. Civil disobedience, as a category of dissent, can accommodate some types of unauthorized disclosures but cannot account for whistleblowing in its generality. These differences led us to argue that whistleblowing is a distinctive category in the genus of democratic dissent. We called a form of civil dissent. Its civil nature owes to its civic and public mindedness, allegiance to constitutional mandates, and an overall belief in the capacity of democracy and democratic citizens to ensure redress of wrongs.

These were the arguments that we presented in the book. Before concluding, we would like to discuss whether a state protection should be granted to whistleblowers.

7.1   Whistleblower Protection as a State Duty

We have not discussed whether whistleblowing should be considered a right.[1] We believe that civic whistleblowers should have a right to the most extensive form of legal protection, rather than a right as such, and such right imposes a public duty to protection in virtue of the public interest function civic whistleblowers play in democratic polities. Many governments and international conventions have recognized the need to protect whistleblowing when disclosures are done with a reasonable belief that a wrongdoing has occurred. However, despite the wide agreement on the positive role played by whistleblowers in exposing corruption, the public perception of whistleblowers is divided among those who consider them to be moral heroes and to those who accuse them of treachery. In the light of these considerations, it is important to highlight that the protection also has important incentive functions. Among them, it makes employees more likely to respond more efficaciously to the professional duty of disclosure in specific cases, and increase one's confidence that civic testimony may reverse the common opinion that individual disclosures are ineffective in the face of widespread corrupt practices.

Governments do recognize acts of civic whistleblowing and provide some channels of disclosure, especially when the information concerns gross mismanagement of funds, abuse of authority, or hazard to public safety and health. However, while such forms of safeguard are directed towards civic whistleblowing, political whistleblowers are still denied any form of protection. It is not uncommon for political

---

[1] We elaborate on the right to protection for whistleblowers in Santoro and Kumar (2018).

whistleblowers to face charges of treason, break of trust, or disloyalty towards one's country.

If the arguments presented in this book are of any value, then political whistle-blowers should also be accorded the same protection when disclosures pertain to public interest and are carried out with the right intent fulfilling proper communicative constraints. Governments and courts should accord them the same safeguards usually recognized to civil dissenters and human right defenders. In this regard it is the duty of the state to protect whistleblowers under a qualified right when disclosures are justifiable. We do not argue for this view in this book but assume that the right to protection is entailed by the justification of civil dissent and the protection of fundamental rights recognized in the main international conventions on human rights.

Whistleblowing is a form of modern parrhesia, an act of fearless speech that stands testimony to wrong. The fact that speaking truth to power is a dangerous business in modern times, often inviting suspicion and retaliation, suggests that the minimum that democracies owe to such speakers is a degree of respect and protection. An absence of such basic recognition would not preclude courageous acts, for individuals would still demonstrate the same conviction to stand for their rights as they have done in the past. But this will be an unfortunate shortcoming for constitutional democracy whose history emerged out of and against the shadows of oppressive regimes to uphold the principle of equality and justice. The innumerable struggles that went into its formation can be lost if we lose those who speak truth to power. It is for the sake of all those courageous, often forgotten, agents of dissent that we ought to support a system of constitutional rights for the safeguard to future dissenters. No matter the direction a democracy may go, individuals will always find ways to resist oppression and wrongdoing. For failing to do so would be failing to stand for what humanity has achieved so far.

Reference

Santoro, Daniele, and Manohar Kumar. 2018. A right to protection for whistleblowers. In *Claiming Citizenship Rights in Europe: Emerging Challenges and Political Agents*, ed. Daniele Archibugi and Ali Emre Benli, 186–203. London: Routledge.

Index

© Springer International Publishing AG, part of Springer Nature 2018
D. Santoro, M. Kumar, *Speaking Truth to Power – A Theory of Whistleblowing*,
Philosophy and Politics - Critical Explorations 6,
https://doi.org/10.1007/978-3-319-90723-9

Printed by Printforce, the Netherlands